AT THE WHITE HOUSE

AT THE
WHITE HOUSE

ASSIGNMENT TO SIX PRESIDENTS

ROBERT PIERPOINT

G. P. Putnam's Sons
New York

Library of Congress Cataloging in Publication Data

Pierpoint, Robert.
   At the White House.

   1.   Pierpoint, Robert.   2.   Journalists—United States
—Biography.   3.   Presidents—United States.
4.   Government and the press—United States.   I.   Title.
PN4874.P49A33   1981   070'.92'4   [B]   80-28142
ISBN 0-399-12281-8

Acknowledgments

In 1951, when CBS flew me from Sweden, where I had been a stringer for its news division as well as a free-lance reporter, to Japan and Korea to cover the Korean war, I stopped in New York to sign my contract and have a chat with Edward R. Murrow. I was a staunch admirer of Murrow's and had done a few simple jobs for him, but I had never met the august dean of broadcast journalists. Ed was disarmingly friendly and full of encouraging words for me, a young reporter about to cover his first war. Had I ever worked as a newspaper or wire-service correspondent? he asked. I replied that my only experience had been in broadcasting. "I thought so," said Murrow. "You write like a broadcaster. One reason we decided to hire you is because we knew we didn't have to retrain you." The thought did not recur to me until many years later, when I began trying to write this book. There is a vast difference between writing for the ear and writing for the eye, and my lack of experience in newspaper journalism came back to haunt me.

Fortunately, in this process of learning to write for the eye, I have had some expert help. Myra MacPherson of the *Washington Post*, one of the finest writers in the field of journalism, first encouraged me to try a book. She also sustained me along the way, with suggestions for editorial changes and additions that have immeasurably improved the final result. Joel Swerdlow did the same, and more. Entering this painful process at a later stage, Joel was my co-author in most aspects of the term. He suffered with me the hardest and longest, and he deserves equally credit and blame for what we have produced.

Publisher David Obst, author-agent Ann Buchwald, and editor Ned Chase all guided me through the early stages, toward a company that was willing to take a chance on a broadcaster trying to write a book, and toward the final form of the book itself. Ann stuck with me until the end, while the rest went on to other things. But all have my grateful thanks for their guidance. At a later stage, Elisabeth Jakab took on the difficult task of acting as my editor, and I am most appreciative of the firm yet sensitive manner in which she aided me in getting down on paper some of the vague thoughts and memories floating in my head, and then made them readable and even interesting.

Susan Zirinsky, a CBS News producer, spent what spare hours she could manage from a very demanding job to do an absolutely priceless job as my researcher. If any of the facts in this book are wrong, Susan gets the blame for my faulty memory.

A special thanks goes to three renowned political-science professors, all specialists in the presidency: Richard Neustadt of Harvard University, Nelson Polsby of the University of California at Berkeley, and Charles Hardin of the University of California at Davis. During oral and written exchanges with these three outstanding academicians, I absorbed a broader view of the office of the Chief Executive and a perspective on the role of the press. I hope that their contributions to this effort will be of some benefit to all students of our political system.

There are many others who deserve thanks for their various roles in helping me to achieve this goal. My CBS News colleague Diane Sawyer, the Associated Press's long-time White House correspondent Frank Cormier, CBS News executives Sanford Socolow and Edward Fouhy all helped in one way or another. So did several friends and sources who prefer not to be named. Respecting their wishes, I thank them anyway for aiding me in delivering an offspring with a five-year gestation period. I hope it was worth the wait.

This book is dedicated to my wife,
Patricia Adams Pierpoint,
who kept me and the family together
with her intelligence and good humor
during the long difficult years in which
I was also married to six presidents.

Contents

AT THE WHITE HOUSE

Introduction

The White House is one of the most demanding assignments a reporter can have. I know, because it has been my home-away-from-home for twenty-three years. On a recent sleepless night, I estimated that CBS broadcasts have included at least 20,000 of my "at the White House" datelines.

I've been around here longer than any other correspondent currently on duty; that's surprising for a television network correspondent, as we are a group with a high turnover rate. What's more sobering is the realization that the only reporter with a longer White House track record than mine committed suicide years ago.

I've covered six Presidents, twelve national elections, one successful and one unsuccessful assassination attempt, two wars and too many crises.

My twenty-three years' witnessing Presidents Eisenhower, Kennedy, Johnson, Nixon, Ford and Carter from close up are what this book is about. The United States is the most powerful nation on earth, and the President of the United States is the world's most powerful leader, but outsiders understand less than they should about how the White House interacts with the press. I would like to share what I've seen and learned.

Before coming to Washington and the White House in 1957, I was a foreign correspondent, reporting political turmoil and social progress in Scandinavia, wars in Asia

13

and the Middle East, and the rebirth of postwar Japan from the end of American occupation to the recapture of world industrial markets. The overseas assignment placed me in a privileged position. Foreign correspondents are their own bosses, thousands of miles from the home office, instant experts on anything they choose to report. Nitpicking editorial complaints arrive by cable or telephone, but can easily be ignored or evaded with the subtle suggestion that superiors are simply wrong. "I am here and you are there," is an unanswerable argument. But back in the States, and particularly at the White House, things are different. For me, a thirty-two-year-old reporter with eight years' experience, the change was awesome. The White House is the news center of the universe. Every important occurrence anywhere in the world eventually generates activity in the White House. If fighting erupts between Chinese and Soviet military patrols along a remote river in southern Siberia, teletypes begin to clatter in the Situation Room one floor below the Oval Office. Within minutes, couriers are dashing back and forth across West Executive Avenue to the Executive Office Building, carrying messages for National Security Council specialists, who have already started a memorandum to the President, complete with background information. Within an hour, the Press Secretary will have a comment, or at least an off-the-record explanation, as to why he cannot comment. Broadcasting correspondents covering these events are responsible to radio editors and television-news producers (who do essentially the same type of work) and to the public, which frequently looks to the White House as the place where their problems are centered and solved. The visibility is high, the pressure is heavy, and the margin for error is practically nonexistent.

One recent crisis began for me about 1 A.M. on April 25, 1980, when my bedroom phone rang. I had just dropped off into that deep first sleep, and I groped groggily in the dark. As so often happens, it was the CBS News Washington Bureau night-desk editor. After a quick apology, he explained that NBC News had broadcast a television bulletin a few moments before, saying that the White House was announcing a failed attempt to rescue the American hostages in Iran. It didn't sound believable. I asked if he had checked with the White House, and he replied that Bureau Chief Ed Fouhy wanted me to do that. Sleepily and in total disbelief, I punched the press-office number. To my surprise, Carolyn Shields, Jody Powell's personal secretary, answered. She quickly confirmed the basic outline of the story and agreed to dictate the statement that Powell had just issued. Sitting on the edge of the bed in my shorts, I took down the tragic confirmation of the aborted rescue operation and the eight Americans who had died in it. The statement was half a dozen paragraphs and about three hundred words long. Taking it in longhand required over five minutes, and seconds later, still sitting on the bed in my shorts, I was broadcasting live on the CBS radio network with a "netalert" bulletin.

As my wife fixed coffee, I showered, shaved and dressed, and then headed for the White House, arriving after 2 A.M. The West Wing was alive with lights and people. Hurrying up the private street that separates the White House from the Executive Office Building, I saw from inside the Situation Room the faint glow from the electronic screen of the "hotline" teletype that is the constant connection between Washington and Moscow. The curtains were pulled, but shadowy shapes were visible behind them. Further up the walk, Presidential Assistant Zbigniew Brzezinski's office lights were on. Walking across the drive by the west portico, I looked into Powell's office, where the Press Secretary, his assistant Rex Granum, and one other person I could not recognize huddled over a table, peering at what appeared to be a large map. Out on the lawn to my left, television crews were working on equipment, strong lights blazing toward the north portico of the White House. I wondered briefly how Amy could sleep on the third floor upstairs, with all those lights and activities.

Throwing off my coat in the press room outside the CBS booth, I notified the Bureau that I was ready to broadcast and then headed quickly back toward the press office to try to get more information than was provided by the formal statement dictated earlier by Powell's secretary. I got only as far as the lower section, around the corner from the Cabinet Room, when one of Powell's deputies politely but firmly informed me that the entire area was off limits to reporters, and that for the time being Powell was answering no questions. Peeking around the corner toward the Rose Garden, I saw a Secret Service agent standing guard in his small glassed-in enclosure. This meant that the President was in the Oval Office. It was 2:20 A.M.

I returned to my booth to report to Fouhy and learned that CBS television could not go on the air from Washington. Primarily for budgetary reasons, we do not keep even a skeleton technical crew at night. This means that under normal circumstances CBS television news cannot get on the air after 11 P.M. from Washington without calling in technicians from around the area. That process, as we soon learned, requires at least a couple of hours. We did numerous radio broadcasts, however, because they require only access to a telephone line to New York.

So instead of television broadcasting, I started gathering more information. Few officials were answering their phones at that hour of the morning, and those who were had little to say. Within minutes, one of Powell's aides revealed that President Carter himself would address the nation at 7 A.M. ABC was to handle the "pool" from the Oval Office, which meant that their technicians and equipment would feed the President's speech to the other two networks. I tried to get permission to watch the speech from the office itself, in the hope of putting a few questions to President Carter afterward. This request was refused, as was a later suggestion that at least one pool reporter be allowed to watch the live broadcast from inside the Oval Office. Almost the only staff personnel we could talk to were aides and secretaries to Powell; they were all tired, nervous, and unable to tell us anything useful. Nevertheless, CBS News wanted a television report from the White House. By about 3:20 A.M., a handful of technicians had set up a Rube Goldberg television operation that got me through to New York. My first TV broadcast, at 4 A.M., was carried on about a half-dozen stations, including the Washington, D.C., CBS affiliate, which had stayed on the air especially for the crisis.

At about 6:30 A.M. another problem developed. CBS services the French and Japanese television networks, and they, quite understandably, were anxious to get on the air. But with the confusion and shortage of personnel, our technicians got their wires crossed. As Bob Schieffer asked me live questions from our studios in New York, I kept hearing French and Japanese in my earphones. This continued for the better part of an hour, often forcing me to guess at what Schieffer was asking. Fortunately for our viewers, only English was going out over the CBS TV network.

I'm not always awakened in the middle of the night. My normal work routine begins as soon as I can grab the morning newspaper, usually the *Washington Post*, along with my first cup of coffee. I watch parts of the *CBS Morning News,* listening carefully to the *World News Roundup* on radio. I usually arrive at my small booth in the White House press room at about 9:30, well saturated with the realities to which Washington has awakened.

During the morning hours the President may hold a meeting with a public figure, and he wants the world to witness it. So, cameras and correspondents are often called into the Oval Office, the Cabinet Room, or the Roosevelt Room. But these events are not always indoors. Foreign heads of state are usually received, weather permitting, on the south lawn with a fancy fanfare from the military drum-and-bugle corps and a review of troops. I usually find these occasions useful as an early opportunity to evaluate the President's mood or spirit, and they sometimes give rise to dramatic events. In 1978, for example, when the Shah of Iran came to visit the Carters, Iranian students received permission to protest on the expansive lawn between the White House and the Washington Monument. Iranian government agents flew in several hundred of the Shah's supporters from around the United States, and they too received permission to assemble on the Ellipse. Each group carried heavy sticks and other makeshift weapons. Park police, some of them mounted, stood between the groups. But, as might have been expected, order disintegrated. What was planned as a routine welcoming ceremony turned into a free-for-all, and police began firing tear gas. The next thing we knew, reporters and dignitaries were coughing and wiping their noses and eyes. President Carter and the Shah tried to ignore the gas, but eventually, they, too, began to wipe away tears. That one scene—of Carter and the Shah crying together on the White House lawn—was a prelude to worldwide headlines that were to dominate the news through the next few years.

Barring such unusual occurrences, the most interesting event of the day is usually the Press Secretary's briefing, where the President's spokesman makes formal announcements on topics ranging from the resignation of a Cabinet officer to the unveiling of a new national health program. If the subject is specialized, government experts also appear, and someone from the National Security Council is almost always on hand to respond to difficult foreign-policy questions. After the Press Secretary finishes, the floor is open to reporters, and it is our opportunity to try to learn what the President may *not* want known. Confrontations can result. For example, it was at a daily press briefing that President Nixon's Ron Ziegler said, "I will not comment on a third-rate burglary attempt." This came in response to a question I asked on a hunch less than twenty-four hours after the Watergate break-in, before any hard evidence linked the White House to the crime.

Press briefings also involve nuances that require strict concentration. For example, some spokesmen will say, "I haven't got anything on that for you now," which is really a clear signal that the story is correct, but the Press Secretary is unable to confirm it. Or the answer may be, "I wouldn't go with that kind of speculation if I were you," which indicates that the reporter is on the right track but not completely correct.

When the press briefing ends, the six telephones in the CBS booth become extensions of my body. Conversations with editors, producers and news sources are vital, because a Presidential Press Secretary rarely provides enough information or explanations for a complete story. In the spring of 1980, for example, President Carter told a group of reporters and news editors invited to the White House from outside Washington that he had received "reports that the Ayatollah Khomeini was threatening to hold the American hostages until after our November elections." We were given a transcript of the President's remarks, and absence of United States liaison with the Revolutionary Council in Teheran as well as the loose manner in which the President spoke, raised doubts that Khomeini had really made such a threat. Further checking was mandatory. A very reliable source with access to all diplomatic cables on the Iran situation said that some of the Ayatollah's *followers* had made such threats. But no intelligence report cited Khomeini himself. So the next night I did a broadcast on the *Evening News* quoting President Carter on the Ayatollah's "threat," but also saying that high officials within his own Administration knew of no evidence for such a charge. I did not directly accuse the President of lying, which would have been explosive and dangerous, but my report did accuse him of stretching the truth a bit.

On a relatively quiet day, I may take off during the lunch "lid" (that is, the observance of a stipulated period in which no news will be released—chiefly for the convenience of correspondents, who are then free to take care of other needs, as in this case eating a midday meal) to dine with a source, usually someone in government.* But frequently the telephone calls or the need to interview Presidential visitors do not permit me to leave the White House.

While all of this is happening, CBS radio carries my live and taped broadcasts, usually once every two or three hours. By 4 P.M., I have also outlined the evening's televi-

---

*The origin of the term "lid" is lost in obscurity. I have heard that Jim Hagerty invented it, and I am happy to give him credit both for coining the term and for conscientiously following the rules. Since then, many press secretaries have observed the custom of issuing a lid, but have frequently ignored their own orders and broken stories while the lid was technically on.

sion story, based on the day's research and events. This television report—by far the day's biggest job—must now be committed to paper, a joint effort by the Washington producer, New York producer, Walter Cronkite and me.

This process of preparing a report for the *Evening News* can require several phone calls just to settle minor changes in the script. When a story is to run only ninety seconds on the air, every word counts. The *Evening News* goes live at 6:30 P.M.; so, as the minute hand moves past 6, the atmosphere both at the White House and in the studios in Washington and New York gets tense. Voices and tempers rise at the frustration over having to cut fifteen seconds out of a story, or to add a fact from somewhere else that forces dropping something from the White House. Occasionally a last-minute development will require that a piece be changed substantially just minutes before air time, and the correspondent can feel the panic spreading through his stomach as he and the producer wonder whether they will make it in time. If a story is to be the first on the Cronkite show, the deadline is about 6:28, or as late as technicians can tape the report, rewind the tape, and have it ready for broadcast. Whenever possible, we like to use tape, but sometimes we miss this deadline and fast-breaking events require me to go on the air live. Just one failure to get the story done properly on tape or in time for a live presentation can end a White House correspondent's career and guarantee transfer to Siberia.

After the 6:30 news, I am free to work on reports for the next morning's CBS television news. Dinner is about eight, or whenever a tired correspondent can make it home to a wife long accustomed to "feeding the kids early."

Being a White House correspondent obviously has its personal costs. But one simple fact always keeps it exciting: Every time a CBS News correspondent goes on the air, millions of people listen and watch. The responsibility to provide them with timely, accurate, fair news coverage continually generates a high-pressure atmosphere.

Of course, covering the White House is not always serious, and I've actually reported from the White House wearing a jacket, tie and tennis shorts.

But playing tennis is in reality part of my job, and I have to confess that I like it better than golf—which in the Eisenhower era was almost a professional requirement. I discovered its (and my) shortcomings soon after joining the White House press corps, and I had gone with President Eisenhower to Augusta, Georgia, where he loved to play golf. After trying it a time or two myself, I realized my lack of ability and—even more important—the fact that it was impossible while on the links to keep up with the constant phone calls that plague a network correspondent covering the President. Being fetched by the club pro in a golf cart, or having to jog all the way back to the clubhouse from far out on the course after someone delivered a message saying I was wanted on the phone, upset everyone playing with me. So I turned to tennis; at least there is always a phone near the tennis court.

Over the years, as tennis became more popular, and particularly as Californians moved into the White House with Richard Nixon, tennis also became a good way to maintain contacts. I had played on the White House court only once or twice during the Kennedy era. But Ronald Ziegler, General Alexander Haig, Bryce Harlow, Secretary of State William Rogers, and even H. R. "Bob" Haldeman enjoyed the sport, and I became an occasional partner. In San Clemente or Key Biscayne, correspondents frequently attended press briefings in a tennis shirt and shorts or warm-up suit. If there was no news, or if only a radio spot was required, we could get quickly onto the courts without having to return to the hotel to change clothes. Eventually Tom Jarriel of ABC, Herb Kaplow of NBC, and I developed the habit of taking a shirt, coat and tie to the briefings. If a television story was needed, we simply put the top of the suit over the tennis outfit. Our cameramen, of course, knew enough not to shoot below the waist—usually!

This pattern continued even through the Watergate days, and I played tennis with Ziegler and Haig almost to the end. Our games provided a curious juxtaposition of the serious and the ludicrous, and occasionally there were some unexpected results, even on quiet Saturday afternoons when President Nixon was at Camp David and the atmosphere was more relaxed. One such Saturday in 1973, a call came from Bernard Collier, a former newspaperman who had interviewed me for a book he was writing on the Washington press corps. Collier wanted to come to the White House later that afternoon and take some pictures of me at work. Somewhat later, Ziegler invited me to play tennis that afternoon at three. At about two, the CBS Saturday News producer in New York asked me to do a story for that evening's 6:30 show, and I found myself in a crunch for time. So I did what we had so often done on the road—I wrote my story and sent it through the Washington producer to New York for approval, and then changed into my tennis outfit in the small locker room right below the Oval Office. (This area is not normally open to reporters or lower-level members of the staff, but if one is playing with an important Presidential assistant, the rules are waived.) Putting my shirt, tie and jacket on over the tennis shirt, I headed for the White House front lawn to do my report. About that time, Collier and his photographer arrived. Quite properly, they asked permission to take pictures while I worked, and without thinking twice about it, I agreed. As a journalist who continually asked others for their cooperation, I felt obligated to help a colleague.

When their pictures appeared on the jacket of Collier's book and later in the newspapers, my superiors were far from pleased, apparently feeling that tennis shorts, a jacket and tie did not provide a dignified image. In fact, our then vice-president William Small demanded that I sue Collier and his publisher. I argued that this would only make me look more ridiculous. Small insisted on the grounds that the photo was demeaning and should not have been used without my permission. I finally sent word that if CBS wanted to sue, it could, but I would not. This was a lucky bluff on my part. Although Small never knew it, strong pleading from Collier had elicited my signature on a waiver allowing him to use the picture. It is almost axiomatic that humorous moments and high-pressure events often run hand in hand.

Indeed, since so much of our time—especially on trips with the President—is spent waiting for something to happen, we make our own fun, which (besides tennis games) can take the form of pranks. For example, Jim Naughton of *The New York Times* once sent my CBS colleague Phil Jones and *Newsweek* reporter Tom De Frank realistic telegrams from the "League of Women Voters" inviting them to serve as panelists for the second 1976 Carter-Ford campaign debate. Acceptances were to be forwarded to "Florence Rathskellar."

At the CBS News Washington bureau, the telegram to Jones caused a minor furor. Everyone knew that CBS News President Richart Salant opposed our participation in the debates because the candidates could veto their potential interrogators, apparently without any explanation. But having made his strong feelings known, Salant had proceeded to tell his employees it was up to individual correspondents to make the decision if invited. Thus, the telegram to Jones precipitated a series of rushed telephone calls between top brass in Washington and those in New York before Jones, sensing Naughton's fine hand, had a chance to say, "Hold everything." At *Newsweek*, however, executives were so excited that one of their boys "made it" to the debates that the corporate hierarchy prepared a public announcement. When Jones and De Frank called the League of Women Voters and discovered the fraud, one *Newsweek* executive was so furious that he even considered contacting the Justice Department to see if Naughton could be prosecuted for sending false information over a leased telex. (He had sent the telegrams via the CBS and *Newsweek* telex machines.) Of course, Naughton got the last laugh. He had obtained the *Newsweek* telex number, and sure enough, a few weeks later the bills for the fake telegrams arrived at the magazine.

Despite such lighthearted breaks in the work routine, we are always aware that any moment may catch us in a story of worldwide importance. Sudden transition from private preoccupation to public sensation becomes a way of life, and those who need time to shift gears don't make it. One essential skill around the White House is the capacity to laugh at one moment and be deadly serious the next.

As my tennis-shorts trauma indicates, life at the White House can go from the sublime to the ridiculous in pretty short order. *At the White House* will take readers behind-the-scenes to see how this happens. I have reported a great many things over the past twenty years—and *not* reported some others. I have seen how television has helped to transform Presidential quail hunts into matters of international concern, at the same time turning every moment of the President's day into an assassination watch. I have seen Presidents openly engage in extramarital liaisons, correspondents drunk on the job, Presidential press conferences become platforms for those who have sharp elbows, strident voices and aberrant political philosophies. I have learned how coverage of the Middle East can inflame the public and endanger a reporter's career, and how reporting on a dishonest President proved that broadcast journalism—the nation's chief source of news—is weak at precisely the point where it should be strong, investigative reporting.

Through such stories I hope to emphasize the need for an informed public in a democratic society, for a press check on public officials and their policies. It is important for officials and public alike to understand the impact of television, and for White House occupants and correspondents to reassess how they can interact more productively. Most of all, the public must understand that politicians and the press are as human and as fallible as anyone else.

This book is written for several audiences. For the general reader, I want to provide interesting insights into what occurs at the White House and how it is reported. I won't be discussing only one specific topic, like Vietnam or Watergate; instead, I'll be presenting an overview covering nearly a quarter century at one of the centers of American political power, involving a wide range of characters and events, the focus of which constantly changes, as the President brings his own personality, style and priorities to the White House.

My second audience is all those starry-eyed, young journalism students raised on the heritage of Bob Woodward, Carl Bernstein and the Watergate scandal, to whom reporters have become what Hollywood actors were in the 1930s—glamorous and eminently emulatable. Future captors of corrupt Presidents are now cramming journalism schools, though not all of them will find that they are qualified for the life they envision. And many lack even a vague idea of what life on the journalistic firing lines is like. Having spent many hours being interviewed by would-be reporters, I have decided that it would be useful (and easier on me) to answer their questions by writing a book.

My final audience is academic experts on the Presidency. Over the years I've read much of their work carefully, and have been privileged to discuss matters of mutual concern with them. Their sharp observations and provocative questions have helped me in my work; now I'd like to return the favor. In particular, my hope is to address their concerns about Presidential power—how it has changed, how it can be controlled, how it can be best used, and what role the media play. These relate directly to the increasing influence—some would argue dominance—of television. As a network correspondent almost since the time television first arrived at 1600 Pennsylvania Avenue, I hope my thoughts and experiences will provide them with material to expand their thinking on these questions.

For each of these audiences, and for my family and friends, I hope *At the White House* will also convey the *emotions* involved. I'd like them to know what it's like to stand in front of a live, coast-to-coast audience and challenge the President of the United States. I want to share the feeling of discussing public policy with the nation's most powerful political leader while he undresses and prepares for his afternoon nap. I want to capture the horrifying immediacy of seeing a President of the United States killed, and another President forced from office because of corruption so pervasive that it took years to recognize. I wish them to understand that covering the White House is not just excitement and glamour, but also frustration, physical exhaustion and fear.

Most important, this book should convey my passionate commitment to a free press and my conviction that democracy cannot survive without it. "Journalism will kill you," Horace Greeley once wrote. "But it will keep you alive while you're at it."

BOB PIERPOINT

The White House
November 1980

1

The White House Press

"Pick up a bottle of bourbon and a bottle of scotch to take to the Press Room tomorrow. It's a tradition the first day on the job. You can put them on your expense account."

It was my boss speaking, CBS News Washington Bureau Chief Ted Koop. Although renowned in Washington for his sense of humor, Koop wasn't kidding. This was his way of confirming rumors that I was getting a new assignment and a much-prized title, CBS News White House correspondent. He was also serious about the liquor.

So, early on the morning of October 7, 1957, feeling slightly nervous and a bit foolish, I entered the White House carrying two bottles in a brown paper bag. In those days the Press Room was a medium-sized office just off the lobby of the West Wing. Jammed with worn desks, rickety typewriters and greasy telephones, it featured, at a window to the rear, one large table and several chairs, which served both as a meeting place and poker center for the White House press corps. I quietly pulled out the two bottles, carefully placed them on this table, and retreated to the lobby, suggesting to the few reporters on hand that early-morning refreshments were available. No one reacted. Slowly, however, the contents of the two bottles disappeared. Drinking on the job was apparently no handicap. Toward the end of the day, several of my fellow journalists congratulated me on my new assignment. If I had not exactly arrived, at least my presence was acknowledged.

To add to my nervousness, the White House and everyone in it awed me. President Dwight Eisenhower was a remote, almost legendary, figure. The nation had not yet undergone Vietnam and Watergate, and just to walk through the still-hallowed White House gates was somewhat intimidating. My new colleagues at the White House seemed more experienced, a shade sharper and a step quicker than any others I had known. Yet even they spoke of their deep respect for the office they covered.

My journalistic training had been entirely on the job, and all of my experience had been overseas, in Scandinavia and the Orient. What concerned me most was my almost total lack of experience of American political life. Although I was familiar with bigotry in many forms, I had never been in a Southern state and was ill equipped to deal with the major running story of that era, the racial and civil-rights problems of blacks. Beyond that, I simply had a lot to learn, a great deal to feel insecure about, and I knew it.

My first trip away from the White House (to Germantown, Maryland, where President Eisenhower dedicated new headquarters for the Atomic Energy Commission*) provided a rather demoralizing initiation.

Six reporters followed the President's motorcade in a rented limousine.† I was sandwiched into a rear jump seat, directly in front of the dean of the White House press corps—Merriman Smith of the United Press.‡ Smitty had a pock-marked face, a natty mustache, and the authoritative air of someone at the top of the heap. His questions invariably dominated Eisenhower's press conferences, and back in the Press Room, just listening to the ease with

---

*In 1974, Congress divided the AEC into the Nuclear Regulatory Commission and the Energy Research and Development Administration, which in 1977 was folded into the Department of Energy.
†Since the late 1960s, the White House has provided transportation for correspondents in the motorcade with the President.
‡It became the United Press International in 1958.

which he dictated his lead and first few paragraphs left more than one toughened veteran feeling inadequate.

Smitty (as everyone called him) looked rumpled and sat rather stiffly in the limousine. While the others read newspapers or quietly chatted, I wondered anxiously what was expected of me and how significant this excursion might be. I was excited, but all too aware of my comparative ignorance.

We had not driven more than a few blocks from the White House when Smitty began to harangue me.

"Why did CBS think a punk like you could cover the White House?" he said with a sneer. The other men in the car looked embarrassed and remained painfully silent.

Although I was too old—thirty-two—to be a complete novice, I suspected that Smitty was asking a very good question. Furthermore, I respected Smitty and the other men in the car and dearly longed for their good opinion of me. No one spoke up to change the subject or to suggest that Smitty was being just a little too rough. This resonant silence served as an explicit reminder that I was not exactly held in the highest of esteem.

Resentment and fear quickened my pulse. Smitty blinked groggily and weaved a bit as the car swerved. Suddenly I realized that he was drunk.

"I guess we'll just have to see if I can do the job," I said, lamely, thinking that I certainly could not broadcast in his condition.

My answer seemed to silence him. While the other reporters resumed their small talk, I retreated into silent anger mixed with bitter self-doubt. When we arrived finally in Germantown, Ike completed the rather perfunctory dedication ceremony without making any news that I could discern, and after taking notes we climbed back inside the limousine for our forty-five-minute return to the White House. No one else mentioned my alleged inadequacies, and I did my best to ignore Smitty in those rather close quarters. But I had been shaken.

I returned to my antiseptic hotel room at the Dupont Plaza, feeling the pressure. CBS had not given me enough time to locate an apartment, so this had to be my home for the time being. As I waited for room service to bring my dinner, I watched television, had a stiff drink, and pondered what Smitty had said. Drunk or not, he had put his finger on the problem: Was I capable of reporting from the White House for a major network? Finally, overcome by tension and anxiety, my stomach rebelled and I ran to the bathroom to vomit. That night I couldn't sleep. This dismal scene of sudden illness repeated itself periodically for several weeks until I made my first extended out-of-town trip with the President and began developing some friendships in the press corps.

Although the run-in with Smitty was by no means my last experience with alcohol-imbibing reporters, it was certainly instructive. But Smitty was above all a brilliant reporter, and I watched him particularly closely as part of my education. Smitty never asked useless or argumentative questions at briefings and press conferences, but deftly elicited the information necessary to fill out his story. I began to realize that he actually wrote in his head as the session progressed. I also noticed that Smitty asked for facts, details and color that revealed he was thinking far beyond the first paragraph of his story, into what we today refer to as background and analysis. Wire-service reporters are under a special kind of pressure, because somewhere in the world at any hour of the day or night a newspaper or radio station is using their material as fast as it comes in. Thus, they are constantly on deadline and always pressed for time. By the time the briefing or news conference concluded, Smitty had the entire story mapped out in his head, and as quickly as he could get to the telephone, he would start dictating it, line by line. Adept at writing under pressure, he won the Pulitzer Prize and several other awards for his coverage of such stories as President Kennedy's assassination.

Smitty's passing (he eventually committed suicide) and the absence of anyone to fill the void he left highlight how significantly the White House press corps has changed since my early days. Bottles and flasks are no longer visible, and I know of no one who drinks while around the White House Press Room. Still a part of the life of a White House correspondent, alcohol is used primarily at the end of the work day. On long trips with the President, the last leg late at night can be a very noisy, wet affair, with stewardesses aboard the charter aircraft moving quickly to keep drinks flowing. In recent years, however, increasing numbers of women reporters have added both beauty and dignity to our group, and they do not drink as hard.

The press corps has changed slowly, but it has changed. Some correspondents have taken to smoking marijuana. I remember the embarrassment of a network correspondent, who must, for obvious reasons, remain unnamed, when in 1978, President Carter fired White House staff member Dr. Peter Bourne for illegally prescribing methaqualone, a powerful sedative more frequently referred to by its proprietary name, Quaalude. Reports circulated that other Carter staffers were using pot, and this particular network asked its reporter to investigate. The problem was that he had not only smoked pot with members of the White House staff, but had actually supplied the weed. To this day, his bosses are puzzled because he never discovered anything on that story.

Without doubt there are those covering the White House who use, or have used, hard drugs. But I have seen no evidence of this. I do remember that during the Eisenhower days, I myself took some of what we called Dr. Walter Tkach's "Little Green Pills." Dr. Tkach, an Air Force officer, was the White House physician for Ike and, later, President Nixon. On long trips with little time for sleep reporters often had difficulty keeping awake. So Dr. Tkach would provide his "Green Jollies." They worked so well that I could go without sleep for twenty-four hours. But when I finally got into bed, I was still so jumpy that I took some of Dr. Tkach's "Little Red Capsules" to put me to sleep. The next morning I found my head fuzzy, and when a shower and black coffee would not help, it was back to the "Green Jollies." After two or three days, I became almost a zombie, uncertain whether I was even functioning properly. Possible failure of judgment on a story worried me, so after a year or so I gave up the pills. Nowadays, however, pills are not noticeable among the White House press corps, although "uppers" and "downers" have become much more prevalent among society as a whole.

Over the years the press corps has also increased enormously in size. When I arrived in 1957, the "regulars"—people permanently assigned on a daily basis to cover the President—totaled only about fifteen. This included one reporter for each wire service (Associated Press, United Press, and International News Service*), one reporter for each of the three major radio-television networks, one for Mutual Radio, reporters for *Time, Newsweek* and *U.S. News & World Report,* and one from each of perhaps half a dozen newspapers around the nation. Many other newspapers and news organizations covered the White House only sporadically. About nine hundred people in all carried White House press passes, including photographers and electronic technicians.

Today, at least three times as many reporters regularly work in the Press Room. Each network has three correspondents, servicing round-the-clock radio newscasts, morning and midday television news broadcasts, evening news, and periodic "instant" specials when a crisis or some other situation erupts. Each network generally assigns two full television crews, plus a radio technician, and on at least one day out of three, a lighting technician. This means the networks alone have eight or nine people in the Press Room on a normal working day. Wire services have also increased coverage and keep three, sometimes four, reporters at the White House. The news magazines have doubled their manpower and significantly more newspapers now boast White House correspondents. Some larger papers, such as the *Washington Post, The New York Times* and the *Washington Star,* now assign two correspondents to the beat, where there used to be only one.

*The INS was merged with the United Press in 1958.

Many broadcasting "groups," that is companies, such as RKO and Metromedia which own perhaps a half-dozen radio stations, provide regular radio coverage as do the radio arms of AP and UPI. About 1700 people*—twice as many as when I first arrived—now hold White House press passes.

This burgeoning of the White House press corps has many causes. The nation's increasing population is an obvious factor. Post-World War II technological and sociological changes have been at least as important. Radio, television, communications satellites and computer technology have given the news an unprecedented immediacy and intimacy. People can now sit in their living rooms and watch the President of the United States order more troops to Vietnam, and only weeks later see their sons, husbands or brothers die in battle. This, in turn, has contributed to a greater desire for information, so that the meager afternoon radio reports whet the appetite for watching the evening television news to see what really happened, and for reading the morning newspapers to find out more about why it happened.

Furthermore, our increasingly well-educated, complex society requires reporters with special training. A general-assignment reporter can usually bluff through any story the first few times the public is exposed to it. But the public and a good editor notice very quickly when a journalist lacks real knowledge of his subject. I learned this early the hard way when Press Secretary Jim Hagerty called us into his office in 1958—shortly after the Soviet Sputnik satellite had been launched into outer space—and presented several scientists to explain the United States space program to us. Even though I had spent two years under Navy orders at the California Institute of Technology, I was totally lost in the maze of scientific jargon that poured from our "briefers." Having deliberately forgotten all that the Navy had forced me to learn, I now needed to know much more about space science and physics than I had time to pick up while covering the White House. So CBS News

*This is a December 1980 figure.

developed specialists to handle such stories. Walter Cronkite became a nationally recognized expert on space science, immersing himself to the point where he could broadcast for hours with knowledge and authority. If Walter switched to me at the White House, I would discuss Presidential reaction to the particular space event, which required special knowledge only about the President.

The White House did have one problem with the early manned space launches. The original idea was to show President Johnson sitting in the Oval Office watching the events on live television. Obviously, LBJ wanted to share the credit for any successes, so CBS proposed that a live, pool camera be placed near Johnson's desk. He could then turn to network correspondents and talk about how pleased he was that his own efforts, and those of the heroic participants, had reached such happy fruition. It was a natural for any President. But Presidential aide Jack Valenti noted a potential flaw in the script. What if the mission had to be postponed for long minutes during a countdown, or worse yet, what if the "bird" blew up? The President probably would be left speechless with horror, and even if words came, what could he say at such a moment? Eventually, the White House decided to reject the live coverage and substituted a printed statement of the President's enthusiastic reaction to successful flights. Later, as subsequent launches proved consistently successful, we were allowed to put a camera in the Oval Office.

Yet many important facets of the White House press corps have not changed at all. A journalist still needs good instincts and the capacity to think quickly under pressure. And, as my first White House crisis illustrates, a little luck also helps.

Reporters who spend a good deal of time in the Press Room can frequently sense a crisis while it is still developing, be it a major international incident, a Cabinet shake-up, or a Presidential health problem. The closer correspondents are physically to the center of activity, the easier it is to detect unusual behavior and eventually to learn what is happening. In 1957 we spent much of our time sitting in the West Wing lobby (a large room, perhaps 80 feet by 50 feet, filled with brown overstuffed couches and chairs, with a huge carved mahogany table in the center. In the winter, the table was usually jammed with the coats and hats of people waiting to see the President or his aides.)

One particular November afternoon, all signs pointed to a crisis. We could see doors to private offices opening and closing. People hurried along the corridors, their eyes turned away. Everyone deliberately ignored us, and the rumor started that Ike had suffered another heart attack. Normally, the person we turn to at such times is the Press Secretary, who, while he might not provide a complete answer, will at least help with a hint or two of the news to come. However, Jim Hagerty was in Paris, arranging for a Presidential meeting with leaders of the North Atlantic Treaty Organization. Left in charge was Deputy Press Secretary Anne Wheaton, a large, friendly, white-haired woman in her sixties. A long-time Republican official, Anne's major qualification for the job was her sense of humor, but that was not particularly useful on this occasion.

As we grew increasingly restive, the time for the regular 4 P.M. briefing came and went. No briefing. Anne stayed in Hagerty's office (or at least out of sight) as rumors of Ike's illness spread. White House regulars sent out speculation, which their editors hardened into hints, which office staffs communicated further as "reports."

Shortly after 5 P.M., Anne summoned reporters into Hagerty's office, a fairly large room, but much too small to accommodate comfortably the approximately 250 now at hand. There was considerable jostling for position, especially from those correspondents on deadline. A wire-service reporter or network broadcaster always wants to be close enough to hear well, but not so far from the door as to be blocked from quick access to telephones or microphones at the session's abrupt end—which comes when the senior wire-service person shouts "thank you" as he heads out of the room. In beating the competition, seconds make a difference. Journalists not near deadline (e.g., columnists and news-magazine reporters) invariably move in toward the Press Secretary at the end of the briefing, hoping proximity will provide more tidbits. The center of the room thus degenerates into chaos, with journalists trying to move in opposite directions.

I grabbed a spot on the side of the room halfway between Anne's desk and the exit, with a fairly clear path to the door. After the last reporter had squeezed in, a visibly upset Anne Wheaton ordered a Secret Service agent to lock the door,* which I had never seen occur before (nor can I remember a similar incident since). This boosted the tension considerably. Anne Wheaton rose, gasping for breath, her voice breaking with excitement, and read a short statement from President Eisenhower's doctor declaring that the President had suffered a "cerebral aphasia." Quickly, someone shouted a question. "Anne, is that another heart attack?" (Ike had suffered his first heart attack in 1956, and almost decided not to run for reelection.)

Clutching her chest, Anne stammered, "I . . . I think so."

Another reporter shouted, "But Anne, isn't that a kind of stroke?" The frantic Wheaton suddenly realized she was in trouble. Almost speechless now, she gasped. "I can't tell you any more. You'll have to talk to the doctors." She waved to the Secret Service agent. "Open the door!"

Over two hundred reporters fought their way out, struggling toward microphones, telephones and typewriters. I had warned CBS that some kind of bulletin would be forthcoming and to be ready to break into the radio network. (Until about 1970, television took its bulletins from the radio news side.) But as I literally ran to reach our microphone, I realized I had a problem. I could repeat the medical bulletin Anne Wheaton had read, but what did it mean? "Cerebral" to me meant some relation to the brain,

---

*In those days, an agent usually attended briefings so he could inform his colleagues about matters of special interest to them, including travel, security or upcoming appointments. Nowadays, Press Room briefings are piped throughout the White House and to various government offices, such as the State Department.

and I had no idea what "aphasia" was. Ignoring Wheaton's confusing clarification, I went on the air with, "President Eisenhower has suffered a 'cerebral asphasia'—which seems to be a mild stroke." This was a mild stroke of luck for me, because my instincts turned out to be correct. Ike *had* suffered a stroke. One less fortunate colleague flashed the highest news priority on his wire and then reported that the President had suffered a "cerebral heart attack." That took several hours and interviews with doctors and other experts to straighten out, while Hagerty sped back from Paris to assume control.

Another contrast over the past quarter century has been the strange, brilliant, funny and impossible people who make up the White House press corps. It is not difficult for most would-be reporters to obtain White House credentials. Basically, all that is necessary is a letter from a recognized news organization to the Press Secretary, who in turn passes it on to the Secret Service. The S.S. (as it is called with a mixture of familiarity and contempt) then conducts a perfunctory security check before issuing a permanent pass. During my early Washington days, this press pass carried one's name and the words "WHITE HOUSE"—which made it convenient for identification in cashing checks. Unable to resist the temptation, less affluent members of the press corps wrote checks that bounced right back to an understandably peeved bureaucracy at 1600 Pennsylvania Avenue. As a result, current passes have only the name and picture of the accredited journalist and his or her employer—all mention of the White House and the Secret Service is gone.

Actually, very few reporters have ever been denied White House passes. And when refusals do occur, the S.S. often refuses to explain why. Writer Robert Sherrill was turned down by the Secret Service, and the only reason given was "security." With the help of the American Civil Liberties Union, Sherrill sued the Secret Service. Eventually, the government had to reveal that he was denied a pass because in his younger years he had been arrested by local police for a couple of fist fights. The pass was still

withheld, so the A.C.L.U. sued again. This time, the Secret Service wrote Sherrill a letter saying that he could
now reapply and a White House pass would be
granted.*

Such incidents, though rare, are extremely dangerous.
A democracy depends upon a free press, and the Secret
Service must *not* have the power to deny access to reporters—it would become too easy to exclude those whose coverage was unfavorable to the White House. At the same
time, the Secret Service has a legitimate right to make
security checks that guarantee the President's safety. But
I have seen only one reporter who posed a potentially vio-
lent threat to a President.

In 1959 a reporter I'll call Dick Jones, who had covered
the White House for several years, began to have severe
emotional problems.

The first time most of us learned that something was
wrong with him came during a trip to Georgia, where
President Eisenhower intended to hunt quail on the estate
of Treasury Secretary George Humphrey. This hunt was a
rather elaborate procedure, involving a mule-drawn wagon with seats mounted on it, several hunting dogs and their
handlers, Secret Service agents, photographers, reporters,
and, perched high on their rolling seats, the host and his
guest armed with shotguns. Just as the entourage was
about to head off toward the nearby woods, a scuffle broke
out between two members of the press corps. It was Jones,
yelling "You dirty son-of-a-bitch" at an astounded Jack
Sutherland of *U.S. News & World Report.* Sutherland,
who had been an amateur boxer of considerable ability,
kept Jones at arm's length while friends and Secret Service agents pulled off his aggressor. This incident occurred

---

*By this time, however, several years had passed. Sherrill was writing
columns and magazine articles, and no longer needed access to the
White House. He never reapplied. When hired by *The Nation* magazine, he was asked what title he wanted on the masthead, and as a joke
on the Secret Service, he told the editor, "White House Correspondent." However, he never goes inside the White House. Sherrill told me
that mail sent to him at the White House sits for weeks before being
sent back, forwarded, or most often dumped into the trash can.

under the surprised gaze of the President of the United States, who was apparently so flustered that he rested his hands dangerously over the muzzle of his shotgun.

President Eisenhower mishandling his weapon made the news, but the fight did not; in those days, reporters felt that stories about each other were not news. Secret Service agents made a few discreet inquiries among Jones' colleagues, but were reluctant to take action. Not long afterward, Jones attacked Sutherland again, this time on a Georgia golf course. Again, Jones was restrained, and again, the Secret Service did nothing. Jones threatened several other reporters as well. Someone should have stepped in, but no one did; and apparently no one informed Jones' superiors, perhaps because no one wanted to cause trouble for a sick but otherwise decent man.

But things inevitably came to a head. A few weeks later, President Eisenhower flew to Seattle to speak at a fund-raising dinner for local Republicans. At breakfast the next morning, Merriman Smith, who was sitting next to me, was called to the telephone, a perfectly normal event. Moments later, Jones sat down a table or so away, and as he casually studied the menu, I noticed blood covering one of his hands. I rushed out to the hall and found Smitty doubled up in pain on the floor, holding his head, blood gushing from his nose. I offered help, but Smitty said calmly, "Help Dick, he's the one who needs it." Eventually we got Smitty to a room, stopped the bleeding, and phoned a doctor, who diagnosed a broken nose. Belatedly, the Secret Service suggested via the Press Secretary that Jones' employers assign another person to the White House. They did so quickly, and eventually Jones was sent away for medical help. In this case, most of us felt that the Secret Service had acted properly. Some of us also suffered guilt pangs. If we had acted earlier we might have saved Jones considerable anguish and embarrassment. Nowadays, if anyone were to go berserk in the presence of the President, it would be reported immediately. But those were much more naïve days before the assassination of President Kennedy alerted us to some very real dangers.

"Dick Jones" was the only reporter I know who might

have been a direct physical threat to the President. But as the size and prominence of the White House press corps have grown, it has attracted some strange people, including a few that the *New York Times Magazine* early in 1977 called "zanies."

Some are pseudo or part-time journalists attracted to the White House for emotional reasons. They receive press passes on the strength of their representation of "news organizations" that they themselves have set up or of small impecunious radio stations or weekly newspapers that, at the cost of a letter of application, are then able to boast of "White House coverage." Although peddling an "at the White House" by-line may occasionally help them sell stories, few major news organizations hire these unprofessional reporters or use their work.

The White House itself can—and should—do very little about these people, even though they are troublesome, disruptive and occasionally even dangerous. But media officials and outsiders have frequently suggested that standards be established to screen out "zanies" or those otherwise unqualified. Yet defining the term "qualified" creates an extremely delicate and difficult problem. The First Amendment to the United States Constitution implicitly forbids government licensing of journalists, and this can complicate noncontroversial government functions, such as protecting the President. In the 1960s, during the heat of the Vietnam war, many so-called underground newspapers sprang up around the nation. When copying machines print thousands of copies in an hour, anyone who can type and press a button could legitimately claim to run a "newspaper." Sometimes these sheets or their editors advocated outright violence against those conducting the war, so the Secret Service was understandably nervous about issuing passes to questionable and possibly dangerous representatives of the underground press. The government has never made public, however, just how many passes were denied for reasons of physical danger to the President.

Denial of press credentials—particularly when it occurs

in secrecy—demonstrates the dangers of government regulation over journalists. To combat these dangers, journalists can and should do more to police themselves. The archaic and stuffy White House Correspondents Association could act as a watchdog *if* it had some simple restructuring. Presently, however, the W.H.C.A. is a self-perpetuating committee* whose chief function is to hold an annual dinner for the President, other high government officials, Association members and their guests. Except for those on the dinner committee, no members may vote on any issue, including membership of the committee itself. Shortly after dessert, the W.H.C.A. leader is retired from the Board and generally fades from sight, ever after to be honored as a past president of the White House Correspondents Association.†

Although the dinner is an obvious anachronism and rather tedious to boot, news editors and publishers around the nation flock to it because it is their one chance to mingle with Washington big shots. They hail the President— no matter how popular or unpopular—as a conquering hero and become quietly depressed should he fail to attend.

The situation is further complicated by the fact that so few people really understand the nature of the organization. Most Presidents and their press secretaries, having heard of the W.H.C.A. before assuming office, mistakenly believe that it speaks for the White House press. They therefore frequently summon its officers to discuss house-

---

*Most members are newspaper, wire-service and news-magazine reporters. In the late fifties, three broadcasters were allowed to join the Association, but not the Board. Anyone can join the Association, but the Board is a closed circle that chooses its own successors. Finally in 1967, Ray Scherer of NBC was elected to the Board, and ten years later three of the ten members were broadcasters, including one woman. In 1976 Helen Thomas was elected president, a decided change over earlier years when women could not even attend the annual dinners.

†In the spring of 1980, I became President of the White House Correspondents Association, a vantage point that has not changed my perspective.

keeping, administrative, or even ethical problems, particularly at the beginning of an administration. These W.H.C.A. officers are in an awkward position. Legally, they speak for no one but the ten individuals who stage an annual dinner, and nowadays they are quicker to point this out. But in the headiness of newly acquired power it can take months or years for the White House to realize it is not dealing with a formal and representative institution.

Obviously, this can lead to problems. In the early years of the Nixon administration, the White House and the W.H.C.A. began discussions over the construction of a new Press Room. Problems were outlined and plans were drawn, and it was not until months of discussion had passed and binding decisions on space and costs had to be made, that Press Secretary Ziegler discovered that he was negotiating with a powerless dinner committee. He then had to repeat much of his negotiation, this time with bureau chiefs for the various networks and news organizations.

Other problems have even higher stakes. Within weeks of taking office, for example, Jimmy Carter started leaving the White House without informing the press. Constant coverage irritates Presidents, especially when they first arrive at the White House and are unaware that any appearance under any circumstances may produce a story. No one knows, for example, when some nut or even an agent of a foreign power may assault a President; so, reporters—especially correspondents for wire services and networks—are duty bound to cover all Presidential forays, even to the theater or a local restaurant.

Carter learned that there was anger and concern over his sudden public appearances without the press corps. Clearly wanting to get off to a good start with White House correspondents, Press Secretary Jody Powell made the mistake of asking W.H.C.A. officers to decide which press representatives would discuss the situation with the President. He should have included at least the major bureau chiefs, who are very jealous of their prerogatives in power-conscious Washington and in any case can overrule almost any decision that reporters make. Egos were bruised, certain reporters loudly objected to the W.H.C.A.'s selections, and at least one organization (CBS News) declined to participate, primarily on the grounds that journalists do not advise Presidents, they cover them. Eventually, negotiation produced an agreement whereby for purely social visits, such as dinner at the home of a friend, a network and wire-service pool accompanies the President. Pictures and the story, if any, are then distributed to all the major news organizations.

This system worked well for the first two years of President Carter's administration. But in early 1979, it became apparent that he was "sneaking out" to attend dinner at the homes of certain staff members, to dine at restaurants, or to jog along the Chesapeake and Ohio Canal. At this stage, the networks (and possibly other news organizations) began to monitor Secret Service and Washington police radio transmissions more carefully. Their simple codes usually give away the President's travel plans. In the fall of that year, Mr. Carter once had to cancel jogging on the Canal because CBS News had learned he was planning such an outing and had placed a camera crew along the towpath. Our crew made the mistake of asking the White House if President Carter was going jogging beside the Canal that day, thus informing the Secret Service that we suspected he had such plans, leading him to change them. The normal reaction of the public to this kind of story is that we should "let the poor man alone . . . he deserves some privacy." But if he should fall into the Canal, for example, it is not a story we would want to miss!

The White House Correspondents Association does provide annual rewards for professional accomplishments in categories such as reporting under deadline pressure, investigative reporting, and in-depth or background reporting. In addition, it occasionally applies pressure on Presidents who have been reluctant to hold press conferences, and has persuaded the White House to rearrange the Press Room facilities so that television gear and technicians do not crowd out reporters. But its undemocratic and unrepresentative nature makes the W.H.C.A. inherently weak. Every correspondent who joins the Association should have one vote, instead of the current ten votes for over one thousand members.

A W.H.C.A. with real power could also help the White House resolve problems generated by foreign powers with different methods for handling the media. One such example occurred in 1971, when Ron Ziegler first started negotiation with the People's Republic of China in preparation for President Nixon's trip to Peking. The Chinese wanted only fifteen members of the American press to accompany the President. With an election approaching, Ziegler wanted extensive coverage, and he knew that fifteen people would not be enough to handle the technical and editorial needs of even one network. He finally persuaded the Chinese to put technicians into a separate category, and to authorize eighty reporters, as well as scores of technicians and a few executives. A total American press entourage of 150 eventually accompanied the President.

This negotiation was long and difficult for Ziegler, especially since he also had to take official responsibility for selecting reporters who made the trip. Everything would have been expedited had some formal organization joined the fight for better coverage.

Furthermore, members of the press should never have to rely on the White House to fight their battles. Presidents have a way of putting their own political interests ahead of the public's right to know, and in instances such as the China trip we find ourselves enjoying access only when it is to the President's advantage.

Of course, not all the burden of 24-hours-a-day coverage falls on an ever-complaining President. The White House press corps is itself continually on call, and one of the least pleasant aspects of the job is to have an evening ruined when word comes that the Chief Executive is on the move. In such instances, our friends, families, and sometimes even our own emotional well-being suffer.

While this has happened to me far too often during the

years in which I've covered the White House, the worst such experience occurred during the early years of the Nixon administration. Late in 1969, a good friend of Dan Rather's told him that President Nixon was about to fire long-time FBI Director J. Edgar Hoover, or at least persuade Hoover to retire. Just how good the source was is not clear to me, but that night Rather aired it quite firmly on the CBS *Evening News*. The date is clear in my mind because it was my tenth wedding anniversary, October 3, 1969. That evening, while we were celebrating, the CBS News office called me to say that President Nixon was on his way to J. Edgar Hoover's house for dinner, and that I should get over there immediately. I protested, first pointing out that I was in the midst of celebrating my wedding anniversary with guests and second that it was not my story. Nixon's gesture obviously was intended to prove Rather wrong, and I suggested that perhaps Rather should rush over to Hoover's house.

In the CBS pecking order, however, I was beneath Rather and had to do most of the night work. Since I was on call and Rather was out for the evening anyway, Bureau Chief Bill Small bluntly ordered me to Hoover's house.

I spent the next hour on a chilly sidewalk in Chevy Chase, Maryland, keeping my camera crew company. Finally, President Nixon emerged and made a predictable denial. My story—a curt statement by Mr. Nixon and aide John Ehrlichman as they climbed into their limousine after dinner—appeared on the CBS *Morning News* the next day. Although the *Evening News* rarely uses a story already broadcast on the morning show, Walter Cronkite also used the piece because he felt compelled to correct Rather's broadcast of the previous evening.

My sidewalk coup—no other network was present outside Hoover's home—seemed to please CBS News, yet it left me with mixed emotions. I was not happy refuting a colleague's story. But Dan Rather is a professional and I knew that he understood. The real problem was that I resented the interruption of my tenth-anniversary celebration for such a nonevent. My professional success did not soothe hurt feelings, nor did it increase my wife's enthusiasm for married life with a White House correspondent.

2

The Press Room

Politicians, Presidents included, look upon the press as there to be manipulated if possible, and tolerated at best. Most Presidents start out determined to win our confidence, and yet most end up believing us to be responsible for publicizing their failures and ignoring their successes. Some even decide that the press itself causes the failures. The end product is an adversary relationship, a constant state of hostility that often borders on open warfare. Much of this action takes place on one battlefield: the White House Press Room.

In the 1950s, reporters and cameramen and the few electronic technicians that were needed at that time worked in a press room the size of an average business or government executive's personal office. (In fact, when Henry Kissinger moved in as Richard Nixon's Assistant for National Security Affairs he later took over the Press Room for just that purpose. His successors have managed to keep it.)

The room was crowded with small desks, each with its own telephone and a few with typewriters. The entire area was scarcely big enough for the dozen regular reporters, so all others spilled over into the public lobby, a huge room in the West Wing, separated by only a hallway from the Oval Office and the offices of top Presidential aides.

Visitors on the President's public schedule or with other White House appointments, went in and out through this lobby, guided by a doorkeeper who sat behind a desk at one end. For many years, this was a tall, bald, bespectacled gentleman with a courtly air, named Bill Simmons. He always rose to greet visitors, and if coats and hats were being worn, he suggested that they be placed on a large, round mahogany table that dominated the center of the lobby.*

Those arriving to see the President were usually escorted into another room, nearer the Oval Office and out of bounds for reporters. Those waiting to meet with Presidential aides, however, were thrown into the lobby with the spillover from the Press Room. They sat as comfortably as possible amid loudly snoring or arguing reporters.

This arrangement obviously had disadvantages for us, but it also offered one great benefit: no one on a President's public schedule could visit him without first going through the White House press corps, and this usually meant that he had to answer our questions. Even a public figure trying to avoid questions could be worth a story.

Such haphazard contact was particularly important in Eisenhower's day, when very few top administration aides ever talked to the press in private. But we did have other opportunities for contact. Journalists were allowed to wander across West Executive Avenue—a closed street entirely within White House grounds—and into the Executive Office Building (EOB), which houses Presidential speechwriters, members of the National Security Council staff, Budget Bureau workers, and others with information of value to reporters. The EOB also has a cafeteria, where we could pick up a quick snack or meal during the long hours of waiting out a national or international crisis. The cafeteria was a good place for meeting and filling out background information for one's next story. For example, when Ike sent Marines into Lebanon, we could call on this relaxed setting and perhaps a cup of coffee or a hamburger to discuss with willing sources what the Administration believed the mission could accomplish.

*   *   *

*This table was a gift from the Philippine government and was made of Narra wood, or Philippine mahogany. It had foot-thick legs, each beautifully carved into a prominent water buffalo head.

In sharp contrast to the military chain of command in the Eisenhower White House, JFK made it relatively easy for us to reach his aides: we simply had to call them on the telephone and request an appointment. Access to Kennedy himself—at least in a cursory manner—was easy, and it often provided him some light moments.

As is now public knowledge, JKF liked attractive women, wherever he spotted them. Frequently he would walk up to the prettiest girl in a crowd and strike up a conversation. This was such a strong habit with Kennedy that I once capitalized on it to please a close friend's wife. Sam Haight, a classmate of mine in college, had married in Sweden a beautiful blond Czech student named Eva. In the early 1960s they were serving with the United States Aid Mission in Laos and came to Washington on home leave. The fact that I worked around the White House fascinated Eva, and she wanted to visit me. Naturally, I agreed—that was easy enough to arrange—but when she arrived Eva asked if she could meet President Kennedy.

A meeting with the President was somewhat harder to manage, but I had an idea. Whenever John F. Kennedy had a foreign visitor in the West Wing, he invariably walked him through the lobby to see him off, and then chatted briefly with reporters before returning to the Oval Office. It happened that during that week of Eva's visit, the President was to receive a foreign head of state. As soon as the visiting statesman had entered the Oval Office with JFK, I stationed the beautiful Eva and her husband in the lobby. After his foreign guest left, the President began to head back inside the lobby, then suddenly veered directly toward Eva! He shook her hand and asked if she worked in the White House. Eva was both pleased and flustered as she explained to the handsome young President that she was actually visiting her friend, CBS correspondent Bob Pierpoint. Kennedy said something to the effect of "lucky Pierpoint," while she tried to introduce him to her husband, who stood quietly beside her. With as much graciousness as he could muster, the President asked Sam a perfunctory question about his job, then wandered reluctantly back toward the Oval Office, visibly disappointed that he could not spend a bit more time with the beautiful blonde in the press lobby.

Most of our informal conversations with JFK were about social matters, such as upcoming trips to Hyannisport or Palm Beach. But even this sort of informal contact proved to be too much for Kennedy's successor, Lyndon Johnson. Early in his administration, LBJ realized that if he brought his visitors through the lobby as JFK had done, reporters would ask questions. Because he believed in very tight control over information flowing from the Oval Office, Johnson initiated two countermoves. First, he started to use the side door to the West Wing of the White House, which faces West Executive Avenue. Johnson was unhappy, however, to see that we covered this door almost as easily as we did the lobby. But bad weather posed a problem, as shelter came from a small overhang that offered protection to only a few; other reporters and television crews had to stand in the rain.

Johnson then initiated his second stratagem: he ordered the White House Police* to keep us away from the West Wing door. Now we could talk to Oval Office visitors only if Johnson wanted us to. Very often he did not, and news organizations had to send reporters scurrying all over town to discover what had just happened in the White House.

In April of 1965, Johnson proceeded to restrict our access even further. A railroad labor dispute threatened to turn into a crippling nationwide strike, so in typical Johnson fashion the President summoned both sides to an EOB conference room, lectured them on their patriotic duties and then suggested that they lock themselves in the room until an agreement was reached. As LBJ left, however, he found the corridor crowded with camera crews and reporters demanding to know what had happened.

---

*The White House Police are uniformed guards assigned to the various entrances of the White House and selected spots inside the grounds. They supplement the Secret Service, whose primary duty is to protect the President and his family. In recent years, the White House Police have been placed under the jurisdiction of the Secret Service and greatly expanded. Now called the Executive Protection Service, they also guard foreign embassies in both Washington and New York.

A frowning, angry President stormed back across the street to the Oval Office and ordered that the press be barred from the EOB immediately. We left unhappily but peaceably. Although Johnson's action was meant only to cut off access to participants in the railroad dispute, the White House Police interpreted it as a permanent order. From that day on, we have been kept out of the EOB and its cafeteria, except when we have a special invitation and police clearance.* It is much easier for us to get into the White House itself than to get into the building across the street.

Johnson repeatedly demonstrated this need to be in constant control. For example, in early 1968 he held a meeting with then Senator Robert Kennedy, who had been considering running for the Democratic Party's nomination. The President had not taken himself out of the race at that time, and he was clearly irritated by Kennedy's implied threat to his own Presidency, as well as by the New York Senator's increasingly critical comments on the war in Vietnam. After the two men had met for about an hour in the Oval Office, Johnson walked into the lobby with Kennedy in tow. Both appeared agitated, but the President was clearly in charge. He introduced the Senator to us with a few bland words about how they had just enjoyed "a little chat," implying they had more or less settled their differences. Then he wheeled about and walked back toward the Oval Office, leaving Kennedy to face a pack of curious and determined reporters. We wanted to know everything that had transpired between the two, but Kennedy would tell us nothing. His face set grimly, he merely echoed the President's empty words and pushed his way out through the crowd of correspondents and camera crews.

Ever since his brother's election to the Presidency eight

---

*I have taken the matter up personally with press secretaries and others in the White House, but I have never directly approached any President, feeling that the Chief Executive should not have to be bothered with housekeeping problems of the press, except through the press secretary. But now I think the President should be forced to consider how our access has been limited since LBJ's time.

years earlier, I had found Robert Kennedy to be open and easily accessible. Thus, his strange behavior made it obvious that the New York Senator was on the verge of a complete break with Johnson's Vietnam policies. After a quick phone call to brief our Washington producer on the situation, I raced to our studio, where I did a short report on that evening's television news suggesting that the nation's two most powerful Democrats were unable to resolve their differences and appeared to be on the verge of a public split. Meanwhile, Kennedy returned to his own office on Capitol Hill, where within hours he made public his decided differences with Lyndon Johnson, which led him a short while later to announce his candidacy in the Democratic primaries.

Johnson's actions were fully consistent with his general attitude. Besides the everyday restraints on the press, very few high-level officials were permitted even to speak with us. They answered our questions only at the risk of facing LBJ's considerable wrath. Marvin Watson, one of Johnson's close aides and a fellow Texan who shared his paranoia about the press, was especially adept at contriving ways to harass and restrict reporters. He ordered that White House switchboard operators demand to know who was calling an Administration official (a task normally left to individual secretaries) and what subject would be discussed before a call could be connected. Answers were logged in and records carefully kept.

Johnson's fear of free-flowing information was so intense that Richard Nixon's Presidency came somewhat as a relief. In fact, despite Nixon's previous history of attacks on the media, relations between press and White House eased significantly during his first year in office.

Nixon even tried to improve our physical comfort. By the time he was sworn in, the West Wing lobby had evolved into a press room, where we worked, relaxed, ate and even slept in big overstuffed chairs and sofas. In the late 1950s, NBC had also successfully negotiated with White House press aides for a small storage closet just off the lobby. When NBC turned this closet into a radio broadcast booth, CBS persuaded officials to let us do the same thing with a public telephone booth. Eventually, ABC followed suit. But these minor improvements did not respond to new demands created by the expansion of the press corps, particularly with the growing importance of television.

When Nixon walked through on his first, informal inspection tour, he was horrified at the conditions under which the press corps was forced to work. (This was not the first time Richard Nixon showed concern for the physical welfare of journalists assigned to cover him. One of his earliest instructions to Ron Ziegler was to make sure the press got comfortable accommodations wherever they traveled—a very smart public-relations strategy.) Now the new President decided that the press needed a new press room.

Immediately an old problem resurfaced. Proximity to power is power itself; the closer, the more clout. Many new Presidential aides wanted offices in the White House, so Nixon considered confiscating our precious space and forcing us across the street into the Executive Office Building. This outraged bureau chiefs, who protested that it would place intolerable constraints on the already-difficult pursuit of information. Ziegler attempted to mollify us by suggesting a closed-circuit television system that would allow reporters to monitor the lobby entrance. Other solutions were discussed—among them, adding a few stories to the existing West Wing of the White House (rejected, as it would change everyone's image of the President's home and would thus antagonize voters), and digging down beneath the White House to add several sub-basement levels (rejected as too expensive, since the ground beneath the White House is solid rock).

Finally, President Nixon himself came up with the solution: he would give up the White House swimming pool, located along a corridor between the mansion* and offices

---

*"Mansion" is the word for the living quarters of the White House as opposed to the East and West Wings, which are working areas open to members of the staff.

in the West Wing, and turn it into a new press room. But this was not as simple as it sounded. For one thing, although Richard Nixon did not like to swim in the White House pool (he preferred the ocean at Key Biscayne or San Clemente), his predecessors had enjoyed the pool since its construction in 1933, and presumably, succeeding Presidents would also want to swim. Furthermore, John F. Kennedy had commissioned a painter to cover the walls with tropical scenes from the Virgin Islands.

It did not seem quite right to Nixon to destroy all this, so he ordered the pool and tiled floor around it covered over instead. A wooden floor was built above the pool, the muraled wall was knocked down and sent to the Kennedy Library in Boston, and the room was expanded. At the end nearest the mansion, some dog kennels and a flower shop were relocated, while a basement addition to the Press Room was dug next to the entrance to the underground heating room for the pool. While working on this basement, workmen discovered artifacts from past White House administrations, including pieces of pottery from several Presidential eras, one positively identified as a century-old plate from Benjamin Harrison's household.

According to Press Secretary Ziegler, the entire project cost $574,000. It was inaugurated, if that is not too pretentious a word, on April 2, 1970, and from a physical standpoint the improvements were tremendous. Instead of the crowded, stuffy and sometimes sweltering office of the Press Secretary, a fairly spacious room directly above the old pool was available for briefings. The room easily holds a hundred or more people, and live television cameras can be installed and activated on short notice.

Another obvious improvement was the increased work space made available to reporters. Each United States wire service received a glassed-in booth about the size of a bathroom. The three networks and Mutual Radio also have small private rooms, including broadcast studios of telephone-booth dimensions, which provide enough space for three reporters to sit at typewriters or telephones. The CBS News White House office, about twelve feet long and five five feet wide, has a waist-high shelf running along one side, on which are two typewriters, plus space for a radio tape recorder as well as for notebooks and newspapers. The shelves above that contain more notebooks, typing paper, a dictionary, briefcase, purses, books, makeup kits, old scripts, other reference material, and even a cadet's cap tossed at the Annapolis Naval Academy graduation in 1977 and captured by correspondent Lee Thornton. (She is a "squirrel" and can't bear to part with anything!) The radio broadcast studio at the opposite end from the doorway contains a typewriter and two microphones, as well as shelves loaded with more of the material described above. There are six telephones on the walls, and one or more of them is ringing most of the time. Most other major news organizations also have at least a desk with typewriter and telephone.

The new press area even provided a kind of recreation room, where several comfortable couches and chairs allow the easing of tired bodies. These are frequently used as temporary beds, since the hours of covering a President are often long, irregular and exhausting. This "rec" room also contains teletype machines from the AP and UPI. In one corner is a coffee-maker, next to the refrigerator where the "brown-baggers" and snackers keep their supplies.* The lunch table is round and thus perfectly suited for poker, although nowadays it is more often used for backgammon, bridge and gin rummy. Participants in these games are usually technicians and photographers. The days of the long poker sessions in the Press Room—when Harry Truman used to drop by for a hand—have almost disappeared. One of the more amusing events around the Press Room is to see a new White House Police officer amble in for a cup of coffee, spotting cards and money stacked all around the table. One technician even used to act as a bookie in the Press Room. But that technician's news organization went broke and so did his White House bookie business.

*The refrigerator was donated to the press corps by Naomi Nover, the widow of Barney Nover, a Washington correspondent for Colorado newspapers and radio stations.

Although equipment storage bins are provided for camera crews, the advent in the middle 1970s of electronic portable cameras and the necessity to be ready at a moment's notice for a breaking story, have brought most of the gear into the briefing room itself. The camera crews have also turned it into a playroom. Televion sets continually blare at opposite sides of the room, and card players dominate the center. Between them are scattered assorted piles of cameras and electronic gear. In fact the entire Press Room is messier now than when Richard Nixon ordered a new one.

In addition to improving our facilities, Nixon at first eased restrictions imposed by his predecessor. But the honeymoon ended when Vice-President Spiro Agnew began to assail the press over its criticism of the Nixon Administration's Vietnam policies. Furthermore, construction of a new press room had caused serious problems. The large West Lobby was converted into several smaller offices, and its entrance was rebuilt into a formal portico, complete with columns and a driveway resembling the front entrance to the White House mansion about seventy-five yards to the east. People on the President's published daily schedule, as well as those seeing his top aides, began to use this West Portico. Since we were confined to the new Press Room, we could no longer see and talk to them freely, unless we stood outside the portico all day. Through architectural transformations we had lost an important vantage point, and we have yet to regain it.

To add insult to injury, White House Police received orders that reporters must stay off the driveway near the portico. We were told to stand instead on the White House lawn, which in winter meant working in mud and snow or, in summer, relentless Washington heat and humidity.

White House visitors who wanted to talk to us now had to leave the driveway and walk onto the lawn. It was a ridiculous situation, but many important stories came out this way. For example, three Republicans—Senators Barry Goldwater and Howard Baker and Congressman John Rhodes—who had just visited Richard Nixon in August of 1974 told us they had informed the President that he would be impeached if he did not resign. This word came to the American public through our vigilant but uncomfortable driveway stakeout.

Probably the only important changes during the Ford Administration also involved lawns. One minor event was that Ford built himself a swimming pool on the lawn just south of the Oval Office, finally making it feasible to incorporate more permanent improvements in the press area over the old swimming pool. So far, however, no further renovations have been made.

A more significant change broke a long White House tradition. During the 1950s, television broadcasters had begun to do "stand-uppers" (or on-camera reports) facing the camera with the White House in the background. These could be filmed or taped across Pennsylvania Avenue in LaFayette Park, or on the Ellipse behind the White House. But the most convenient spot was just north of the Press Room, on the lawn in front of the West Wing. (This is about fifty yards away from the area of the lawn where we were forced to stand when the driveway became off limits.) Although it made no sense, reporters had to get special press office permission for each story, apparently on the unstated theory that stepping on this part of the White House lawn would harm the national interest. Each time permission was granted, someone from the press office had to give formal notice to the White House Police. This silly routine was repeated three or four times daily for at least fifteen years. Finally, President Ford's press secretary, Ron Nessen—himself a former White House television correspondent—persuaded the White House police to permit "stand-uppers" on the White House lawn at any time.

The same bad-weather problem, however, persists to this day. Rain or snow makes it almost impossible for a reporter to write in his notebook, and winter cold can cause a camera to malfunction. A few stories have even been missed because we gave in and retreated to the Press Room instead of keeping the outdoor vigil. White House visitors often refuse to stand in the wet or cold to talk with reporters. Those wise to the ways of Washington and desiring press attention schedule press conferences at a nearby hotel or other public place, indoors.

The Carter Administration further eased restrictions by instructing police to allow reporters to move closer to the West Portico, although not actually to the door itself. As a result, our shouts to departing visitors make it more awkward for them to avoid questions—although it is not impossible. The one man who persistently foiled our attempts to pump him was the late George Meany, who as AFL-CIO president, came to the White House frequently to meet with each President from Eisenhower to Carter. Meany would never talk to us afterward, except to grunt "No comment." This became increasingly frustrating, so sometimes we would follow him to his limousine, continuing to ask even though we knew he would never answer. We even shouted to him that as members of one of his own unions, AFTRA (the American Federation of Television and Radio Artists), we deserved to make a living just like other union members, and that, therefore, he should help us by answering our questions. But that never seemed to impress the tough old New York plumber.

Business and industrial executives are among the worst people to try to cover, because they normally attempt to avoid or ignore us. When the auto industry's top executives come in to see the President, for example, they almost always refuse to talk to us. I have tried to reach them by telephone after their visit, but I am always switched over to a public-relations officer who has not seen the President of the United States and therefore cannot answer my questions.

The President sometimes sees people who disagree with his policies, and the White House rarely provides such people with a road map to the Press Room. They are courteously and quietly ushered out. But some visitors want to find us. This group includes foreign envoys who understand the Western press and covet its attentions, as well as representatives of minorities and other interest groups who want the public to know what they have just said to the President. One frequent visitor to the White House who knows his way around and is not intimidated by the surroundings is the Reverend Jesse Jackson. Whenever he comes in to see the President, Jackson seeks out and talks to reporters. For example, early in 1980, after President Carter had revealed the outlines of his new "tight" budget, Jackson came to the White House to try to save some of the funds for minorities and the urban poor. Jackson ambled into the CBS booth to volunteer quite forcefully that if Carter cut back heavily on the federal aid to poor blacks, "we'll just have to take to the streets again!" It was not a threat, but a statement of fact as Jackson saw it, and he was not about to stand for protocol that might prevent him from talking to reporters wherever he could find them.

Unfortunately, such willing interviewees are rare around the White House. To add to our frustrations, news people are traditionally restricted to the general vicinity of the Press Room and press offices. We are not allowed to wander freely and knock on doors. In order to see anyone in the White House, a journalist must either make an appointment, or be escorted by an official. With all the police and Secret Service around, it is also impossible for anyone to enter the Cabinet Room or Oval Office without permission. However, that did happen once. In 1977 a White House visitor who had an appointment with a lower-level Carter aide got lost and wandered from the visitors' lobby into the Roosevelt Room, from whence it was but a short stroll acoss the hall to the Oval Office. The President was very startled to see a total stranger walk in, and the man was at least as surprised at this easy access to the Chief Executive. After a brief chat it was determined that the visitor had made an innocent mistake, and a red-faced Secret Service agent escorted him to his original appointment.

Our own dealings with security personnel are not always so friendly. The White House Police occasionally order me out of certain areas, and if I believe the matter to be sufficiently important, I refuse. The police then threaten me and my camera crew with arrest, and I order that our cameras be turned on the police. As a result, the officers back down and save face by demanding the names of those participating in the "disobedience." They then report us to the press office, which never does anything.

A typical example of this situation occurred at a meeting called in 1979 by President Carter to discuss the Soviet combat brigade in Cuba. Having first declared the Soviet brigade's presence in Cuba to be "unacceptable," Carter needed to explain his inability to force the Russians to withdraw. In the midst of this, Walter Cronkite called me to say that he had received a tip from a person who had been invited to serve on a group of special private advisers regarding Carter's self-imposed Cuba problem. Cronkite suggested that I phone around and find out whether such a group existed, and if so, who else was included. I phoned such obvious possibilities as Dean Rusk (who would not talk to me about it, and by his very reticence confirmed the group's existence and his presence in it), Clark Clifford, Henry Kissinger, William Scranton, and Sol Linowitz. When I got this far, a White House source confirmed that Clifford was to serve as chairman, and we put this story on the *Evening News* that night. Then I kept in contact with a few of the members and was told in advance when they were meeting with the President at the White House. Although this meeting was not on Carter's public schedule, we subsequently discovered a number of unfamiliar cars and limousines parked on West Executive Avenue. Now I had a problem. While we are allowed to come through the gate that leads into that private street, we are barred by the police from taking camera crews down there for interviews.

Assuming that the advisers would emerge from that private White House exit after their meeting, I stationed my camera crew within shouting distance up on the main driveway to the Northwest portico, while I walked up and down West Executive Avenue to wait for the visitors to leave. About an hour after they had gone inside, they suddenly appeared in a group. After a quick shout to the camera crew, I stopped Clifford, the chairman, and held him in conversation while camera crews and correspondents ran through the gate past a protesting policeman, and down the steps to the West Executive exit. There we managed to do a few brief interviews with Clifford and others, while an angry guard attempted to shoo us back to the normal press area. We ignored him until we had finished our work, then we headed back to where we supposedly belonged. He took down a number of names and threatened to report us to the press office. As usual, nothing further happened.

The fault for this ridiculous and recurring situation does not lie with the White House Police or the Secret Service. It lies directly with the Presidents and press secretaries who have refused to consider our access problems. The President obviously has a right to privacy. But just as obviously we have an obligation to dig out as much of the news as we can. Minor inconveniences and silly impediments—like scrambling on forbidden sidewalks after Clark and his colleagues—do not protect the President's privacy. They only make everyone feel a little foolish. We should be granted freedom of movement around those doors through which visitors regularly enter and leave. Playing cops-and-robbers on the White House grounds doesn't help anybody. And while Presidents and the press will always have their differences, a more rational system of handling them would benefit both sides—as well as the American public.

3

The Press Conference

One of the best ways to judge a President requires no special access, no network credentials and no White House press assignment. It is the live televised Presidential press conference—an avenue open to observation by everyone.

Short of an impeachment proceeding, these press conferences are the only times our Chief Executive must publicly explain and justify his perception of the nation's needs.

After watching many of these Presidential performances, I have devised a rough rating system. But before sharing my informal report card, I'd like to discuss how this political theater has evolved.

The press conference is entirely the creature of the President, who may use it for his own purposes or discard it altogether if he feels this will best serve his political interests. Still, the American people and the world at large have come to expect that the President of the United States will periodically expose himself and his policies to questioning by reporters under the close scrutiny of a watching public.

It was not always so. Few people realize that the press conference has no legal standing and only a relatively short tradition. During the first century of the republic, certain newspapers, editors and even correspondents had special relationships with various Presidents. It was not until Theodore Roosevelt spotted several reporters standing in the rain outside the White House gates, waiting for tidbits of news, that a formal Press Room was set up inside.* Woodrow Wilson initiated the first formal Presidential press conference on March 15, 1913, and held regular sessions with correspondents until America entered World War I. Then he abandoned the idea as too fraught with possibilities for slips that could affect the war or foreign affairs. At that time, journalists were not allowed to quote the President directly, a rule that was strictly enforced throughout the twenties and thirties. Unless he gave specific permission to quote him, the President was only to be paraphrased.

Although Presidents Harding, Coolidge and Hoover occasionally met with reporters *en masse*, none was particularly entranced with the press-conference format. It was left to Franklin D. Roosevelt to capitalize on its public-relations potential. He began regular semiweekly sessions in the Oval Office, where he would fence with journalists, chide them and even insult those he disliked. But Roosevelt also provided plenty of news, and what was more important, he offered the opportunity for the press to question him closely. Neither Roosevelt nor his successor Harry Truman, however, permitted direct quotations. No matter how lively the sessions, the rule remained the same: only indirect or paraphrased attributions to the President could be made. This permitted the President to deny any statement that caused trouble later on because he could always insist that he had been misinterpreted and misquoted.

While it had distinct advantages for the President, the no-quote rule had several disadvantages for the public. First, it forced reporters to inject some degree of personal interpretation between the Chief Executive and the nation. Good journalists tried faithfully to reflect the nuances of his words, but newspaper readers and radio listeners had to decide for themselves what the President had really said. (This reminds me of an incident years later, when reporters were trying to decipher the meanderings and musings of Republican Presidential candidate Barry

*See Chapter 2, "The Press Room."

Goldwater. During that 1964 campaign, an agitated Goldwater supporter admonished one journalist, "Don't write
what he says, write what he means.")

Second, the no-quote rule removed the "feel" of the
press conference. A President may have been trying to
conceal either the truth or his own uncertainty about
whether the truth would prove too harmful politically. But
when the words were cleansed and filtered through pa-
raphrases, his state of mind was hidden from the public—
unless, of course, a journalist reported that the President
stumbled, hesitated or jumbled his words.

Dwight D. Eisenhower, under the astute guidance of
Press Secretary and former *New York Times* reporter
James Hagerty, initiated the policy that press conference
answers could be quoted directly. By the time I arrived at
the White House in late 1957, radio microphones and television cameras were recording the entire press conference.
Yet neither the radio tape nor the television film could be
broadcast until Hagerty had cleared the transcript. Even
direct quotes had to be held while the Press Secretary
completed his checking. The process took about two hours
and essentially gave Hagerty the prerogative to purge the
record. Hagerty would "clear" the transcript without
scrutiny on stories that the White House wanted out immediately. For example, when Ike announced plans for a
summit conference with Soviet Premier Khrushchev and
explained what he perceived as the purpose of that meeting, we were allowed to quote the President without further clearance.

During the eight years Ike was in office, however, Hagerty made no transcript changes that had major domestic
or international implications. He rarely intervened, and
then only when the President's garbled syntax made his
sentences almost unreadable. While I admired and respected Hagerty for his restraint, on one occasion I was so
embarrassed for the President I secretly wished his Press
Secretary had been more aggressive.

In late 1958, the President appointed Admiral Lewis
Strauss as Secretary of Commerce. Strauss, a Jew, had

served as Chairman of the Atomic Energy Commission, and was a bright but difficult person. He did not suffer fools gladly and clearly believed many members of the United States Senate to be fools. Predictably, Strauss ran into trouble during his 1959 Senate confirmation hearings. As the confirmation struggle dragged on and became increasingly bitter, some Congressional Republicans began to accuse certain Democratic Senators of anti-Semitism in their opposition to Strauss. These accusations broke into the news on the morning of a Presidential press conference, so I decided to ask Eisenhower about them. Hagerty normally briefed the President on every subject that might conceivably come up. But this time, his system failed.

I stood up and Ike pointed at me, indicating that I was permitted to ask my question.

"Mr. President, do you agree with the charge of some of the Republican Congressmen that anti-Semitism may be a factor in Admiral Strauss's confirmation difficulties on Capitol Hill?"

"Well, I didn't know this charge emanated from Republicans. I will say this: If it is brought forward seriously, this is indeed tragic. We have here a man of the highest type of character, ability, devoted many years of his life to public service; and to see such a false charge thrown at him in order to belittle him or hurt him would be very, very sad, I think."

Both the puzzlement on Ike's face and his words showed that he did not understand either the question or the situation. Somehow the President had inferred that the Admiral was being charged with anti-Semitism! My first reaction was to try to straighten out the confusion. But on second thought, this seemed hopeless. It would have required too much explanation, placing the President in the role of a not very bright pupil, behind in his current-events homework. I sank slowly back into my seat while Ike moved on to the next question.

Hagerty could have changed the official transcript to save his boss, but that would have shown poor judgment and dishonesty. With or without the direct quote, report-

ers in the room could have recounted the story as it actually happened, and cleansing the record would have drawn
too much attention to the whole interchange.

Although in this case Ike's confusion was only a foot-
note in the day's news, significant—even history-mak-
ing—answers can emerge from such exchanges between
correspondent and President. During the 1960 Presidential campaign, Charles Mohr (then with *Time* magazine)
was curious about Ike's claim that the Republican candidate, Richard Nixon, had been a great help as Vice-President.

> One of the issues in this campaign [Mohr
> said] is seeming to turn on the question of Mr.
> Nixon's experience, and the Republicans to
> some extent almost want to claim that he has
> had a great deal of practice at being President.
> Now, I wonder if it would be fair to assume that
> what you mean is that he has been primarily an
> observer and not a participant in the Executive
> Branch of the Government. In other words,
> many people have been trying to get at the de-
> gree that he has—I don't want to use that word
> "participated"—but acted in important deci-
> sions, and it is hard to pin down.

The President was unhappy, squinting and wrinkling his
face in a manner that made him look more like the angry
general than the smiling, good-natured father figure the
public was used to seeing. He did not want to hurt Republican chances of retaining the White House, but he also
did not want to give Richard Nixon credit for his own
accomplishments with which Nixon had little or nothing
to do. So he replied:

> Well, it seems to me that there is some confu-
> sion here, haziness, that possibly needs a lot of
> clarification. I said he was not a part of decision-
> making. That has to be in the mind and heart of
> one man. All right. Every commander that I

have ever known or every leader, or every head
of a big organization, has needed and sought
consultative conference with his principal subor-
dinates. In this case, they are normally cabinet
officers. They include also such people as the
head of G.S.A. (General Services Administration), the Budget Bureau, and the Vice-President as one of the very top. So the Vice-President has participated for eight years, or seven
and one-half in all of the consultative meetings
that have been held. And he has never hesitated,
and if he had I would have been quite disappointed, he has never hesitated to express his
opinion in terms of recommendation as to decision. But no one, and no matter how many differences or whether they are all unanimous—no
one has the decisive power. There is no voting.

It was a long answer, but Ike wasn't finished yet.

It is just—you could take this body here, and
say, "Look, we are going to do something about
the streets down here, about parking around
here, you people." All right. Now, around the
White House, and so who is going to decide—I
am; not this body. So Mr. Nixon has taken a full
part in every principal discussion.

Mohr, a towering blond Nebraskan of Danish descent,
could be as stubborn as any Army general. Instead of sitting down dissatisfied, as most correspondents would have
done, he stayed on his feet. "We understand that the power of decision is entirely yours, Mr. President. I just wondered if you could give us an example of a major idea of
his that you had adopted in that role, as the decider and
final. . . ."
"If you give me a week, I might think of one. I don't
remember."
The President of the United States was saying that he
needed a week to think of one single contribution made by

his Vice-President during nearly a decade in office. Gleeful Democrats seized on the quote, and the apparent criticism of Nixon by the ever-popular Eisenhower may ultimately have had some influence on the outcome of the extraordinarily close 1960 election.

Such incidents are a continual reminder that reporters are needed at the White House. News emerges, not through the meticulous recording of everything a President plans to announce, but through his interaction—frequently adversarial—with men and women whose job is to dig for the news.

Perhaps with potential mistakes like the Nixon incident in mind, Eisenhower's Press Secretary Hagerty in the late 1950s rejected the suggestion of broadcasting press conferences live. "It's not that we want to censor any of his remarks," Hagerty argued. "What we are actually trying to do is prevent a human fluff that the communist propagandists can use to a good advantage."

Although Hagerty's explanation dated back to the accepted philosophy of the Wilson Administration, there was talk around the Press Room that this President simply could not express himself easily, that under tough questioning he sounded confused and distracted, and that he had a particular fear of television. In retrospect, I think this judgment a little harsh. Ike would have done as well as most Presidents in live press conferences, and his genial personality would have been a definite asset.

Shortly after the election of John F. Kennedy, the new Press Secretary, Pierre Salinger, approached me and a few other correspondents with the idea of a televised press conference. I endorsed it immediately, and almost as quickly referred Salinger to my bureau chief for further exploration of policy and technical considerations.*

---

*Bureau chiefs and other broadcast executives are extremely sensitive about such conversations between correspondents and government officials. For instance, network reporters are generally kept uninformed about negotiations over whether and when to broadcast a news conference or Presidential speech. This shields them from involvement in company-versus-government arguments that might compromise either their job or their reporting role.

Kennedy began to hold live-broadcast Presidential press conferences less than a week after his January 20, 1961, inauguration. More than four hundred reporters attended. CBS was assigned a seat in the second row on the right-hand side, facing the stage of the new State Department auditorium, which still smelled of the fresh cloth-covered seats. JFK stood on the stage, perhaps twenty feet from the front row. This was quite different from the old crowded Indian Treaty Room of the Executive Office Building, where President Eisenhower had held his press conferences. There I sat only about ten feet from the President, and directly in front of him. He could not avoid me when I rose to ask a question. But to get President Kennedy's attention in the new setting, I had to bob up and down until he glanced my way. Excitement was high at these early live-televised sessions, and there was heavy competition to be recognized.

Kennedy's live conferences were an instant success. He was completely at ease, and he clearly enjoyed the combative give-and-take, triumphing in the informal debates much more often than he lost. White House correspondents provided him with a challenge, a chance to match wits in public with not-unfriendly adversaries. Frequently I came away chuckling over some Presidential thrust or parry, but just as frequently found myself wondering what I, and the public, had really learned.

For example, five months after the Cuban Missile Crisis, Kennedy was asked the following: "Do you have any accurate information on the number of Russian troops that have been removed from Cuba? Are you satisfied with the rate of troop removal? And was there in the Russian *aide mémoire* any suggestion or provision for verification of troop removal?"

His smiling answer, so simple and disarming then, would be hard to get away with now.

"No."

That was the President's full response, and the official transcript confirms what we all remember so well. At his answer, the audience, packed with tough, hardened professional journalists, burst into laughter.

Kennedy's answer had, however, carried a kernel of

hard news: the President of the United States was admitting that he had no accurate information about Soviet troop removals and that he was dissatisfied with the rate of removal. He did not wish to elaborate, however, and he used his charm to avoid being asked to do so. The ploy was successful: the next questioner asked for Kennedy's impression of his own administration, and the President quite predictably approved of his own accomplishments and proposals.

Covering the White House can be intimidating, and the televised conferences made it even more frightening. A journalist probing at a President and his policies employs a powerful weapon, but it is a double-edged sword and, if wielded improperly, can be deflected to wound its user. The worst experience for a correspondent is to be turned aside either by a Presidential quip or have the President say, "I'm glad you asked me that." Furthermore, the President and his aides, news executives, colleagues, and the public are constantly searching the reporter's questions for signs of inaccuracy, bias or dishonesty (as well they should). Pressure is greatest when you stand up during a news conference, and for one intense moment the reporter and the President spar one-on-one.

Being on live television in prime time is not all that difficult for network correspondents. We've done it too many times. Nonetheless, the presence of a vast audience magnifies the significance of any possible errors in questioning or in commentary afterward, and I always feel a slight sickness in the stomach and a sweatiness of the palms and forehead.

After more than twenty years, I still go through a "psyching up" period, similar to that of a professional athlete before the big game. I read the morning newspapers and follow the news on radio and television, concentrating on the questions I will ask and the issues that could emerge at that day's conference. This means writing down a half dozen questions which the President should answer that day. I try to anticipate how each might be answered, phrasing the question carefully so the President cannot evade it. At the same time, questions must be designed to elicit genuine information or reactions of national importance. A reporter should not ask anything simply to further his or her own interests (as one correspondent did when he kept asking about Federal disaster relief for those, himself included, who had lost beach homes in a hurricane). And finally, the question cannot be so obscure or so simple as to risk making me look foolish or to waste my colleagues' and the public's limited press-conference time.

As the hour approaches, my concentration becomes more intense and I lose interest in mundane matters such as lunch or the fact that my car is suffering a terminal breakdown and the mechanic has telephoned to speak to me.

Sitting in that room waiting for the President to appear, I am acutely aware of the personal power and prestige of the office he holds. Journalists who have felt the angry heat of public opinion know that a nationally broadcast conference can easily become a confrontation in which they generally lose.

My uniform of the day, a bright tie, pale-colored shirt, and light suit, is consciously designed to attract the President's attention. This may sound superficial, but everybody except the wire-service reporters—who are automatically granted the first two questions—must fight to be recognized. After the wires finish their initial questions, the free-for-all begins. Since President Kennedy's first televised conference, my strategy hasn't changed: I take notes on what a President is saying, mentally crossing out my own questions as they are asked by others. At the same time, I listen for possible follow-ups; that is, queries in areas the President has evaded or only partially answered. Last and far from least, I carefully watch the President's eyes, so that when he finishes an answer I can leap to my feet and catch his attention. Audiences at home don't realize the complicated factors involved. For example, the President may ignore a correspondent whose recent stories he considers to be unfavorable or he may focus on a woman reporter he considers to be sexually attractive. Sometimes, tricks are useful. One of my favorites is the false start, whereby I blatantly move to stand up while the President is still speaking, catch his eye, and then jump to my feet the instant he finishes an answer.

It makes no sense to ask a question for the sake of asking a question, and one of my greatest concerns is that I might say or do something that will embarrass myself or my organization. Yet top network executives put heavy pressure on their correspondents to be recognized by the President. It is one of the criteria they use in judging how well their White House correspondents are doing. Their reasoning has more to do with show business than with news; it is an emphasis on visibility, not quality. But network news is always, to one degree or another, show business. Still, sometimes a reporter gets so anxious about gaining the President's attention that he can temporarily "black out." I have myself fought this tendency to sudden panic. One of the best reporters I know once fell victim to these pressures. Sitting in the front row—networks get the best reserved seats in the house—my colleague quickly got to his feet as the conference began, and the President soon called on him. Suddenly his mind went blank. We all sensed something was wrong, and with a nervous laugh the correspondent explained that he had forgotten what he meant to ask, and he sat down. The public, watching on television, probably thought it was funny. But I didn't. It could happen to me, and I doubt that my bosses would be very amused.

The stakes are also high at press conferences because they generate a high percentage of the White House news. Of course, the particular pattern depends largely on the personality of the President involved. Lyndon Johnson, for example, frequently initiated "impromptu" conferences in response to his own notorious aversion to unplanned leaks. One classic example occurred early in 1966, when Murray Marder of the *Washington Post* learned from his sources that the new American ambassador to Japan would be career diplomat U. Alexis Johnson. Since the host government must clear ambassadorial appointments before they can be officially announced, such premature leaks are not unusual.

Marder's story appeared on page 22 of the March 30, 1966, *Washington Post*. Poorly displayed as the report was, President Johnson read it and was furious. Later that day, during a Roosevelt Room briefing of reporters by Agriculture Secretary Orville Freeman on food aid to India, Johnson suddenly burst into the room. To startled reporters he angrily denied that he had decided on a new ambassador to Japan. Since Marder was not present, LBJ's anger seemed to be directed primarily at the *Post*'s Carroll Kilpatrick, a mild-mannered and gentlemanly Alabamian, who was as intelligent as Johnson, but quite opposite in personality. Pointing and jabbing with his finger, Johnson said that the *Washington Post* had printed a story that was wrong, and that he did not understand where they got such incorrect information or why they had printed it.

The more Johnson ranted at a man who had absolutely nothing to do with the story, the more we knew it must be true. His attitude was that until "yo' President" announces his decision, it has not been made. This response was not unique to Johnson. Decisions that appear in the press prior to formal Presidential announcement frustrate and anger all Oval Office occupants, occasionally inducing them to change some aspect of their decision, just to make the reporter appear wrong. But in this instance, Johnson was trapped. The name had already been submitted to the Japanese government, which soon signaled its approval. Recalling the name and starting the process all over again would have been complicated and embarrassing; so, instead, LBJ delayed the appointment for several months. When he had cooled down somewhat, it was duly announced.

Gradually, White House correspondents began to suspect that Johnson would even change decisions in order to avoid confirming leaks. The President and his aides stoutly denied such pettiness, but one day LBJ inadvertently confirmed that he might be capable of just such behavior. The

President was expressing to some reporters his dislike of the speculation (he strongly disliked all speculation) on who would replace Nicholas Katzenbach as Attorney General after Katzenbach had moved at the President's orders to the State Department, as Undersecretary. Suddenly Johnson glanced at me, and with some anger in his voice, declared, "When you see on the ticker that Oshkosh says that Bob Pierpoint may be Chairman of the Joint Chiefs of Staff, you don't necessarily need to give much credence to it, because the very fact that it is on there is the best indication that it is not likely to happen." From that time on, whenever a premature story on an appointment was published, we asked ourselves whether the "Oshkosh Rule" might be invoked, robbing the appointee of the job.

One time that the Oshkosh Rule was fortunately not applied involved Johnson's appointment to replace John McCone, head of the Central Intelligence Agency. By April of 1965 the post had been vacant for some months and I asked a friend who had been high up in the Kennedy and Johnson Administrations, whom Johnson might choose. As it happened, my friend knew. However, to protect himself, all he felt comfortable giving me were two clues, which didn't help me very much: "He's a retired admiral," my source said, "and his nickname is 'Red.' " I knew few retired admirals, either personally or by reputation, and none nicknamed "Red." So I waited and hoped. The second weekend in April President Johnson was, as usual, at the LBJ Ranch, and we White House correspondents, also as usual, drove from Austin to Johnson City to watch him go in and out of church. He had some guests along and after the service, as happened frequently, he took them to his boyhood home to display what we irreverently called "the shrine." As the press corps stood outside the fenced yard, we tried to identify some of the guests. Suddenly I heard Bill Lawrence of ABC say, "Why, I know that guy. That's Admiral Raborn, 'Red' Raborn, I play golf with him at Burning Tree."

As unobtrusively as possible, I told my radio technician to come with me, and we headed for the nearest pay telephone. A quick call to my friend in Washington confirmed my conclusion: the President was about to name Admiral "Red" Raborn to head the CIA. "You've got it, that's the guy," my friend said. So I went ahead with the story, calling New York to set up a radio broadcast over the phone line for the next hourly news report. In those days the only Sunday television news was late at night, and because I suspected that LBJ would announce his appointment before then, or that someone else might figure it out, I wanted to get on the air with it as soon as possible. (One almost unbreakable rule in journalism is "Never sit on an exclusive story or you'll see someone else publish it.") I then rejoined the press corps, and not wanting my beat (journalistic slang for what used to be called a "scoop") to go unnoticed by my colleagues, suggested to several that they listen to the next CBS hourly news. They did, but so did someone else—Lyndon Johnson!

As I soon learned, the President exploded in fury at almost everyone around the LBJ Ranch. This, after all, was a somewhat more serious leak than most, since it involved the appointment of the highest intelligence agent in the country. Press Secretary George Reedy, fortunately for him, was not in Texas that weekend, so most of the President's wrath was directed at another White House aide, Jack Valenti. Johnson had apparently seen me speaking to Valenti outside church that morning and accused him of leaking the story. Valenti was completely innocent, but Johnson was in no mood to listen. He even ordered a Secret Service agent to take away my White House pass.

The President stormed off to a nearby schoolhouse, where he was scheduled to sign the first bill providing federal aid to education. (He had attended the small frame elementary school as a child.) I was already there, basking in congratulations from my colleagues, and nervously trying to convince some of the more skeptical, such as ABC's Bill Lawrence, that my surmise was correct. Suddenly President Johnson arrived on the scene, looking like a black cloud about to loose a bolt of lightning. I had a suspicion whom he wanted to strike. The bill-signing ceremony was more abrupt than usual, after which LBJ strolled over to the roped-off press area, followed by several White House aides, Admiral Raborn, and a man I could not immediately identify. But Lawrence could, and did; he was Richard Helms, the Acting Deputy Director of the CIA, formerly in charge of the Agency's plans and operations, and a fairly well-known career intelligence officer.

With what I interpreted as a malevolent stare in my direction, Johnson began a long introduction praising the career of Helms. I felt queasy, and the sweat on my forehead was not just from the Texas afternoon sun. The President's tribute to Helms continued for minutes that seemed like hours to me, concluding with the announcement that Helms was being named "Permanent Deputy Director of the CIA." The President added one more abrupt sentence, to the effect that he was naming Admiral "Red" Raborn to head the organization; then he strode off to his limousine, trailed by a string of unhappy aides and the pleased but somewhat puzzled new CIA Director. I breathed freely for the first time in some minutes, thinking that the S.O.B. had deliberately put me through hell.

A moment later Valenti dashed over and grabbed my arm. Frantically, he demanded why I had "fingered" him for leaking the story on Raborn. Startled, I explained as calmly as I could that I had done no such thing. The Presidential aide, in a state of near-panic, said that Johnson had implied that I had actually named Valenti as my source. I felt sorry about Valenti's awkward position and explained that my source would remain secret, which seemed to satisfy Valenti. In the meantime, Secret Service Agent Arthur Godfrey (no relative of the broadcaster) informed me very soberly that he had been ordered by the President to lift my credentials. Then Godfrey grinned and told me that the President had "blown sky high" when he heard my broadcast about Raborn's appointment on an Austin radio station. Godfrey did not intend to take away my White House pass. The President often gave such orders in a fit of rage, always rescinding them later. Johnson himself never mentioned the incident to me, although I heard that he discussed it with his staff for some time afterward.

Despite his difficulties with the press, Richard Nixon continued the pattern of Presidential control over press conferences. Little hard news emerged that he did not want to reveal. However, a different side of his political personality gradually revealed itself.

A classic example occurred in the spring of 1971. The Nixons were enjoying an Easter vacation at their San Clemente home when a military tribunal, convened at Fort Benning, Georgia, convicted Lieutenant William Calley of multiple murder. His fellow officers, all of whom served in Vietnam, found Calley guilty of the premeditated killings of at least twenty-two Vietnamese children, women and old men in the village of My Lai. The verdict rocked a nation already torn by the mounting tragedies of the Vietnam war. Richard Nixon, sensing that his natural political constituency of conservatives might rally around Calley, ordered that the young lieutenant be freed from prison and permitted to live in his private apartment at Fort Benning while an appeal, publicly backed by the President himself, worked its way through the military courts and up to a final review by Nixon.

Three weeks later, after his return to Washington, Nixon tried to justify this unusual intervention in a murder case. In a press conference, televised live across the country on May 3, ABC's Tom Jarriel asked, "Mr. President, you have said that you intervened in the Calley case in the national interest. I wonder if you could define for us in greater detail how you feel the court-martial verdict endangered the national interest and how you feel it was served by your intervention in the case?"

"Well, Mr. Jarriel," he answered, "to comment about the Calley case, on its merits, at a time when it is up for appeal would not be a proper thing for me to do. Because as you know, I have indicated that I would review the case at an appropriate time in my capacity of final reviewing officer.

"In my view, my intervention in the Calley case was proper for two reasons: one, because I felt that Captain Calley should not be sent to Leavenworth Prison while waiting for the months and maybe a year or so that appeal would take. I thought that he should be confined to quarters. I think that was proper to do in view of the fact that under civil cases where we have criminal cases we grant the right of bail to people that are charged with crimes."

Nixon didn't seem to notice that he had given Calley the wrong rank, and continued: "Second, I felt that it was proper for me to indicate that I would review the case because there was great concern expressed throughout the country as to whether or not this was a case involving, as it did, so many complex factors in which Captain Calley was going to get a fair trial.

"I believe that the system of military justice is a fair system. But as part of that system is the right of the President to review; I am exercising that right. And I think that reassured the country and that is one of the reasons that the country has cooled down on this case. I will review it."

The President's claim that "we grant the right of bail to people that have been charged with crimes" startled me. I knew of no case where convicted murderers had been let out on bail, and I knew of one very prominent case just two months earlier where no responsible judge would have allowed it—the conviction of Charles Manson and his followers for the murders of actress Sharon Tate and six other people in California. It seemed to me that Richard Nixon was distorting the law and deliberately misleading those watching his press conference, in order to justify his political efforts on behalf of Lieutenant Calley. But how does one get such a message across? I decided to put it in the form of a question:

"If I may follow up with a question on Lieutenant Calley? I am not a lawyer, but I inferred from what you said that in this country men who are convicted of multiple murders get out on bail. Is that actually the case, and if so, would you recommend that someone like Manson be out on bail, as you seem to imply that Lieutenant Calley should be?"

I had acted quickly with a follow-through question, and relying more on instinct than on knowledge—a dangerous but occasionally necessary strategy for a press conference. For all I knew, some courts might indeed have granted bail to convicted murderers, and lawyer Richard Nixon would be able to demolish my implied argument. (Lawyers familiar with both the Calley case and laws relating to bail later told me that bail—although an important constitutional protection in our judicial system—is rarely granted for anyone convicted of, as Calley was, mass murder.)

The President looked nervous and irritated; I had clearly made a valid point. He answered almost reluctantly:

"No. I am not going into the specific laws of each state, and they do vary, of course, and you, even not being a lawyer, would know that they vary according to every state—and some states are much more strict than others where capital crimes are concerned—there are many states that do not allow any bail at all if they feel that the individual is one who is a danger to society."

Perspiration broke out on Mr. Nixon's upper lip, as it frequently did when he was under pressure.

"What I am simply saying is this: That the real test for granting a bail in any case is whether or not the individual concerned is considered by the judge to be one who will be a danger to society. Now Captain Calley, let me point out—he's not getting out on bail in the usual sense. He is confined to quarters on the base. He is, therefore, not free in the sense somebody getting out on bail is. I am simply saying that I feel that a man who has a long process of appeal ahead of him, and who is going to be confined to quarters in any event, that this was the right thing to do under the circumstances."

The viewing audience probably didn't understand the risk of incurring Presidential wrath and subsequent retribution. If my question had been poorly phrased, the President could have ridiculed me, which would be particularly embarrassing for someone in a profession where clear articulation is supposed to go with the job. There was also the possibility that news executives watching the broadcast would not approve of my question or of the manner in which I had asked it, and that could provide other unpleasant consequences. Finally, there is the risk of the audience's reaction. Americans do not like to see their President put in an embarrassing position. Although the nation has no monarch, many Americans like to treat Presidents as if they were royalty.

Even more important than my personal role, however, was the mirror in which the Calley case permitted America to see its Vietnam involvement. Richard Nixon, the President of the United States, was granting to the murderer of defenseless Vietnamese civilians precisely the special treatment he abhorred for those who committed similar crimes at home.

Another point must be emphasized. In print, my question may look somewhat unfair. Nixon wasn't really advocating bail for Calley; civilian life has no equivalent to "confinement to quarters," so the analogy to Manson was strained. But the President's tense facial expressions and tone of voice strongly suggested that he knew he was distorting the law and the truth to satisfy his own political needs. In the case of such exchanges, the written record offers only a partial view. For this reason, historians and future generations must turn to the filmed record and to eyewitness accounts when attempting to interpret these events.

Another press-conference situation involved a minor incident that reflected a major conflict. On October 26, 1973, as Watergate pressures mounted, Mr. Nixon lashed out at what he called "outrageous, vicious, distorted, frantic, hysterical" reporting by television news. "I am not," he added with a typical twist, "blaming anyone for that."

As I sat stunned at this wholly unexpected emotional outburst, I tried to fathom exactly what television coverage or which television reporter might have aroused such anger. I suspected that he was especially incensed over a story ABC's Bill Gill had put on the air a few days earlier, which had implied that evidence existed in Key Biscayne,

Florida, of some special Presidential "slush fund" being held by Charles "Bebe" Rebozo's bank. In damning all television coverage indiscriminately, Nixon was hurting innocent people, and I believed that if he had accusations he should be more specific. As in the case of the Calley question, I acted instinctively.

As I stood before the Presidential seal on his podium, I sensed the tension within Richard Nixon and concluded that he might be pushed to reveal another side of himself.

Courteously, I noted that he seemed to be angry. "Mr. President, you have lambasted the television networks pretty well. Could I ask you, at the risk of reopening an obvious wound, you say after you have put on a lot of heat that you don't blame anyone. I find that a little puzzling. What is it about the television coverage of you in these past weeks and months that has so aroused your anger?"

He replied curtly, "Don't get the impression that you arouse my anger." The official transcript shows laughter from my colleagues—but to my ears it sounded like a collective sigh.

Still on my feet, I broke with regular protocol and continued. "I'm afraid, sir, that I have that impression." Again, the transcript shows laughter, but again, it was much more an expression of nervous concern.

"You see," the President replied, looking right at me, "one can only be angry with those he respects." His tone was sarcastic: he obviously intended to insult us. The room erupted in sounds of shock and dismay.

Astounded by the quiet ferocity of his attack, I sat down. Nixon seemed to realize that he had betrayed more than he had intended. Seconds later, he broke off from another questioner to turn back to me with an explanation: "Let me say, too, I didn't want to leave an impression with my good friend from CBS over here that I don't respect the reporters. What I was simply saying was this: that when a commentator takes a bit of news and then, with knowledge of what the facts are, distorts it, viciously, I have no respect for that individual."

Initially, I did not take his remark personally, and later that night, I asked my wife if by chance the White House had called. I half expected the President to apologize and I later learned that Julie and David Eisenhower told him that he had made a mistake. However, members of the White House staff eventually explained that his remark was in fact deliberately directed at me. Nixon was furious about a mini-series of three Cronkite *Evening News* broadcasts I had done with Producer Ed Fouhy describing how Rebozo had used his friendship with the President to enrich himself.* Our investigation, which stretched out over eleven months, had not unearthed any illegal activities on Rebozo's part, but had made it clear that he was engaging in some questionable banking practices as well as playing his well-publicized Presidential friendship for all it was worth. Nixon, a White House aide told me, saw nothing wrong with Rebozo's behavior, and he bitterly resented our reports.

Such tense confrontations were not unusual during the Nixon years. Most visible and acrimonious were the run-ins between the President and my CBS News colleague, Dan Rather. As reports on Watergate made Mr. Nixon's position increasingly vulnerable, these confrontations took on added importance. Both men were clever, tough and aggressive, both knew how much was at stake, and viewers knew that every time Rather stood up the situation was explosive. While the President had reason to fear that Rather might hit an exposed nerve, Rather had to cope with the deep-rooted feeling of most Americans that their President, whoever he is, is always good and wise.

The managers and owners of many CBS affiliate stations around the nation complained that our attitude was causing problems with local advertisers, who thought we were too consistently antagonistic. This made network executives nervous, and anti-Pierpoint, anti-Rather pressure within CBS management mounted. The affiliates' dissatisfaction could not be judged; in the long run, networks

*See Chapter 9, "Anatomy of an Award."

cannot operate without their affiliates, which are free to join a competing network. To their credit, CBS executives shielded us from the complaints. But we knew what was happening. For one thing, there was Vice-President Spiro Agnew's energetic attack on the networks, which began in the fall of 1970 with a speech to the National Association of Broadcasters in Des Moines. In this speech, actually written by Nixon's own speechwriter, Patrick Buchanan, with the full approval of the President, Agnew charged network news organizations with conspiracy against the Vietnam war. Many NAB members, businessmen who were hostile toward the press in general, agreed.

What followed was a well-orchestrated campaign that focused attention and pressure on the network correspondents covering the White House. Periodic newspaper stories brought to our attention the fact that the White House had contacted CBS Chairman William Paley and News Division President Richard Salant to complain about CBS News coverage of the war and the President.

But by far the most direct pressure came from the affiliates themselves. In those days, whenever the President traveled around the country, the network channeled coverage of his activities through the most convenient local television station, usually an affiliate.* During such out-of-town "feeds," the correspondent and the producer often encountered affiliate executives who were unhappy with CBS News coverage of the Nixon Presidency. Local newsroom personnel generally posed no problem, but higher executives such as the station manager would occasionally suggest—not without anger—that the station might not cooperate in feeding the story to the network. While I do not believe we ever missed airing a broadcast this way, several times I sweated over engineering delays that could have been deliberate disruptions. One station official in Montana told me in 1973 that he and his business friends

---

*Technological developments since then, particularly the change-over from film to electronic tape, have circumvented this procedure. Now most television stories can be assembled and fed into the network news program directly from a local telephone company relay station, or even a hotel room.

were actively working to get rid of Rather. He refrained from saying they were also trying to eliminate me from the White House beat, but that was a safe assumption.

It was in this atmosphere that a particularly provocative press conference occurred.

The date was March 19, 1974; the location was Houston, Texas; and the scene was the annual convention of the National Association of Broadcasters, the same conservative group of radio and television station owners, executives and salesmen addressed by Agnew four years earlier.

Dan Rather, Tom Brokaw of NBC, and Tom Jarriel of ABC were asked to sit on a panel that would question the President. Knowing that many members of the audience believed that the press was unfairly persecuting Nixon, Rather indicated to me that he was somewhat hesitant about his role, fearing that the President would use him as a foil. But Dan had little choice, although he was clearly nervous that this time the conversation could become personal.

After the easy "softball" questions served up by local stations' news executives, Rather rose and was greeted by the audience with a mixture of applause and boos. In his book, *The Camera Never Blinks,* Rather writes that he heard only the applause, which may also have been true of the President. Here, in any case, is the official transcript of what was said:

RATHER:	"Thank you, Mr. President. Dan Rather, CBS News. Mr. President. . . ." (Applause, mixed with jeers.)
THE PRESIDENT:	"Are you running for something?"
RATHER:	"No, sir, Mr. President. Are you?"

Watching on a television monitor in the Press Room, I could see the President's face much more clearly than could Rather, who stood about twenty-five feet from Mr. Nixon. The President looked tense, perhaps even more so than Rather. I'm convinced that in his awkward way, Nixon was attempting to ease a difficult situation with a joke. But Rather had misunderstood, apparently feeling he had been challenged, and he had quickly lashed back.

This public exchange, brief as it was, hurt both men. Some members of the audience may have agreed with Rather that the President was taunting him for having done his job only too well in recent months. On the other hand, Rather had addressed the President of the United States with a rude and unprofessional remark that belied his usual cool. His mistake provided an opening for his enemies.

In any case, five months later, and only five days after Richard Nixon resigned from office, CBS removed Rather and myself from the White House assignment. No one at the network explained, either then or subsequently, why this decision was made. If anyone at CBS was unhappy with our performances, no one ever said so. But it is fairly clear why they waited until after Nixon's resignation: to have acted earlier would have made it appear that CBS was caving in to White House pressure.

CBS News executives in New York delivered the news to Rather, and in Washington, bureau chief Sanford Socolow called me to suggest lunch. We met at the International Club, in a shiny new building on the corner of Nineteenth and K streets. Socolow is one of my oldest friends, and I knew he was tense. Skipping the usual banter, he came straight to the point: "How would you like to cover the Pentagon?"

Startled, I replied that I would not.

"What would you like to cover?" Socolow asked. "You're being taken off the White House."

I was shocked and angry. I pressed Socolow as to why I was being removed at this particular time, and he simply insisted that I was being reassigned. His instructions clearly came from higher up. I vividly remember my reaction: If so ordered, I will report to the Pentagon, but only long enough to find a new job.

As news leaked that both Rather and I had been removed, circumstances changed. The print media and some of our broadcast colleagues roundly criticized CBS News, and several weeks later word came from New York that Rather and I had been successful in our efforts to maintain our professional reputations. He was promoted to a bigger job at a higher salary in New York and I was allowed to stay at the White House (I had actually never left) so long as I agreed to the terms of a new contact. With two children in college, I deemed it wise to sign. Besides, I was curious about what sort of President Gerald Ford would turn out to be. Shortly after signing the new contract, I was demoted to the third position at the White House, behind correspondents Bob Schieffer and Phil Jones, newly assigned to the beat.

Press-conference formats under Ford largely reflected the decisions of his Press Secretary, former NBC White House correspondent Ron Nessen. For one thing, Nessen institutionalized the so-called "follow-up" question. President Ford, Nessen announced, would permit each reporter one follow-up after his or her initial question. This system worked quite smoothly and was continued by President Carter.

Another of Nessen's innovations succeeded brilliantly and should be revived on occasion. During some of the press conferences that President Ford held outside Washington, Nessen devised a method of mixing the questions from White House correspondents and local reporters, assuring each a fair chance. A day or two before the scheduled conference, one list would appear in the White House Press Room and another in some place convenient to the out-of-town reporters. Any White House correspondent who wished to ask a question of the President could sign up. The question or topic was not listed, just the individual's name, and that of his organization.

The day of the conference, the names of about fifteen from each group would be drawn from a hat. The order of withdrawal became the order of press-conference questioning, and the reporters lined up behind two microphones. The President alternated, recognizing first a local reporter, then a White House regular, moving down the line as time permitted.

The new system had the advantage of being orderly, allowing the questioners to concentrate on their interrogation, and permitting other journalists to focus more attentively on the exchanges. The main disadvantage was that press conferences became more haphazard than before, with absolutely no follow-up questions beyond that of the original questioner. But this was a minor problem compared with elimination of the jack-in-the-box jumping, arm-waving and raucous shouting that usually mark sessions with recent presidents. On March 6, 1981, President Reagan tried the lottery system, despite the vehement protests of some White House correspondents (particularly from the networks, which insist that their reporters try to ask questions and be seen on the screen). The new President was carrying out an experiment suggested by a commission set up by the White Burkett Miller Center of Public Affairs at the University of Virginia on ways to improve communication between presidents and the public. Having been a member of that commission, I admit to some bias, but I thought the lottery press conference worked fairly well. It was certainly more orderly than some in the past, and the President could not simply call on his favorite people. On the other hand, it lacked spontaneity and focus, since many reporters asked questions they had decided on beforehand, without reference to what President Reagan was saying. However, that defect is not limited to lottery-style press conferences! Most such sessions lack real focus.

President Carter, who was probably the best at handling press conferences since JFK, added still another wrinkle. On his way out of the room after the session was over, he would stop and talk with reporters, primarily about personal matters, such as where he and the family planned to spend Christmas or summer vacation. Sometimes he would also let drop a word or two of truly national importance. The networks normally switched back to their studios for summary and commentary immediately after the last answer. But Carter—intentionally or through simple informality—forced them to change.

Whichever network was the pool—that is, covered the conference and fed it into all three network systems—instructed its camera and sound technicians to keep their equipment focused on the President while he remained in the room. This way, the audience caught some spontaneous personal glimpses of Carter. Eventually, however, the President became cautious, hurrying from the room and disappearing without the customary chats. This was unfortunate and perhaps misguided, since the personal asides had added a pleasant human note after the formality of the conference.

Carter, like Nixon, was highly reluctant to conduct press conferences. What makes this astonishing is that whenever Mr. Carter did hold a press conference, most correspondents agree, he did very well. He adhered to his policies and defended them with vigor and conviction. His facts were accurate, and he was exceptionally precise with details.

While first campaigning for the Oval Office, Carter seemed to sense this strength, and promised to hold conferences at least every two weeks. He kept his word for the first two years. But when his standing in the polls plummeted and the Washington press corps became critical, his confidence apparently faded. During the crucial summer of 1979—after United Nations Ambassador Andrew Young resigned, following the President's seemingly self-imposed crisis over Soviet troops in Cuba, and when Senator Edward M. Kennedy had made clear his intention to seek the Democratic nomination—Carter let more than two months elapse before holding a press conference. Intense pressure built up as the Presidential silence continued, and when Carter finally broke this silence, I felt very strongly that this would be an important press conference.

As usual, I had prepared about a half-dozen questions and was seated in the front row, at one end of the room. A few rows behind me were a number of what we call "the zanies," individuals with strong opinions, which they invariably hope to express on national television.* Their

*See Chapter 1, "The White House Press."

usual strategy is to shout raucously at the President, hoping that he will be forced to recognize them.

Sometimes this ploy works, but on this occasion President Carter seemed determined to ignore them. The more obvious this became, the louder they shouted. In the meantime, I had not been able to get him to call on me, probably because he was carefully avoiding my part of the room. But toward the end of the session, as I stood yet again to catch his attention, he turned to me and nodded.

The din behind me, however, became so ear-splitting that I could not even begin my question. One of the zanies kept shouting his question even though everyone in the room knew that President Carter had recognized me. Frustrated and angry, I turned around, fully intending to tell him—despite the national television audience—to shut up. Apparently, however, my outraged expression was enough, because he broke off in midsentence. I thanked him sarcastically and turned back to the President, who, in the meantime, had realized what was happening and started to laugh. The television audience never knew why the President appeared so amused, since the camera remained on him and not on the incident.

The zanie's behavior that day convinced me that the format for press conferences—which are, after all, an outsider's only opportunity to question the nation's leader— must be dramatically changed. However, not everybody agrees on what should be done. One faction maintains that press conferences, particularly in their televised versions, simply are not the best vehicle for obtaining information. "The necessary thing is to provide an adversary whose questions the President must answer and whose analysis of situations and proposals for policy the President must consider. With all due respect to reporters in press conferences, they are incapable of performing this function," writes political scientist Charles Hardin.*

Some, myself included, disagree. In *The Twilight of the Presidency*, former LBJ Press Secretary George Reedy writes that "of all the few social institutions which tend to

Presidential Power and Accountability (Chicago: University of Chicago Press, 1974).

keep a President in touch with reality, the most effective—and the most resented by the chief beneficiary—is the press. It is the only force to enter the White House from the outside world with a direct impact upon the man in the oval room which cannot be softened by intermediary interpreters or deflected by sympathetic attendants."

Both Hardin and Reedy, however, have given up on the press conference as an institution that can be counted on to provide information and Presidential accountability; they prefer the interpellation or question time of the parliamentary system, in which the prime minister and his cabinet must regularly answer questions posed by other members of the legislature—usually representatives of opposition parties—forcing a prime minister to explain and defend his policies. The public thus has an opportunity to learn about and influence the workings of its democracy.

This may have merit in theory, but I see absolutely no prospect for the constitutional changes in executive-legislative relationships that would be required for a parliamentary question time. Therefore, the only option is to leave the press with responsibility for improving Presidential accountability through an improved press conference.

Numerous procedures have been proposed for reform of this all-important institutional tradition. President Carter wisely retained the Ford Administration's initiative that permits one follow-up question. Certain crucial conferences could be limited to a single broad subject, and the current jumping match to attract the President's attention might be replaced with something more orderly.

Two important obstacles block reform. The press itself is fiercely competitive and bound by tradition—and perhaps even by antitrust laws—not to agree upon a common line of questioning. After all, we do represent competing news organizations and networks. Our only cooperative association, the W.H.C.A., has little real power. Most of my colleagues prefer it that way, and efforts to organize more formally always fail. On September 12, 1970, for example, thirty White House correspondents met to discuss two basic issues: how to convince the President to hold more regular sessions with the press, and how to encourage more follow-up questions on a single subject. It had been over two months since President Nixon had held a press conference, even though his communications director, Herb Klein, had promised shortly after the inauguration that Nixon would meet with reporters every few weeks.

Despite a 1968 campaign pledge to end the war in Vietnam, Nixon had ordered the invasion of Cambodia and then refused to discuss it. We had numerous questions to ask. One would expect that the White House correspondents—men and women not known for their lack of aggressiveness—would do something decisive at the meeting. Such was not the case; they merely concluded, quite predictably, that the President should hold more conferences and that reporters should ask more follow-up questions—conclusions both unenforceable and totally meaningless.

The second obstacle to reform is the President's absolute control over press conferences: how often they occur, when and where they are held, whether questioning can be limited to a specific subject or subjects, and most important of all, whether he wants to be responsive to questions. Presidential behavior can be bitterly frustrating to the press and the public, but there is little we can actually do about it.

This was particularly true during the Nixon Presidency. *New York Times* reporter Hedrick Smith, one of the most respected members of his profession, wrote a bitingly critical article in *Atlantic Monthly* on the May 8, 1970, press conference.

> The nation was in agony [Smith wrote]. The campuses were aflame. The stock market was plummeting. Secretary of Interior Walter Hickel's letter of distress to President Nixon had exposed a split high within the Administration. Members of Congress, angered at not having been consulted about sending U.S. troops into Cambodia, were rising to challenge or limit the President's war-making powers. Within hours, the White House itself would face a siege of protesters.
>
> Rarely has a news conference promised so

much but, alas, produced so little. That session
in the East Room was a pale shadow of the passion and trauma in the nation. It was as real-life
as a minuet, as illuminating as a multiplication
table. President Nixon held the assembled reporters at bay as easily as Cassius Clay dabbling
with a clutch of welterweights.

Smith went on to charge that "the cream of the Washington press corps are viewed by many young skeptics as
lapdogs rather than watchdogs."

Most participants in the press conference shared his
frustrations. Yet there was nothing wrong with most of the
questions asked that day, or on similar occasions. We
asked the President point blank about contradictions in his
statements on Vietnamization, about his scathing comments on college students, about whether he had influence
over South Vietnamese troops in Cambodia, and about
why South Vietnamese President Thieu had a different
version of what the Cambodian venture meant. None of
these questions was easy, but Mr. Nixon had, as usual,
prepared well. Our job was not to reflect passion and trauma. It was to get the facts. And if the President didn't
want to provide them, then it was incumbent upon us to
expose his reticence to the nation.

The ideal way to improve press conferences and Presidential accountability is to mobilize public opinion for frequent regular gatherings. Presidential candidates should
be put on the record with firm pledges to hold live broadcast sessions at specified intervals. If such a pledge is later
broken, both the President and the public should be constantly and forcefully reminded of this breach. Congress
can help to enforce the pledge, perhaps passing a resolution to express its disapproval, should Presidential silence
continue. Reporters and opposition party members could
also query members of the President's own party about his
failure to answer questions.

The isolation of the Oval Office and the sycophancy of
those who work in the White House can best be combatted

through regular exposure to energetic adversaries whose commitment is to facts and the news, not to the President and his policies.

It was no accident that the President who had the greatest difficulty governing honestly was the President with the least respect for and contact with the press.

"Well, he doesn't get very good questions at press conferences," Nixon aide John Ehrlichman once complained. "Newsmen are sort of like insecure young ladies, and they keep asking us if we love them."

In the lighthearted spirit so evident in Ehrlichman's misunderstanding of us, I'd like to offer my Presidential Report Card. Although highly subjective, it is based on nearly a quarter century of close contact by a group of distinguished journalists, with the several Presidents at exceptionally exposed and volatile moments.

PRESS CONFERENCE RATINGS: 1 TO 10

	DDE	JFK	LBJ	RMN	GRF	JEC
Candor	8	5	2	5	7	8
Informative Value	7	6	3	6	5	7
Combative Skill	4	9	6	8	4	6
Humor	3	9	4	4	6	7
Total Overall	22	29	14	23	22	28

The veteran President-watchers who participated in this joint assessment of the qualities of the six most recent Chief Executives included John Chancellor of NBC, Frank Reynolds of ABC, Don Irwin of the *Los Angeles Times,* James Deakin of the *St. Louis Post-Dispatch,*

Charles Roberts (formerly of *Newsweek* and now with the National Wildlife Foundation), Ray Scherer (long-time White House correspondent for NBC and now a Washington executive with RCA) and myself. The individual ratings, based on a scale of 1 to 10, were then averaged, producing this report card. From the journalists' point of view, John F. Kennedy was clearly at the head of his class, followed closely by Jimmy Carter, while Lyndon Johnson came close to failing.

4

The Press and the Presidents

John F. Kennedy once said that the White House is not a good place to make new friends. But JFK had friends among the press corps before he went to the White House, and he maintained most of them while he was President. This was not unusual. Presidents generally acquire at least a few journalist friends during their climb up the political ladder, and although it is not always easy to retain these relationships in the Oval Office, they try. But most reporters assigned to the White House—no matter what their own popularity or professional prestige—are not personally close to the President. The system simply does not encourage such friendships. Instead, the nearly daily contact forms a tenuous link whose components are physical proximity, shared experience (especially in time of crisis), shared scenery while traveling, and shared disillusionment at failure to achieve the nation's domestic and international goals.

I covered President Eisenhower for more than three years, often wondering whether he knew my name, even though I repeated it once every two weeks when I asked a question at his news conferences as was required in those days. I don't even know whether he ever heard my broadcasts or how he reacted to them. Eisenhower carefully avoided personal contact with most reporters. When I first arrived, for example, I asked Press Secretary Jim Hagerty if I could meet the President, thinking this to be a normal request since I was to cover him for the next few years.

Hagerty was affable but noncommittal, saying, "Oh, sure, I'll arrange that some time." He never did. I think Ike viewed us somewhat like soldiers; he had a pretty good idea what we were there for, but he never took much interest in us as people. The only reporter I ever saw Ike pay much attention to was Larry Burd of the *Chicago Tribune*. Tall and friendly, Larry represented a publication that strongly supported Republicans, but more importantly, he was a good golfer. Whenever possible, Hagerty put Burd in situations that required a pool reporter. The rest of us approved, since Larry got much more from Ike than we would; and since he was also an excellent journalist, we knew we would get a good pool report after the eighteenth hole.

As he neared the end of his Presidency, however, Eisenhower hosted several stag dinners for White House correspondents. These were relatively informal affairs attended by several close aides, a few Cabinet members, and about a dozen reporters. An incident at one such dinner provided an insight into Ike's character and helps explain his enormous public appeal.

It was a warm evening in the late summer of 1960, and Richard Nixon had already been chosen as the Republican candidate to succeed Eisenhower. But there was not much talk of politics. We started with drinks in the private quarters on the top floor of the White House, in what Ike called the Trophy Room, filled with bejeweled swords, gold-encrusted scabbards, and similar expensive gifts from Arab potentates and other world figures. Eisenhower had been collecting these since the war, and he now worried aloud about which should go to the museums at West Point, and which might legally be passed on to his family without burdening his son, John, with heavy inheritance taxes.

We walked to the State Dining Room, where one long table had been elegantly set. The atmosphere was relaxed and convivial, considering the usual gulf that existed between the press and the President. Ike positioned himself in the center of the table, with Secretary of the Treasury Robert Anderson at one end, Hagerty at the other, and reporters scattered between. I sat almost directly across from the President. The discussion soon turned to the failure of Admiral Lewis Strauss to receive Senate confirmation as Secretary of Commerce.

Most of us at the table believed that Strauss's abrasiveness had so incensed the Democratic majority on the Commerce Committee that they simply refused to extend the usual courtesy of automatically confirming a Cabinet nominee. But some reporters expressed the view that certain Senators demonstrated latent anti-Semitism by opposing Strauss primarily because he was a Jew. Eisenhower said little as our opinions flowed back and forth across the table, although he frowned a bit now and then. Finally he broke in, clearly bothered by the thrust of the conversation and more specifically by the charges of anti-Semitism.

"I never question a person's motives," the President said. "I always assume he does what he does for good motives, not bad ones."

There was a brief silence while we considered this gentle rebuke. It was impossible to tell whether Ike was being naïve, or whether he simply thought it best not to dwell on ulterior motives in a case that was already past history. I later decided that he was much more astute than we. It is good politics to assume that someone acts for the best motives. Believing the opposite can destroy important political and personal relationships. Here was a side of Eisenhower that I had not previously appreciated, and it helped me to understand why members of his staff were so loyal. Ike's wise generosity may also have been sensed by voters in a way that had escaped the cynical reporters around the table.

Ike's attitude toward women was not so benevolent. He preferred that they all behave like ladies and officers' wives, as did his own Mamie. A humorous manifestation of this attitude occurred after the 1960 Presidential election, when Ike took his annual autumn pilgrimage to Augusta, Georgia.

Although he was now a lame-duck President, a sizable number of White House correspondents accompanied him.* During the trip, these reporters decided to hold a farewell dinner for Ike, Hagerty, and some of the White House staff. One of the few women reporters who covered the White House on occasion was Anne Chamberlin, then with *Time-Life.* A liberated woman before the term became fashionable, Anne was seated across the dinner table from the President (in the special way reserved for women in those days). All went smoothly until cigars were passed around, and Anne took one. Ike looked surprised, and as she lit up and started puffing away with the complete nonchalance of experience, the President's jaw dropped in astonishment. Eisenhower was clearly offended, and although he never said a word, those famous furrows in his brow were eloquent signals of his shock. Anne coolly ignored the President's stony silence, but she came in for considerable kidding and even some angry verbal abuse from a few of her colleagues afterward.

Unlike Eisenhower, his successor, John F. Kennedy, sought out companionship from the press.

As a reporter for the Hearst publications in 1946 and then as a politician, Kennedy had learned the value of constant open communication between public figures and the fourth estate. He felt comfortable with us; some reporters were among his best friends, including columnist Charles Bartlett, who had introduced him to Jackie, and Ben Bradlee, then with *Newsweek* and later the editor of the *Washington Post.*

JFK's easygoing informality became evident during the 1960 campaign. Whenever a new reporter was assigned to cover Senator Kennedy's drive for the Presidency, Press Secretary Pierre Salinger immediately introduced him or her to the candidate. This was usually accompanied by inviting the reporter along on the next flight of the Caroline, the Kennedy family's private two-engined Convair. Although campaign plans and speeches kept him very busy, the handsome young Senator always took time to chat with the reporters aboard, paying special attention to

---

*I was already in Palm Beach with President-elect Kennedy.

the women. Sometimes he would ask for our opinions on how the campaign was going, and he seemed genuinely interested in our criticisms. When it appeared that he had a good chance to defeat Richard Nixon, Kennedy began talking about possible Presidential appointments for our friends and contacts.*

One one occasion he asked me about two men already in government. One was Ted Clifton, a brigadier general at the Pentagon, in charge of Army public relations. As a young officer during World War II, Clifton had worked with many of the war correspondents, including several of my older CBS colleagues. I had come to know and respect him through them, and I strongly recommended him to Kennedy, although I had no idea what Kennedy, if he won, had specifically in mind for the General. Kennedy also asked me about Lincoln White, a spokesman for the State Department under John Foster Dulles during the Eisenhower administration. White was both liked and respected by the correspondents who covered State and foreign affairs, and I said so. Kennedy later made Ted Clifton his Chief Military Aide, and it worked out well for everyone concerned—including me, since I then had a good source close to the President. White, a Southern conservative, was deemed unsuitable for the Kennedy Administration, at least as a spokesman for the State Department. Nevertheless, he received a pleasant assignment as Consul General in Melbourne, Australia.

Shortly after winning the 1960 election, Kennedy flew to Palm Beach to recover from the grueling campaign. The next day, CBS News ordered me to switch my coverage to the incoming President. Palm Beach was a dream assignment. The November weather was warm and balmy. Each correspondent had a comfortable apartment in the Palm Beach Towers Hotel, with plenty of time for tennis or golf after the day's light work.

One morning during the daily briefing, the portly, cigar-chomping Pierre Salinger announced that Senator

*The ramifications of this type of situation are discussed in Chapter 8, "Press Ethics."

Kennedy was inviting correspondents and their families to a garden party a few days later. Nothing like this had ever happened in the Eisenhower years, and we were all pleasantly surprised. The party would be held at the Kennedy beachfront rented mansion, and we could swim, play tennis on the private court, drink and dine. He mentioned that members of the Senator's staff would also be there, and I sensed a unique opportunity to get acquainted with the people who would soon be running the nation. My wife, Pat, had stayed in Washington with our children, but I immediately phoned to suggest she find a live-in sitter and join me in Palm Beach. With the garden party coming up, the social scene was too good to miss.

Pat arrived the next day, a bit bewildered by this new and different White House routine, but as delighted as I was. On the afternoon of the garden party, the weather was perfect, and we brought our bathing suits and tennis rackets. I was playing tennis with Charles Roberts, of *Newsweek,* when JFK suddenly appeared. He was tall and slim and moved gracefully. To my wife, he looked "gorgeous," sporting a white outfit of slacks and jacket, with a bright-red ascot tie, all set off magnificently by a deep bronze tan.

I walked over to shake hands and introduce the ladies, saying, "Senator, I don't believe you have met my wife, Pat." But it was already too late. He had given her what we called "the double whammy." Gazing down with those bright-blue eyes and appraising her from top to bottom, he very deliberately said, "How do you do, Mrs. Pierpoint." Then he added with a mischievous smile, "But haven't we met before?" A sophisticated thirty-five-year-old woman, my wife reacted like a schoolgirl, stammering in her flattered surprise. "I—I—I don't believe so, Senator," she said, noticeably flustered as she tried to carry on a normal conversation. His mission accomplished, Kennedy moved off to meet other guests. But it was clear that he had conquered yet another woman, using what Pat called "the oldest line in the world."

This incident demonstrated one of Kennedy's greatest assets—his extraordinary personal charm. He had a quick wit and a self-deprecating sense of humor. His open flirtation with my wife was kidding both her and himself, but JFK knew he had a devastating effect on women and enjoyed it to the fullest. When he traveled, we actually counted empty shoes along the route of the motorcade, abandoned by women who had literally leaped out of them when they glimpsed JFK waving and smiling from his limousine. What this charm and his other political talents could have meant to the country will never be known. Certainly they held much promise. But at the same time, Kennedy had great difficulty marshaling press and public support for his specific policies.

Kennedy's successor possessed none of this charm. In fact, my first experience with LBJ got us off to a bad start and from then on, it was downhill.

In 1959, the CBS Washington Bureau was temporarily short-staffed and asked me to cover Senate Majority Leader Johnson's press conference on Capitol Hill. When I arrived at the announced room, his aides told me that television cameras would not be allowed, but that the Senator would answer our questions later in the Senate Radio-T.V. Gallery. Separate press conferences for the print and broadcast media were common in those days, so I went along with the arrangement. After attending the session for the print journalists, I walked up to the studio to make sure the camera crew was ready, while some of the broadcast correspondents who knew him escorted Johnson to the gallery. I let the "regulars" from Capitol Hill start the questioning. Nothing very newsworthy was said, so I decided to begin a new line of questioning designed to elicit for film the most colorful quotes from the session just held for the print media.

Suddenly Johnson stopped talking, stared at me, and declared, "I didn't agree to answer any questions on that subject." Startled, I retorted that I had not agreed to limit my questioning in any way. This was met with awkward silence from my competitors. I repeated the question, whereupon Johnson started to leave, angrily claiming that I was breaking the rules. The other network correspondents requested that I order my crew to turn the camera off. I reluctantly agreed, and they explained that Johnson did not allow television cameras in his regular press conferences, and would come to the studio to answer questions only if the network correspondents would limit their questions to certain issues. It was a disgraceful situation, one that would never be tolerated by the networks today, but as the new kid on the block, I was forced to agree.

The next time I spoke to Lyndon Johnson, he was President of the United States and had clearly forgotten the earlier episode. But I had not. It was December 8, 1963, and the nation was still mourning John F. Kennedy. The new President had flown to New York for the funeral of that state's former Governor and United States Senator Herbert Lehman. On the way back to Washington that evening aboard Air Force One,* Jack Valenti invited three White House correspondents to join him and LBJ in the President's airborne bedroom for a private talk. The four of us sat on the bed with Johnson, drinking and exchanging generalities. As we were about to land, Jack Valenti stood, and we caught the signal to return to our seats. I was the last one out the door, and was just thanking the President when he clasped my arm, looked down squarely into my eyes, and said, "Ah'm a good friend of yo' boss, Frank Stanton. Anything Ah can do for you, just let me know. Ah know we're going to get along just fine." He released me, and I walked to my seat, feeling somewhat disgusted. Lyndon Johnson apparently thought I could be bought, intimidated, or both, and it seemed highly possible that if neither could be accomplished, he might try to get me off the White House beat.

Johnson was a man of extremes. He could be as kind as he was crude. At his best and his worst he was overbearing, full of energy and power, like an enormous engine operating nearly out of control. In any mood LBJ was awesome, especially to children. But not always victorious,

*For that particular trip it was a Convair; any Air Force plane on which a President is traveling automatically becomes Air Force One.

as shown by a brief difference of opinion he once had with our youngest daughter, Marta.

In July of 1965, the President invited the press corps out to the small farmhouse where he was born. This was not his boyhood home in Johnson City, but a less pretentious frame house that Johnson rebuilt, refurnished and then pronounced his birthplace. He filled it with pre-World War I furniture, some of which, he asserted, had originally belonged to his family.* On this occasion Johnson was in a particularly expansive mood, playing the kindly school-teacher as he greeted wives and children lined up at the entrance to the "birthplace." Suddenly he spotted my wife holding the hand of three-year-old Marta and invited them both on a personally conducted tour. While the three of them strolled through the house, LBJ proudly told the story of his family background and his own birth. Marta was impressed with this big, enthusiastic man until we came to a high chair in the kitchen, which he explained had been "Lady Bird Johnson's baby chair." Then LBJ suggested that Marta climb up to have her picture taken in the "baby chair."

"I'm not a baby," the three-year-old responded, firmly refusing all his entreaties. Neither parent wanted to interfere, and Johnson finally gave up, retreating from the scene with a hurt look on his beagle-like countenance. For once Lyndon Johnson's famous persuasive powers had failed.

During the early years of his Presidency, Johnson twice invited my wife and me to social affairs. Parties at the White House are not exactly wildly informal affairs, even when given by the Lyndon Johnsons. Guests are greeted at the diplomatic entrance by a bevy of military aides, who check invitations and explain how the evening is to proceed. A table place card is given each guest, and male military officers, usually handsome young Marines or

*LBJ had once claimed that his "Granddaddy" fought at the Alamo, and a check by reporters found this to be another Johnson "whopper." After this, we never accepted anything he said about his family history as accurate unless we could actually verify it.

Army lieutenants, escort the women into the East Room, where cocktails are served while everyone awaits the arrival of the President, his wife, and the guests of honor. Upon their arrival, a long line forms, and a White House aide introduces each of the hundred or more guests to the President, who then introduces his wife and the honorees. These introductions are always an ordeal for everyone involved.

Dinner is then served in the State Dining Room. Ten people usually sit at each round table, with one person—normally a Cabinet member or some recognizable member of the President's staff—designated privately by the White House as the "host." Husbands and wives are separated, and one of the best parts of the evening comes afterward, when you and your spouse can compare notes on who at your table said what about whom. But first, the President and the guest of honor exchange toasts, long and frequently boring speeches.

After dinner, guests move back to the East Room, where formal entertainment is presented. Usually this is either a famous singer or instrumentalist performing a few solos, or a small group presenting a musicale or parts of a play. Afterward comes the dancing, often to the accompaniment of a big-name guest orchestra or the U.S. Marine Band's special dance group.

But our first invitation from LBJ—a dinner for Great Britain's Princess Margaret—promised to be different. Word went out to the press from the White House Social Secretary that some of Washington's more refreshing young couples were to be invited, so we were quite flattered to be included. But it turned into a personal disaster for me, and I cannot remember anything other than my acute embarrassment. We had been told that after the formal dinner and a brief program, there would be dancing. Before we left for the party, Marta asked if I was going to dance with the Princess. I said I would try, and remembering that look of awe on her face (Princesses are evidently more important to some three-year-olds than Presidents), I decided I had to do so. Late that night, as the dance grew livelier, Princess Margaret allowed herself to be cut in on by a steady stream of men, most of them handsome, young military escorts provided by the White House as "extras" for such occasions. I made my move when I spotted her dancing with a man about my age, who looked vaguely familiar. In full view of several eagle-eyed society reporters, I crossed the wide expanse of the East Room to tap the Princess' escort on the shoulder, and was completely humiliated when she turned me down flat! As I crept (slunk?) back toward the comforting presence of my amused wife, a woman reporter asked if I had not realized that Princess Margaret was dancing with one of her favorite actors, Kirk Douglas. I hadn't, but I never forgave the Princess anyway!

The second invitation from the Johnsons came a few weeks later, when India's Prime Minister Indira Gandhi visited the White House. Since LBJ liked to dance, it was once again a dinner dance, though with a somewhat more subdued gathering. Toward the end of the evening, after Mrs. Gandhi had left, some of us clustered around the grand piano with Mrs. Johnson in the big entry hall to sing, while the President continued dancing in the East Room. Suddenly I noticed a white feminine undergarment lying beneath the piano. I simply couldn't believe my eyes, and bent down to pick it up. Sure enough, it was a woman's slip. No one at the piano volunteered to claim it. Months later, I learned that it belonged to one of the women reporters who had lost it during the evening (I was never quite sure how), but it makes me believe that I may have been missing the full story of what happens at White House receptions.

President Johnson looked upon these social occasions as small bribes, to be dispensed as favors to the press. I learned this through a friend on the White House staff, a bright young lawyer named Harold Pachios who was usually assigned the duty of accompanying the President to Texas on weekends, to act as liaison with the press corps. Among other tasks, he was to report to LBJ precisely what various reporters did with their social time, and with whom they were doing it. One evening Pachios and I were making the rounds of the few bars in Austin. We had arrived back at the motel where I was staying, and were headed through the lobby toward the bar when the clerk said, "Mr. Pierpoint, I have a call for you." It was a White House Signal Corps operator, who wondered if I knew where Harold Pachios was, since he had left word he would be dining with me. I said he was right there; she asked me to put him on, and I did so. The next thing I knew, Pachios was running down a list of the reporters he had seen that night. The Presidential aide spoke softly into the telephone, clearly uncomfortable about the whole situation. Prodded by the person at the other end, he would answer, "Well, I think he's with that young coed from the university," or "Doug Kiker is with his local friend." It didn't take too long to identify his inquisitor since everyone knew of LBJ's penchant for gossip.

Pachios was quite embarrassed when he confessed afterward that indeed it was the President, and that he received similar calls fairly often. I asked what LBJ said about me, since I knew he made biting comments about everyone around him, including the press corps. Pachios told me that Johnson was quite upset by my recent broadcasts. This was 1966, and the Vietnam war was an increasingly controversial domestic issue. Information on the degree of American involvement was clearly being withheld from reporters and the public, and I had openly criticized Johnson's lack of candor. LBJ had called Pachios into the Oval Office one day and grilled him on why Pierpoint seemed so ungrateful—". . . after all Ah've done for that boy." He obviously meant the dinner invitations!

My disagreement with Johnson over the war evolved from the unusual perspective I had on Communism while covering Scandinavia in the late 1950s. During several visits to Finland between 1948 and 1951, I watched that tiny nation fight courageously to keep the Communists from seizing control. At that time, Finnish Communists commanded about twenty percent of the vote and received strong support from their powerful neighbor, the Soviet Union. My first CBS News broadcasts in the summer of 1949 reported an attempted coup by Finnish Communists, who already controlled several important Cabinet posts, including the extremely powerful Ministry of Interior and its National Police Force. But the Finns had united, and through democratic, rational means had thwarted the Soviet efforts.

In contrast, it was a shock to return to the United States at the end of 1949 to find the nation traumatized by an almost irrational fear of Communism in America. McCarthyism was rising, even though the Senator from Wisconsin could find few real Communists among the voters, and even fewer in positions of power or influence. A decade later Fidel Castro drove many Americans into an even deeper anti-Communist hysteria when he set up a Marxist regime in nearby Cuba. In the meantime, the French had been forced out of Indochina, and America steadily assumed the burden of "saving Asia from Communism." This, in turn, gave rise to the policies that Johnson inherited and expanded. They were based upon an oversimplified view of Communism as a monolithic worldwide conspiracy, and of the United States as the perpetual would-be savior of democracy in foreign lands.

As the Vietnam war escalated, relations between LBJ and the press grew worse, but he never stopped trying to influence us. He and Bill Moyers had parted company, and Johnson brought in a fellow Texan, George Christian, to be his new Press Secretary. A protégé of John Connally, Christian had been Governor Connally's press secretary. Softspoken, conservative in both politics and manner, Christian was respected by reporters. He quickly earned the confidence of Lyndon Johnson as well, in large part because he was very careful never to tell journalists more than the President wanted them to know—which, as the Vietnam War went grinding on, was less and less. LBJ began inviting Christian to small lunchtime planning sessions on the war; these were attended also by such officials as Secretary of Defense Robert S. McNamara (later Clark M. Clifford), Secretary of State Dean Rusk, and National Security Adviser Walt W. Rostow.

Occasionally, Johnson had Christian invite various White House correspondents up to the private quarters for lunch, though usually without the other war planners. In the fall of 1967, Christian asked Ray Scherer of NBC, Frank Reynolds of ABC, and me to one of those private luncheons. At this time, heavy United States bombing of North Vietnam had become an international issue which turned many friends and allies against the United States. Critics were also asking whether the bombing was really helpful in winning the war. Tempers were running high on both sides of the issue.

The luncheon was awkward, at least for me, because Johnson knew I considered the war in Vietnam a national disaster. I sat on Johnson's left, and throughout most of our conversation, he vehemently defended his war policies and punctuated his remarks with complaints that the press refused to see things his way. When the meal was over and the topic of the bombing came up, the President began boasting about the great job of "licking the Communists" his Air Force was doing. At one point he said proudly that the North Vietnamese "have got two hundred thousand people today cleaning up the mess I made yesterday."

This was more than enough for me. I had been silently berating myself for not taking direct issue with Johnson's more outrageous statements; now, I had to make at least one point. "Mr. President," I interjected politely, "the North Vietnamese keep saying that if you stop the bombing, they will negotiate a peaceful settlement of the war. Why don't you try it, and then if they don't seriously negotiate, you could resume the bombing but with the monkey on their backs?" It was not exactly a thunderous disagreement with his conduct of the war, but it was sufficient to cause a small explosion. Johnson leaned over and declared angrily, "You're just helpin' ma enemies, the Communists!" He went on to denounce me and everyone else who questioned his war policies. We were "aiding the enemy," he said. Warming to the task, the red-faced President then offered the astonishing statement that FBI Director J. Edgar Hoover had warned him about "five thousand Communists inside the U.S. Government." No one said a word—we were all too stunned.

That a President of the United States could actually quote such a ridiculous charge was disgraceful—and worse if Johnson really believed it. Afterward, Scherer, Reynolds and I discussed the remarkable outburst. Johnson obviously felt that the Viet Cong, the North Vietnamese Communists, Moscow, and Americans who opposed the war were all tied together. But we could not decide whether the President actually believed what he had said or was just trying to intimidate us. Unfortunately we could not report the incident, because under the rules of the luncheon, everything was off the record.

Although antiwar rallies and domestic violence were on the upswing in 1968, Johnson could probably have defeated Richard Nixon. It would have been a bloody election, figuratively and literally, and his decision to withdraw was at least partly based on placing the nation's interests above his own. But Johnson was unable to go one necessary step further and allow Vice-President Hubert H. Humphrey the freedom needed to win the Presidency. During the 1968 Chicago convention, LBJ vacillated back and forth between relinquishing leadership of the party (as he should have done)—thus permitting Humphrey to take a different line on Vietnam—and insisting that the Vice-President follow the Johnson war policies. The President could not even decide whether to attend the Chicago convention. For several days during that hectic August, we White House reporters with him in Austin kept our bags packed because LBJ aides warned us that we might leave at any moment for Chicago.

The politics of the convention ebbed and flowed, as did rumors on whether the President would fly up for a personal appearance on the last day. That day was also LBJ's sixtieth birthday. The rioting, the assaults on newsmen, and the bitter in-fighting between delegations were over; Humphrey had been selected to lead the party in its struggle with Richard Nixon. As we waited in the Press Room to board the buses that were to take us to the airport for our flight to Chicago, a deputy Press Secretary announced "off the record" that LBJ was instead going to his daughter Luci Nugent's house for a birthday celebration, and we were to join him.

That birthday party was one of the strangest episodes of my career. Some twenty reporters, by now completely alienated from an embittered Lyndon Johnson, stood around a small living room self-consciously singing "Happy Birthday, Dear Lyndon." We munched on store-bought cake and mumbled embarrassed small talk with LBJ and his family, carefully avoiding any hint of politics. But everyone was painfully aware that LBJ really wanted to be in the Chicago convention hall accepting cheers from a thousand delegates.

Outsiders used to ask me about the monumental Johnson ego, which I generally viewed as a manifestation of deep self-doubts and insecurity. LBJ constantly abused aides and reporters, insulting them behind their backs— and sometimes even in their presence. If he particularly disliked someone, Johnson would deliberately mispronounce the name. For example, he always referred to NBC correspondent Ron Nessen, who later became President Ford's press secretary, as "Neeson" or "Messon."

In some strange way, Richard Nixon shared the same ego problem. Each man came from a family where the father considered himself a failure and the mother's puritanical Bible reading dominated home life. This appears to have affected Johnson and Nixon in a very fundamental way. Both were determined to rise to the top of the heap, and when they did, both frequently referred to their mothers as being largely responsible for their success.

Basically, however, Nixon disliked people and was especially ill-at-ease around strangers. Yet initially he managed to fool many observers into believing just the opposite. The first day after Nixon's inauguration, Press Secretary Ron Ziegler invited a pool of four reporters, including me, into the Oval Office. As we entered, Nixon stood up behind his desk, smiling and shaking hands while he accepted our congratulations. Then he began showing off his recent handiwork as an interior decorator. He was particularly pleased with the huge red, rather ornate wood desk, which had apparently belonged to Woodrow Wilson and was called the "Wilson desk." Nixon emphasized that

Wilson was his favorite President.* I was surprised to hear the anti-intellectual and highly partisan Richard Nixon praise a former college professor and Democrat. But even more surprising was his demeanor. He had never before been quite this comfortable and candid with journalists, and it occurred to me that Nixon was relaxing now that he had achieved his long-time ambition of the Presidency. He even kidded us a bit, pointing out that he had removed the two wire-service teletypes and the three television sets that Lyndon Johnson had installed in the Oval Office to monitor every word written or said about him. "Don't take it personally," joked the new President, "but I'm not going to pay that much attention to you."

Another incident also led me to believe that Nixon had learned to relax and enjoy his job. In late February and early March of 1969, the new President took his first trip abroad. Ziegler put me in the pool aboard Air Force One, which carried the Presidential party to Paris. On landing at Orly Airport, as the plane slowly taxied up to a long red carpet, I looked out to see the French and American flags flapping in a brisk breeze. It was obviously quite chilly, since the welcoming crowd wore heavy overcoats, scarves and gloves; all, that is, except one person. At the other end of the red carpet, flanked by two aides, stood the tall, austere figure of French President Charles de Gaulle, sans overcoat. President Nixon walked through our compartment of Air Force One on his way to the exit, putting on his overcoat. "Mr. President," I said, "it looks cold out there, but President de Gaulle does not have on a coat." Nixon ducked down for a quick look out the window, then tossed me his overcoat with a carefree "Viva la France," and out the door he went. It was the new Nixon, happy and apparently secure—and one I never saw again.

Shortly after those first two months in office, Nixon appeared to become increasingly dissatisfied with the way

*Later it turned out that the Wilson desk had actually belonged to Henry Wilson, an obscure Vice-President under President U. S. Grant. I think someone probably once said to Nixon that this was the "Wilson desk" and he just assumed that it belonged to Woodrow Wilson. I doubt that it was a deliberate deception on his part.

the press—and the nation—were treating him. Even his landslide in 1972 didn't change this. On the night of the election, a few correspondents were sitting in the Press Room following the returns. After Nixon's overwhelming victory became clear, we waited for him to leave for the Republican rally at Washington's Sheraton-Park Hotel, where he could savor his triumph with hundreds of supporters. An aide informed the press pool that Nixon was about to leave the Oval Office, where he had been watching the television coverage of the election results. I started to walk through the Press Room toward the waiting cars in the motorcade behind the mansion, when I glimpsed someone heading in the same direction. Our paths crossed just before the corridor opened onto the colonnade beside the Rose Garden. It was Richard Nixon hunched over and staring at the floor; he was followed silently by Bob Haldeman, Ron Ziegler and some Secret Service agents. I stepped back to allow him to pass and, overcoming the incongruity of the gloomy scene, forced myself to say, "Congratulations, Mr. President." Almost without looking up, Nixon grunted a quick "Thanks," and hurried on.

I was astounded at this ill-humored response and wondered about it for some time. At first, I attributed Nixon's odd behavior to his increasing dislike of the press, but I have since concluded that he was still worrying whether the Watergate cover-up might begin to unravel now that the election victory had given the conspirators less of an incentive to remain disciplined.* From that moment, Nixon retreated more and more into a private world. He even cut himself off from members of his staff and from politicians in his own party—and the only people who had been able to get close to him during his first four years in office.

Nixon's choice as Vice-President during this period †

---

*My CBS colleague Diane Sawyer, who then worked for President Nixon, says that he also was suffering from a toothache that day.
† Vice-President Spiro Agnew resigned in 1973 pleading *nolo contendere* to the charge of income-tax evasion. He had been accepting bribes while holding the nation's second-highest office.

was Gerald R. Ford, a popular Republican Congressman and Minority Leader, whose conservative beliefs coincided with the President's. After twenty-six years in office, Ford had introduced only one notable piece of legislation, the highly unpopular call for the impeachment of Supreme Court Justice William O. Douglas. Nixon's resignation then propelled this rather unlikely prospect into the nation's highest office, and Ford's Presidency reached its high point on the first day, when the new President made a memorable speech declaring that the nation's long nightmare of Watergate was over. Ford was not quite correct, however, since he himself soon prematurely pardoned Nixon, creating a partisan controversy and causing the Republican party even more severe losses than they had expected in the 1974 Congressional elections.

Although personally and politically Ford never aroused much passion from the public, his Presidency did bring two assassination attempts, one of which I broke to the public. It was in San Francisco in 1976. President Ford had spoken to a group at the St. Francis Hotel and was leaving to fly back to Washington. Normally CBS has three correspondents on such a trip, but for some reason only Bob Schieffer and I were present. Schieffer was at the local television station preparing an insert for the Cronkite *Evening News,* and I was trying to finish up my radio chores in time to join the motorcade to follow the President to the airport. This was not considered essential, since the other media personnel flying on Air Force One back to Washington with the President constituted a pool, and their material was available to all of us. Nevertheless those reporters who had finished their work early liked to board the press bus in the motorcade, partly to be sure that the President got off safely, and partly to get aboard the press plane and begin the "relaxation process" at the end of a long trip.

This motorcade was to depart at 3:30 P.M. San Francisco time, and as I gathered up my typewriter and hand luggage I thought I would make it with a few minutes to spare. But as I walked out the door of the hotel I could just see the last of the motorcade pulling around the corner through a haze of what I thought at first was exhaust fumes. Then I noticed an acrid smell, well-remembered from the Korean war, and heard a woman say "I think someone shot at the President." Looking around at the stunned faces, I could see that something had happened; several people were talking excitedly of hearing a shot. At that moment I spotted a San Francisco police officer standing a few feet away, and I moved up to ask him if a shot had been fired. He looked almost as surprised as everyone else in the crowd. "Yes," he said, "I think someone fired at the President."

"Did he get hit?" I asked.

"I don't think so," the cop answered, and as I was about to ask him to explain in more detail just what he had seen, another male voice spoke up. "This just hit me in the stomach," a chunky, shabbily dressed man in his thirties said. "Maybe you want it," he added. I looked down and saw he was holding what appeared to be a .45-caliber bullet badly mashed on one side. It had obviously hit him without much force, after ricocheting. While the policeman took the bullet, someone nearby told me that other police had hustled a suspect back inside the hotel.

That was enough for me. I rushed back to the Press Room and the nearest telephone, meanwhile assembling the facts in my head. As nearly as I could tell, one shot had been fired at President Ford, but it had not hit him. The Presidential motorcade was presumably en route to the airport—or a hospital; I could not be sure which—and a suspect had been captured. I tried not to run too fast, aware that a breathless announcement on the air can be both alarming and unintelligible. The one piece of information I badly needed was whether the President had gotten safely away.

Entering the Press Room, I looked around for either a Secret Service agent or a press aide. They both keep in constant contact with the President's motorcade through miniature radio receivers and transmitters worn on the body. I spotted John Carlson, deputy to Press Secretary Ron Nessen. Staring at John as hard as I could without revealing to my competitors scattered through the room that I knew someone had tried to kill the President, I said, "John, is the President okay?" At first Carlson seemed reluctant to talk, apparently because he was not sure either just exactly what had happened, or how much he should say. I decided that accuracy was more important than the scoop, and I blurted out quickly, "Someone shot at the President, John. I know that. What I want to know is did he get away in the motorcade okay?" Carlson nodded Yes, as I picked up the phone. Immediately my colleagues gathered around, trying to ask questions, which I refused to answer. "When I get New York on the phone," I told them, "you will hear the story as I broadcast it."

Less than a minute later, I was on the air for CBS radio with a brief bulletin, reporting what I had seen and heard. Since this was in the middle of Walter Cronkite's evening newscast, he then came on the line to interview me live on TV. In the meantime, other reporters had begun spreading through the hotel, trying to locate the police and the suspect that I said had been taken. The Associated Press put out a bulletin, saying that CBS News correspondent Robert Pierpoint had reported that an unknown assailant had fired a shot at President Ford, "Who . . . Pierpoint reported . . . had escaped unharmed." A short while later one of the local reporters came in with word that the San Francisco police had captured a woman (eventually identified as Sara Jane Moore) who had fired at the President with a .45 pistol. It was another fifteen minutes before we had final word from the airport that President Ford was safely on his way back to Washington aboard Air Force One. That night I stayed in San Francisco, cleaning up the "crisis coverage" and doing radio and television broadcasts until dawn, when I caught the first commercial flight back to Washington. Months later, I learned from John Carlson that he had not really been sure what I was asking when he nodded to me just before I went on the air. He had actually known nothing about a shot fired at Ford and had meant only that the motorcade had left the hotel for the airport.

Ford's Presidency was generally lackluster and suffered from the same lack of new ideas as had marked his Congressional career. In fact, the most innovative Ford action I covered ended up as a disaster.

Sometime in 1976, an epidemic of swine flu broke out in various parts of the country. It threatened to become nationwide and serious. One day in early autumn, reporters and photographers were suddenly summoned to the press briefing room in the White House, and President Ford appeared, flanked by several top aides. As the television cameras recorded the scene, the President discussed the dangers of swine flu, disclosed that a new vaccine had been developed, and then announced a massive inoculation program, designed to reach every American. It was a mind-boggling undertaking unveiled in dramatic fashion, and it caught us all off guard. But brief reflection reminded me that the target date for completing the inoculations just happened to coincide with the finish of the Presidential campaign. It did not seem to me that the timing could be purely coincidental.

In my first broadcast for radio that day I merely pointed out the coincidence. But within an hour or so of the President's announcement, I received a call from the CBS News bureau chief in Atlanta, Zeke Siegel, telling me that some experts at the Federal Center for Disease Control did not support the new inoculation program. From Zeke and one of our CBS correspondents in Atlanta I learned that a split had developed within the scientific community involved in the project. Some thought the flu virus was so threatening and the vaccine so efficient that every American should be inoculated as soon as possible. Others were not sure of either the dangers of the virus or the efficacy of the vaccine. They were also worried that the vaccine might produce unknown, but harmful, side effects. In any case, the inoculation project had been pushed strongly by the bureaucracy and by White House aides who finally persuaded Ford to put it into effect.

For my broadcast that night on the Cronkite show I related some of these facts. My story raised serious doubts about whether this massive new vaccination program was medically sound, and how it might have been politically motivated. This incensed the Ford White House, and several top Presidential aides complained to me that I was simply being too cynical.

Shortly afterward, the project itself failed. The vaccine was found to cause paralysis in some individuals, and as word of this spread, people by the millions declined to be vaccinated. Although my broadcasts probably had some effect on the public's antivaccine attitudes, neither Ford nor his aides held a grudge. Their reaction was typical of the Gerald Ford White House, reflecting the President's good-natured ability to roll with the political punches.

This capacity was not contrived. Gerald and Betty Ford were two of the nicest people that ever lived in the White House. Both were always gracious with the press corps. At first, President Ford's staff was largely a holdover from the Nixon Administration, and that made for difficulties and lack of communication. But the Nixonites were gradually phased out; Ford replaced them with more congenial people of his own choosing, and the Ford White House became a pleasant place to work in. Even during the 1976 campaign, when press and President were tired and sometimes snappish, President Ford never quite lost his good humor. I felt that he had one marvelous quality as a politician: Gerald Ford genuinely liked people, even reporters. Despite a faltering economy and a heavily Democratic electorate, this quality brought him breathtakingly close to defeating Jimmy Carter in 1976.

Carter was another matter. He had a self-righteous air that seemed to alienate other politicians. Shortly after he took office, for example, Carter invited a group of Democratic Congressmen to the White House. As one of them told me later, "He invited us down for four o'clock tea. And you know what he served? Tea!" A President who wanted to convey the image of a good Baptist teetotaler (he does take a mild bit of alcohol now and then), Carter could not bring himself to serve his colleagues what they wanted, hard liquor.

But Carter's problems ran far deeper. A hard-driving overachiever, he nevertheless seemed unable to persevere with other politicians well enough to accomplish his long-term goals, always moving off abruptly in another direction. Carter got into the White House by capitalizing on the nation's distress over Vietnam and Watergate, with such slogans as "I will not lie to you" and "America deserves a government as good as its people." But, once there, he did not know how to use the power he had acquired.

Carter's inability to wield the powers of his office was noticeable even before he moved into the White House. In the period between the 1976 election and the Inauguration, he began announcing appointments to his incoming administration. One of the first was that of Theodore Sorensen, a former JFK aide who had helped Carter in the campaign, to head the Central Intelligence Agency. A brilliant writer with strong humanitarian instincts, Sorensen had also been a conscientious objector during World War II and presumably (although not demonstrably) retained some of his aversion to the use of force to resolve international problems. In my view, this made him a somewhat doubtful candidate for the job of CIA Director. That was also the view of several members of the Congressional committee that had to approve his nomination, the Select Committee on Intelligence, and specifically of the Committee's Democratic Chairman, Senator Daniel Inouye, of Hawaii. Within hours of Jimmy Carter's announcement, word arrived in Plains, Georgia, that Inouye was unhappy with Sorensen's nomination. Then something incredible happened. Carter and his aides simply began to back down. Press spokesman Jody Powell equivocated when we asked if the President-elect would insist on Sorensen's approval by the Senate. Eventually Carter completely capitulated; Sorensen's name was withdrawn, at considerable embarrassment to all parties concerned.

At the time, I thought back on how Lyndon Johnson would have handled the same situation. First, he would have made sure that the number of Senators required for approval (especially the committee chairman) were already on board before he made the nomination public. If the chairman had then publicly balked, as Inouye did, I can very well imagine LBJ picking up the phone for the following one-sided conversation:

Good mornin', Mr. Chairman, this is yore President. . . . Not too well, thank you. I'm a mite unhappy that you don't seem to like my new Director of the CIA. At least that's what I read in the press. . . . Yeah, Senator, I know all that. Knew it before I nominated him. Senator, I want to tell you something I been thinkin' about. You know all them military bases you got out there in Hah-wai-ee? Well, I been wonderin' if some of them bases might not be better off somewhere else . . . say Alaska . . . or Gu-Wam. . . . No, Senator, I haven't made any decisions yet. But I do know those bases are pretty important to your people out there. . . . Oh, is that right, you've changed your mind about my appointment to head the CIA? Thank you, Senator, I thought you'd see it my way!

Now that's the kind of power a President has, and that's also the kind Jimmy Carter either never understood or never used. For some reason, Carter strongly disliked confrontations. In 1979, for example, when he wanted to fire Bella Abzug as head of his women's advisory panel, he called the feisty former Congresswoman in for a personal chat. They talked amiably for some time, and after leaving the Oval Office she told reporters she thought they had patched up their differences. While she was speaking to us, a minor functionary handed her a note. Bella excused herself and walked back into the White House, where she had been asked to check with Hamilton Jordan. It was Jordan who told her President Carter wanted her resignation.

The ability of a President to use the power and influence of his office determines to a large extent his eventual success. That means a President must be able to talk to members of Congress, particularly key leaders and committee chairmen, with both authority and knowledge. He must know their needs and wants, what their constituents demand of them, and how they can be manipulated. Jimmy Carter seemed unable or unwilling to play politics with the

Congress and therefore had serious trouble getting through some of his most important legislation, at least in the form he wanted it.

Another factor that hindered Carter's effectiveness and appeal was a streak of hostility that would surface from time to time. My colleagues who had covered him during the 1976 campaign spoke of the way his steely-blue eyes would transfix questioners with a cold glint when he did not like their questions, or became angry. It was never the words, they said, so much as the expression on his face— jaw set, lines tense, and especially those hard eyes. After he became President, those of us who covered the White House began to see the same thing.

One graphic illustration occurred during the 1980 primaries at a Philadelphia rally for President Carter, a so-called "town meeting" in which ordinary citizens got to ask him questions. This one took place a few days after Secretary of State Cyrus Vance, a man of impeccable honor and integrity, had resigned following Carter's overruling of his objections to plans for the abortive raid to rescue the hostages in Iran. Senator Edmund Muskie, equally respected by his countrymen, had been appointed to take Vance's place, a clever political move by the President. The "meeting" proceeded routinely, until suddenly, in answer to a fairly innocuous question, Carter lashed out at Vance, comparing him most unfairly and unfavorably with Muskie. A shocked White House Press Corps immediately ran for typewriters and telephones, only to be intercepted by a surprised and upset Jody Powell. The President's Press Secretary tried to undo the damage by explaining that Carter had meant no insult to the former Secretary of State, but it was too late. The negative impression we had all received from Carter's unprovoked attack on Vance was too strong to be erased.

In the end, this less-publicized, unpredictable, hostile side to Jimmy Carter hurt him most critically in his final drive for reelection. As the 1980 campaign drew to a close, the Democratic and Republican Presidential nominees agreed to debate. All public opinion polls showed Carter and Reagan running very close, and many political observers—including myself—thought the debate would be crucial. One question uppermost in my mind was how the Carter personality would fare against Mr. "Aw Shucks," nice-guy, Ronald Reagan. That night, the President clearly tried to keep his temper under control—which in this case meant keeping the anger out of his voice, face and eyes. But he did not quite succeed. At two or three key points during their debate, Carter shot hard, vindictive looks at his opponent, which the television cameras clearly picked up. Reagan, the consummate political actor, played his role perfectly, perhaps typified best by that quick smiling glance at one Carter accusation, and the words, "There you go again." More than anything substantive said about domestic or world problems, the difference in personalities shown by such exchanges cost Jimmy Carter the debate.

The resultant landslide brought to the White House a new and untested commodity—a former movie actor, an advocate of public-policy positions sometimes regarded as extreme, and a former governor with no foreign-policy experience. Covering the Reagan Administration promises to be anything but dull.

5

Press Secretaries

At 6 A.M. on July 14, 1958, I sat down in my office at the local radio station where CBS rented its Washington quarters. The only other people in the building were an early-morning disc jockey and a technician. The clatter of the teletypes echoed through the empty room as I glanced at the front pages of the *Washington Post* and *New York Times,* sleepily deciding that they had nothing from which I could borrow a story for the 8 A.M. World News Round-up. Suddenly over the chattering of the AP, UP and INS wires I heard the unmistakable sound of a clanging teletype bell. It is similar to the *ding* a typewriter makes before it hits the margin, only slightly louder, and it means the wire service is starting a special bulletin. Walking quickly to the noisy machine I read the dateline, Baghdad, and the lead; a military coup had overthrown the King of Iraq, and raging mobs of Arabs were dragging his body and those of other government officials through the streets. A full-scale rebellion against the pro-Western government was underway.

Iraq was then a member of the American-backed Baghdad Pact, and this was serious. I needed an immediate reaction from the Eisenhower Administration, so I called the home of State Department spokesman Andrew Berding, awakening him. His involuntary response was a shocked, "Jesus Christ!"—hardly a useful quote for my morning broadcast. Berding suggested that I call Ike's Press Secretary Jim Hagerty. Since it was 6:10 in the morning, and Hagerty would most likely have nothing different to offer, I decided to broadcast my report without waking anyone else.

Later that day, when I did discuss the matter with Hagerty, he was upset that I had not phoned. "I'm here to help reporters," he explained. "After all, you're my boys."

This attitude helped make Hagerty an extremely effective Press Secretary and fit right in with Ike's White House. As might be expected, it was run in a military manner, and each official within the chain of command was assigned a carefully delineated area of authority. We reporters were Hagerty's "troops," and he took the care and feeding of us very seriously. He always made sure that his "boys"—no woman regularly covered the White House in those days—got good food, a decent night's sleep, and the best possible communications facilities whenever Ike traveled.

This was smart press relations. Hagerty would not allow us to be hauled halfway around the world over a twenty- or thirty-hour work day, then force us to work at the other end without time for sleep or meals—as subsequent press secretaries have done. He knew that an overtired journalist, away from his family for too long, is going to reflect exhaustion and dissatisfaction in his stories.

Of course, Hagerty's approach also had its drawbacks for us. We were seldom, if ever, allowed to interview White House officials unless we had first "cleared it with Jim," which involved the painful process of explaining to Hagerty just what you were after and what specific questions you wanted answered. Unless Hagerty thought there was no potential danger to the Administration, he would refuse permission. For example, whenever I tried to talk directly to the President's economic advisers, Dr. Arthur Burns and Dr. Paul McCracken, or to members of the National Security Council, they always suggested that I "clear it with Jim," and Hagerty would then handle my questions himself. And, when I wanted to question White House Chief of Staff Sherman Adams about his relations with financier Bernard Goldfine and the infamous vicuña coat—a gift that raised conflict-of-interest questions and precipitated Adams' resignation—Hagerty blocked my inquiries.

In his role of Press Secretary, Hagerty also conducted daily briefings. As I soon learned, they are as often long, boring and frustrating as they are eventful, exciting and raucous. The official function of these encounters is to brief the press on the actions and attitudes of the President, and, in turn, to answer questions about them. The exchange may be friendly, but it is also adversarial. One side always wants more information than it receives; the other always wants to provide less than it knows. Members of the press can be often unpleasant, but press secretaries learn early that we come with the territory, and they must find some way to cope with us.

Like other aspects of news coverage, the press briefing has changed through the years, although a few undesirable elements have unfortunately remained. When I first came to the White House, Jim Hagerty held two briefing sessions each day—at 11 A.M. and 4 P.M. This offered numerous obvious advantages for the press. Reporters might raise an important issue during the first briefing, and Hagerty could supply the answer during the second, before most of us had to file our stories. This system also left correspondents several crucial hours in which to investigate an announcement or disclosure by Hagerty, so that they could return to the second session armed with pertinent details or background. At the second briefing Hagerty could also be asked about developments that had arisen earlier that day on Capitol Hill or around the world. If, for example, Congress passed an important measure in the early afternoon, correspondents could obtain Presidential reaction, including hints of vetoes or plans for implementation, in time for their evening deadlines.

Briefings are often somewhat stressful for press secretaries, and Hagerty managed to cut back to one per day whenever he could—which was whenever President Eisenhower was away from Washington. Reporters who accompanied Ike rarely objected, especially when he took "working vacations" to places such as Palm Springs or Newport, Rhode Island. At such times, no one liked to spend an entire day around the Press Room, especially those reporters who had brought their families with them. So Hagerty held one morning briefing and—to pacify the press, which was usually not difficult—he simply had to hand out one fairly good White House story per day, anything from reaction to an international event like China's first atomic device to the establishment of a new Presidential commission to investigate a potential railroad strike. After the briefing, Hagerty would put on a news lid. This usually meant that around 12:30, Jim or someone from his press office would come into the Press Room and say, "The lid is on for the day"—meaning that the White House would release no new information that day. Reporters could then join their families for golf, swimming or tennis without worrying that they would miss something.* In Washington a lunch lid was usually on from 12:30 to 2:30 P.M. In the evening the lid was put on in the same way, except that it was then announced as a "lid for the day," meaning that the lid was on until the President's first public appointment the next day, or until some event scheduled by Hagerty. If something occurred during the night that required the lifting of the lid, a "call-out" was arranged, and the White House telephoned regular White House correspondents to tell them the news or to summon them to the Press Secretary's office. This system still exists, both for lids and call-outs. The only noticeable change is that banks of two star-shaped lights have been placed at two places in the press area. One light is for reporters, the other is for photographers and sound technicians. Occasionally, the lid light goes on for camera crews and photographers around 5 P.M., which means that they may go home while the rest of us stay. This is the Press Secretary's way of saying that no further on-the-record information that

---

* The origin of the term "lid" is lost in obscurity. I have heard that Jim Hagerty invented it, and I am happy to give him credit for coining the term and for conscientiously following the rules. Some of his successors have not been equally conscientious.

could be photographed or filmed will be forthcoming that day, but that a background briefing may still be in store.

Hagerty and Eisenhower made the best Press Secretary-President combination I've seen, although Powell and Carter came close. From our standpoint, Hagerty's intimate relationship with Ike was wonderful. It gave us a clear channel to the President's thinking and permitted Hagerty to advise the President about how reporters would react to or interpret a particular story.

Hagerty used his influence to good advantage, but on at least one occasion gave, or at least concurred in, advice that backfired badly.

In 1960 the superpowers scheduled a summit conference as a follow-through to the Geneva disarmament summit of 1956. Soviet Premier Khrushchev had steadily acquired more personal power since the Geneva meeting, and President Eisenhower, who had not done too well in gaining any concessions from the Soviet leadership in Geneva, wanted to try again. Khrushchev himself seemed more willing to discuss East-West problems, although this may have been a maneuver to show the world—as well as rivals within the Kremlin—that he was now in firm control. In any case, it was a hopeful time for Ike, who wanted progress toward disarmament for its own sake as well as to smooth the transfer of power to his designated Republican successor, Richard Nixon. But the hopes that built up toward the Paris summit quickly collapsed when a Soviet missile shot down the American "U-2" spy plane carrying Francis Gary Powers over the Soviet Union on May 1, 1960, on the eve of the summit.

At first, the State Department issued a CIA cover story claiming that Powers was a civilian on a NASA weather mission and got lost. But the Soviets then produced Powers himself, who confessed that he was a spy. Nevertheless, the Soviet leadership apparently did not want to destroy chances for a productive summit and for Ike's scheduled visit to the Soviet Union. Khrushchev gave Eisenhower an obvious "out" by hinting that perhaps the United States President had not had advance knowledge of the flight.

The Soviets also demanded an apology, and Ike could very easily have seized their tacit offer of "forgiveness" by denying that he had known about or authorized the flight, and adding his regret that it had been carried out without his instructions. But this strategy, while it could have improved relations between Moscow and Washington, ran directly counter to a domestic political problem of which Hagerty was acutely aware. Considerable criticism had been leveled at Eisenhower for being a President who did not do his homework. Later I learned that Ike and Hagerty decided that the President should announce that he had originally authorized the spy plane's flights, and that he had specifically ordered them to be continued during the preparations for the Paris summit. Their goal was to enhance Eisenhower's image as a leader in complete control of the nation.

Eisenhower made at least two serious mistakes. First, if he actually knew about each flight in advance (and I am not convinced that he did), he should have considered the consequences of a mishap at such a crucial time. The fact that as yet no U-2's had either crashed in the Soviet Union or been shot down was certainly no guarantee that such luck would continue. The Kremlin had never publicly acknowledged them, but it had to be assumed that they were aware of the high-altitude spies. Therefore Ike should have canceled all such flights for several weeks before the Paris summit.

The second mistake was the manner in which Eisenhower handled the incident after the Russians revealed that they had shot down the aircraft. He should have lied if necessary and said he did not know of the plan for the flight, would have canceled it had he known, and was happy to apologize to Khrushchev and the Soviet people—in short, he should have met Khrushchev halfway in smoothing the way for the summit. The Soviet Premier gave the United States President every opportunity to back off. The thought of an American President apologizing to a Soviet Premier might have bothered many Americans, but Eisenhower was ultimately responsible for the mission, and thus for the fact that it failed. Probably more than any President in recent memory, he could have survived such an apology with the affection of the American people intact. The result of his inflexibility was a resumption of the cold war, including construction of the Berlin wall, and a speed-up of the international arms race that continues to this day. Who knows what might have been the positive results if the Paris summit had succeeded?

When John Kennedy succeeded Eisenhower, the press-office atmosphere relaxed perceptibly. Instead of acting as intermediary between the press and government officials, Press Secretary Pierre Salinger simply let reporters fend for themselves (although he was always willing to help out when asked). A simple phone call could usually produce an appointment, even with powerful Presidential aides. In keeping with this less formal atmosphere, Salinger tried to cut the regular twice-daily White House briefings back to one; but after a week's trial run, he gave in to the objections of the press and returned to two briefings.*

Despite Salinger's best efforts, relations between Kennedy and the press were not always pleasant. In the spring of 1962, the *New York Herald Tribune* ran a number of editorials, and a few news stories of doubtful authenticity, all criticizing the President. In exasperation, JFK ordered Salinger to cancel the White House's twenty-two *Tribune* subscriptions and to order instead the *St. Louis Post-Dispatch,* a paper that generally supported him. Salinger clearly considered this a public-relations mistake, done hastily and in anger, and decided to leak the story. The next morning, he called me into his office for what I thought was just one of our usual chats. In those days the Press Secretary's office was like a Western bar with a swinging door. White House regulars would drop by at will, unless the door happened to be closed for a private conference. Thus, there was nothing unusual about Salinger's invitation.

Salinger was sitting behind his big desk, rolling his

---

*On the road, however, press secretaries since Hagerty have held only one daily briefing unless special circumstances required more.

At a press conference with Ike in 1959 (Jim Hagerty and Anne Wheaton also present). *The Ollie Atkins Photograph Collection, Special Collection, George Mason University Libraries, Fairfax, Virginia.*

With President Kennedy at Cape Canaveral, 1962. *Official White House photograph.*

President Lyndon Johnson briefs White House correspondents aboard Air Force One on Vietnam War developments, September 14, 1967. *Okamoto, The White House*.

On the steps of the Capitol, 1967. Left to right: Congressman Robert Eckhart of Texas, Robert Pierpoint, Mrs. George Bush, Mrs. Eckhart, Jessica Catts, George Bush (then a Texas Congressman), Bill Hobby (then editor of the *Houston Post;* in 1980, Lieutenant-Governor of Texas). *U.S. House of Representatives photograph.*

With President Nixon in Vietnam, 1969. *Official White House photograph.*

Robert Pierpoint's most famous—and most controversial—portrait, 1971. © *1971 by Maggi Castelloe, from* Hope and Fear in Washington (The Early Seventies).

With William Simon, President Nixon's Secretary of the Treasury, on the steps behind the Oval Office—January 11, 1975. *Official White House photograph*.

With President Ford at the 1976 White House Correspondents Association dinner. *Stan Jennings*.

With President Carter and daughter Marta Pierpoint at the White House Lawn Party—May 29, 1978. *Bill Fitzpatrick, The White House.*

usual cigar. He greeted me with a jovial smile as I took the seat beside his desk and asked a couple of questions about the President's schedule for the next few weeks. Since White House correspondents' private lives are guided by how, when and where a President spends his time, we often try to get advance private information on travel plans and public appearances. Even such information given "off the record" can ease a reporter's relations with his wife and children, since he may know in advance of one weekend that he'll be away with the President.

With the smile still on his face, Salinger off-handedly told me about the newspaper cancellation. But between his casual manner and my general disinterest it slipped by me completely. It did not take Salinger long, however, to "chat" with other reporters, and the cancellation became a front-page item. Kennedy looked foolish, the White House resubscribed to the *Herald Tribune,* and I had the good sense to keep quiet about how I had missed a story.

Salinger was one of the more colorful characters of my years at the White House. In the tradition of most Presidential press secretaries, he could drink and carouse with the best—or worst—of the correspondents, and frequently did. But his free-wheeling, quick-witted attitude reflected JFK's own self-confidence and sense of humor. When assassination brought LBJ to power, it was obvious that Salinger's White House days were numbered. Sure enough, Salinger left in 1964, and Johnson brought in George Reedy, an intelligent, introspective man who well understood the function of a free press in a Democratic society—something that his boss never really did. Reedy also understood that reporters could not do their job properly without cooperation from the White House on basic matters such as the President's travel plans and his thoughts about key appointments. Reedy's attempts to help us invariably incurred the wrath of the President. Leaks made Johnson especially ferocious, and he usually blamed Reedy, even though most leaks came from others within and outside the White House. To compound his problems, the Press Secretary was honest and felt obliged to confirm stories when he was not the original source. As a result, Reedy was constantly pulled to one side by the President and the other by the press. Finally, his health failed and he resigned less than a year after becoming Press Secretary. In a sense it was probably the best thing that ever happened to George Reedy, who left the White House to become a widely respected author and professor of journalism.

The next Press Secretary was Bill Moyers, who had already been working with LBJ for thirteen years, as a reporter for Johnson's radio-TV stations in Austin, as a Capitol Hill aide, and as a speechwriter and later Chief of Staff during Johnson's first couple of years in the White House. He could speak with authority for the President, and was also unfailingly polite and personable with reporters. If anyone had a close working and personal relationship with LBJ it was Moyers. But even he reached his Waterloo with Vietnam.

Moyers persistently tried to put a humane face on an increasingly inhumane war, explaining the President's Vietnam policies in the most acceptable terms possible, just as he tried to make LBJ appear more reasonable, human and flexible and less stubborn and egocentric than he often was. However, normally Moyers was only as forthcoming as LBJ would allow; thus, he was more pleasant than he was informative. But he did know how to handle his tyrannical boss. One morning I walked into the press office and was told by one of Moyer's secretaries to go to him immediately. I quickly learned that my morning radio report had so outraged the President that he wanted to see me.

"Was the story wrong?" I asked.

Moyers remained very calm. "No, that's not the reason he's upset. He's just very angry, wants me to bring you up to the Oval Office right away. He wants you to tell him the sources for your story."

I told Moyers that I would be happy to tell Johnson personally that I would never divulge a source. The Press Secretary, skillfully protecting his boss from an unpleasant confrontation, then told me to ignore the Johnson request. Subsequently, LBJ launched an internal investigation to discover my source, but it was unsuccessful.

Such incidents inevitably took their toll on Moyers, and he told me that Johnson's war policies and Johnson's temper eventually became too much. Moyers decided to accept an offer he had received months earlier from Harry Guggenheim, publisher of the Long Island, New York, *Newsday*. During a seven-hour drive around the LBJ ranch, Johnson tried to dissuade Moyers from leaving, and when this failed, the President never forgave him. After Moyers left the White House, Johnson spread ugly rumors that Moyers had failed at his job and had tried to build himself at the expense of his employer. Although he had been in most respects like a member of the family, Johnson cut off all communication with Moyers, and did not even invite him to Lynda Bird's wedding. Johnson's attitude hurt Moyers, who twice wrote conciliatory letters to the LBJ ranch after Johnson retired. The former President, who appeared to be too proud to admit that he had been wrong in his treatment of Moyers, never answered. Yet in 1972, five years after Moyers had left his side, Johnson spent considerable time during a three-hour meeting with Senator George McGovern, then the Democratic Presidential candidate, discussing his former press secretary in terms of a much-missed prodigal son.

But, in many ways, Johnson had only himself to blame, because he had forced Moyers to become Press Secretary. In fact, even before he accepted the position, Moyers had privately sought out suggestions for a substitute. And after only a few months on the job, Moyers was already seeking a replacement.

I found this out the hard way, one early spring day in 1965, as my wife and I sat down to lunch. The telephone rang. It was Moyers, who knew Mondays were my day off and that I'd be at home.

"Have you had lunch yet, Bob?" he asked, and he hastily added, "because if not, the President would like you to come down and join him for lunch." Needless to say, I arrived at the White House in record time.

The Press Secretary greeted me with a quick handshake and a smile and said, "The President is waiting." Until that moment, I had assumed that LBJ was having several

White House correspondents in for lunch—a bit suddenly, perhaps, but something he had done before. Johnson, by now securely installed in the Oval Office—having swept the 1964 election—was settling down to run the place in his own special way. Among other things, he maintained close, personal contact with reporters. This was fine, except when Johnson did not like your latest reports, in which case he could unleash fearsome personal verbal attacks.

As Moyers escorted me up the hall toward the big oval-shaped office that looks out over the Rose Garden, I became increasingly afraid that I might be in for trouble. When Bill opened the door to announce me, my apprehension increased. None of my colleagues was in sight; there was only the tall Texan, looming large over his big desk, a formidable figure silhouetted against the windows.

But for the moment at least, LBJ was in an affable, "schoolteacher" mood. (White House regulars frequently listed the various roles of great actor Lyndon Johnson, ranging from the fiery Southern preacher, through unctuous undertaker, to angry drill sergeant. The fatherly schoolteacher was one of his more likable personas.)

"Have you had lunch, Bob?" he asked.

"No, Mister President."

"Well, let's go outside and take a little walk, and then we can go up in the mansion and get a bite to eat."

I flung a somewhat panic-stricken glance at Moyers as we headed out the doorway and down the driveway, but this was apparently to be a one-on-one confrontation. I steeled myself for a Presidential outburst.

During a quick two laps around the circular driveway behind the White House, I had trouble keeping up with LBJ's long strides and his disjointed conversation about his family and trivial matters back at the LBJ ranch. He switched back and forth from his daughters' performances in school, praising Lynda as a "real scholar," to problems that he and his ranch foreman were having with the cattle. Most of this was of no interest to me, but every time I tried to bring up another subject, such as the burgeoning war in

Vietnam, he would brush me off with a nonanswer and go back to his personal musings. Then we headed for the ground-floor Diplomatic Entrance in the rear of the mansion. Once inside, the President, his ever-present but silent Secret Service agent and I turned left and entered a small elevator which I had never known was there. In an awkward silence, the three of us slowly ascended to the third floor. I had no idea what to expect as we entered the sacrosanct private family quarters of Presidents. I had been there briefly a few times before—most often when President Kennedy used the private upstairs den to receive the credentials of new ambassadors.*

The unexpected came quickly, as LBJ stuck his head into one of the rooms off the main hall and shouted, "B . . . I . . . R . . . R . . . R . . . D! Bob Pierpoint's here to have lunch with us."

A high-pitched Southern voice called back, "I've already eaten, Lyndon, but I'll come set awhile!" A moment later, Lady Bird Johnson joined us in the private upstairs dining room.

Elegantly furnished with nineteenth-century American Federal pieces, this room looks out toward the fountain on the front lawn and Pennsylvania Avenue. The table is easily long enough to seat ten people, but on this more informal occasion the President sat at the south end near the door, Mrs. Johnson sat on his left, and I to his right. The early conversation was memorable, to say the least. Mrs. Johnson apparently did not know that I was a reporter, and she began to discuss how happy Lyndon would be to know that more tourists had inspected the premises that day than on any day when the Kennedys lived there. This might have been welcome news to Lyndon Johnson, but he

*All ambassadors must present their credentials directly to the President. It is a meaningless, time-consuming formality, and Presidents usually devise Oval Office or Cabinet Room ceremonies that will move quickly and make for good news photographs. In accepting the credentials upstairs—an experiment he eventually dropped—Kennedy was simply trying to find a more convenient, informal way to perform this chore.

was not about to gloat in the presence of a newsman, so he glanced at me to see if I had noted his wife's slip and quickly changed the subject.

LBJ then seized the conversational initiative in typically unsubtle fashion. He yawned. His wife looked at him with concern and said, "Lyndon, you look tired; I think you ought to take a nap this afternoon." His trap was set. Stretching somewhat deliciously, LBJ answered, "Yes, Bird, ah am tired." Then with a bawdy wink in my direction, he added, "What time was it ah got into *your* bed this mawnin!" The first Lady replied with complete composure, "I believe it was about 4 A.M."

Lady Bird excused herself shortly afterward, and the President and I spent another forty-five minutes in endless, meaningless discussions of LBJ's family affairs. By this time, I was trying to decide just what LBJ wanted with me, presuming it to be either heavy-handed criticism, or, if I was lucky, a "leak" of an exclusive story. I probed at several points, asking about the escalating war in Vietnam, changes in the Cabinet, and Capitol Hill maneuverings, but got nowhere. The President kept returning to problems at "the ranch," (which really consisted of scattered land and cattle holdings around Johnson City, Texas, where he went almost every weekend), and his daughters, Lynda Bird and Luci, including their relative intellectual abilities, personalities, affection for him. At one point LBJ expressed irritation at several recent stories speculating that one of his private advisers, lawyer Clark Clifford, might become Secretary of Defense, vigorously denying that Clifford was his adviser on anything except "the girls," and Lady Bird's legal problems, their estates, and that sort of thing. With a completely straight face, Johnson proclaimed that Clifford was really closer to them than to him.*

By about 2:30 P.M., we had finished lunch and I thought it time to leave. I tried, but LBJ wouldn't allow it. First he insisted on coffee, then more conversation. By this time I had run out of questions, and our dialogue had deterio-

---

*Later, Johnson did appoint Clark Clifford Secretary of Defense.

rated into a Johnson monologue. I began to suspect that the President was just lonesome. At 3 P.M., I again tried to leave, but this time the President suggested that we move across the hall. I followed him to where a young man stood in front of an open door. Startled, I saw that the medium-sized room was dominated by a huge bed, the canopy and matching spread of formal blue-and-white French design. Again I attempted a graceful exit, but the President simply ignored my effort, instructing the young man—apparently a valet—to usher me back to the Press Room when we had finished talking. In the meantime, LBJ began to undress. At first, I did not quite know how to act as the President took off one piece of clothing after another and handed each one to the valet. But as I stood in the doorway trying to figure out what to do, and Johnson kept on with his monologue, the humor of the situation struck me. There was the President of the United States, the most powerful man in the world, standing in his underclothes and later, as he would have put it, "bare-assed nekkid," while I tried to discuss serious issues and he tried to avoid them.

Still chatting unconcernedly, the President donned his pajama top, then moved past me into the small bathroom near the entry, where he proceeded to relieve himself while speaking loudly over the sound of passing water. I wished I had a camera, if only to convince my friends that this had actually happened. When LBJ put on his pajama bottoms, crawled into the canopy bed, and stuck his reading glasses on his nose, I could only think of the big bad wolf masquerading as grandma. Although I don't think I betrayed my thoughts by so much as a smile—in fact I was very fearful of doing so—it was an hilarious picture.

By that time, I was experiencing a combination of fatigue, fascination and shock. Except for occasional brief interjections such as, "Yes, Mr. President," and "No, Mr. President," and, "Isn't that interesting," I was simply watching the passing parade.

Once President Lyndon B. Johnson had crawled into bed, the valet handed him the afternoon newspapers. But, try as I might, I still did not escape for another fifteen minutes, when the President finally turned on the reading light. As I walked back to the Press Room at last, I noted that it was 3:45 P.M., nearly three hours since I'd arrived.

Looking back at this strange episode, I concluded that LBJ was simply lonely, that he could feel those walls closing in on him and he was reaching out for human contact. In that regard, I failed him because I deliberately avoided sympathetic conversation. I was a reporter—not a confidant—and wanted to keep it that way. However, I also learned a few weeks later that Bill Moyers was searching for someone to take over as Press Secretary, and had wanted LBJ to look me over. Moyers rather guardedly asked if I would consider the job if the President were to ask, and I replied that I did not want it. I opposed Johnson's increasing military involvement in Vietnam, and I disliked the way LBJ often treated his staff. Finally, I am not sure that LBJ was very much impressed by our long session together, since I dropped my end of the dialogue after the first hour or so. In any case, President Johnson never invited me to take Moyers' job, so I never had to say No. It might not have been easy, since he was one of the best persuaders in the business.

After Moyers' departure in early 1967, LBJ found the press secretary who suited him best in George Christian. Christian would tell the press as much as Johnson wanted and no more. Furthermore, like Johnson, he believed the Vietnam war was a justifiable necessity, and he was unfailingly supportive of the President's policies. But I never knew Christian to lie or mislead the press. His calm personality also helped counterbalance Johnson's frequent emotional outbursts. Even under mounting public dissent over Vietnam and during the roughest sessions with the White House correspondents, Christian maintained his quiet credibility.

Although LBJ's unwillingness—or inability—to tell the truth about Vietnam exposed his press secretaries to continual firestorms, Richard Nixon's Ron Ziegler had the toughest job of any press secretary I've seen.

Nixon's first few months in office were easygoing, and

Ziegler's dealings with the White House press seemed to be off to a good start. The President, his Chief of Staff H. R. "Bob" Haldeman and Ziegler comprised a kind of team for dealing with us. At the most basic level, they maintained excellent relations. During the 1968 campaign Nixon had given instructions that the traveling press corps should be provided the best possible hotel rooms, transportation facilities and food. This was wise on Nixon's part, since he knew that the reporters themselves do not pay for their "keep" while on the road, and that we are happier when more comfortable—a fact sometimes reflected in our reporting.

Early in 1969, on President Nixon's initial trip to San Clemente, Ziegler's staff booked the press corps into a middle-class motel, with all rooms opening to outside corridors, therefore providing the privacy of a beehive. It was also not large enough to accept the entire press corps, so the owner-manager—who just happened to be a friend of Nixon's—gave only reporters private rooms and forced the photographers and electronic technicians to double up. This was a serious mistake. In the pecking order of the White House press corps, correspondents may think they are at the top, and since the press secretary must deal primarily with them, he may make the same error. But photographers and technicians are extremely important. For example, without technicians to provide and operate the equipment, no broadcast correspondent would ever get on the air. They also have very strong unions. So on this occasion, the photographers and technicians simply picked up and walked out, heading for a better motel.

They found what they were looking for about ten miles north of San Clemente, at the Surf and Sand Hotel in Laguna Beach. Although some of the President-elect's staff initially objected to the move, there was nothing they could do about it. Ziegler quickly got the message. As glowing reports of the comfort and convenience of the Surf and Sand came rolling in, Ziegler investigated. The next time Richard Nixon returned to San Clemente, this time as President, the White House press corps and the staff of the Press Secretary happily settled into luxurious surroundings at Laguna Beach. The Surf and Sand was our California headquarters for the next six years, although, to mollify the President's friend, some of the staff stayed in San Clemente. Ziegler kept the press briefing room at the San Clemente Inn, and sometimes we used it, but most briefings were held in Laguna Beach.

However, Vice-President Agnew soon began to attack the television networks, clearly under orders from the White House, and the long-smoldering feud between Richard Nixon and the media flared up again. The feud went back to Nixon's early years as a "Communist baiter," and his smear campaign against Jerry Voorhis and Helen Gahagan Douglas. Many members of the press criticized his tactics, which exacerbated what seemed to be Nixon's innate dislike and distrust of all but the most pliable journalists. The simmering hostility between Nixon and the press broke into the open after his 1962 defeat in California's gubernatorial election with Nixon's famous farewell: "You won't have Richard Nixon to kick around any more."

Ziegler was squarely in the middle, a "no-win" position that he was forced to maintain throughout the Nixon administration. Ziegler himself was not particularly anti-press, and occasionally he did try to alleviate problems. During the early years of Ziegler's service, it was not quite clear how much, or how little, real power he had. I believed at the time that he functioned like most spokesmen for Presidents, meeting with the man in the Oval Office and relaying his views to the press, and vice versa. But as Watergate became an increasing problem for Nixon, the truth emerged: Ziegler and the President rarely ever met, and the Press Secretary was merely a mouthpiece for his true boss, White House Chief of Staff H. R. "Bob" Haldeman. Haldeman had hired Ziegler for the 1962 gubernatorial campaign, then employed him at the Los Angeles office of the J. Walter Thompson advertising agency, and finally made him the press spokesman for Nixon's 1968 drive to the Presidency. So, perhaps it should have been obvious that Ziegler was not what his title implied, but really a press secretary once-removed.

Nevertheless, a spokesman for the President, even one with limited powers, must be able to think on his feet and answer without damaging his employers, and Ziegler could do both. He had the saving grace of a quick sense of humor, a rare commodity in the Nixon White House. Toward the end of Nixon's Presidency, when Haldeman had left the White House, Ziegler actually assumed the role he had been playing as stand-in before. As Nixon's resignation approached, Ziegler did meet with the President daily and probably became Nixon's closest associate, with the exception of General Haig, Haldeman's replacement as chief-of-staff.

Ziegler generally followed orders, whatever their source, and in the face of mounting accusations against the Nixon Administration, he confronted daily attacks from an increasingly aggressive, restive press.

"Stonewalling," an expression first used to describe the White House approach to questions on Watergate, was his chief weapon. As stories of the involvement by Presidential aides became more embarrassing, Nixon (or perhaps Haldeman) ordered Ziegler and his deputy, Gerald Warren, to answer questions in a way that conveyed no real information. Ziegler was especially talented at appearing to respond to questions but not, in fact, giving out anything beyond a denial that the President or his staff had done anything wrong. At other times he filibustered or simply refused to provide answers.

But such tactics seldom stopped questions. As every press secretary eventually learns, unanswered questions generally turn into news stories. For example, questions such as "What does the President remember having discussed with Haldeman during that gap in the tape?" were transformed into stories that began with leads like, "For the third day in a row, White House Press Secretary Ron Ziegler refused to answer questions about how that eighteen-and-a-half-minute gap appeared on the tape of the President's conversations of June 23, 1972." This so upset Ziegler that he began to make himself available for only one daily briefing, usually about eleven-thirty in the morning.

Even with this limited exposure, Ziegler sometimes said enough to get himself into trouble. Such an incident remains in my mind for a particularly frustrating reason. On June 19, 1972, I triggered a story that was used nationwide by other journalists, but that my own organization refused to broadcast.

Richard Nixon had been at Key Biscayne for the weekend, when the report broke that burglars had been arrested in the Democratic National Committee headquarters at the Watergate Hotel. During Ziegler's one regular briefing that day I asked if he had any comment on the break-in. His answer: "I'm not going to comment from the White House on a third-rate burglary attempt."

The Press Secretary's words, as well as his aggressively defensive manner, indicated to me that there might be more to the story than Ziegler cared to tell us. But the CBS Saturday *Evening News* producer in New York did not agree, and I never got the exchange on the air. I was upset, but I was not as forceful as I have been in other circumstances. I had no knowledge that Ziegler was lying; I had only instinct. In any event, Ziegler's response to my question received extensive attention from other journalists and rapidly became an important phrase in the jargon of the unraveling Watergate revelations. As new bits of data and truth emerged, commentators repeatedly noted that the White House considered Watergate to be a mere "third-rate burglary."

Years later, Ziegler asked me why I had addressed that question to him, since I had had no evidence that the White House was involved. I told him frankly that almost every reporter in the room shared my suspicion that, given Richard Nixon's history of dirty tactics during his campaigns for Congress, the Senate, and Governor, some kind of involvement by the President or his agents seemed quite likely. I had simply asked the question before anyone else did.

Whether Ziegler actually knew the truth is hard to determine. He must have felt very suspicious, to say the least, when Haldeman told him to keep insisting that the President knew nothing about Watergate until he was informed by John Dean in March of 1973. Ziegler's staff was eventually assigned to work on the tape transcripts— it was in his office that transcripts were first altered before being given to the press. Most of the changes were to eliminate profanity or irrelevancies, although at least one alteration removed evidence of the cover-up. It is not clear that Ziegler ordered or condoned this effort at whitewash, but he had borne some of the onus ever since.

Ziegler's experiences should be a warning to future press secretaries about the possible pitfalls in the job. A press secretary's first loyalty is, by the nature of his job, to his President. But a press secretary also owes something to the public, which pays his salary and expects him to perform with honesty and integrity. These are judgment calls, of course, and the best press secretaries are those who display the best judgment in serving their employer, the public and themselves.

Perhaps President Ford had Ziegler's experience in mind when he chose Jerry terHorst, a well-respected reporter for the *Detroit News*, as Press Secretary.

Short and rotund, terHorst was always respected among his colleagues for both his warm personality and his reportorial skills. On his first day at work I walked into his office to offer my congratulations. He asked me to sit down. "You've been around here a long time, and you know I have a tough job," terHorst said. "I'll need your help." But for reporters, even general advice is hard to give. Old friendships notwithstanding, a wall exists between staff members and reporters.* He quickly realized this, especially when rumors about a deal to pardon Nixon began to spread.

Several correspondents had picked up reports that a lawyer representing the President had gone to San Clemente to work out the terms of the pardon. TerHorst tried to check the reports, and others in the White House lied to him saying that it was not true. Jerry in turn told his former colleagues what he thought was the truth, that the rumors were false. Then came the surprise announcement

*See Chapter 8, "Press Ethics."

of the pardon, and terHorst's resignation came quickly thereafter. He felt that his own integrity was more important than a new career. TerHorst had not spent long enough on the difficult job of press secretary to have made enemies among his former colleagues, so he could return to journalism without much trouble.

Ford's next choice was NBC White House correspondent Ron Nessen. Although Nessen had been a fairly popular "regular," he apparently longed for the "respectability" of the Republican White House. In any case, Nessen made the transition from reporter to staff aide almost too easily. For example, the press corps followed Ford to Japan shortly after he assumed office. The night of the arrival, after an exhausting flight from Washington through Alaska and across the western Pacific, tired and rumpled correspondents were working on their stories while Nessen sipped cocktails at a Japanese reception next door to the Press Room. Within earshot of our Japan-based colleagues whom he did not know, the Press Secretary was heard to remark, nodding in our direction, "And to think, a few weeks ago I was one of them."

The atmosphere around his office was further poisoned by his running feud with my CBS colleague Phil Jones, who had been his rival in covering Jerry Ford as Vice-President. When Nessen took over as Ford's Presidential Press Secretary, the feud spilled over into public. At least once a week, the two men exchanged bitter personal barbs during briefings. The rest of us just stood there somewhat embarrassed as we waited for both men to calm down.*

Nessen's successor as Press Secretary, Jody Powell, brought with him none of this personal animosity. Although he was quick-tempered as well as quick-witted, Powell never held a grudge. In many ways he reminded me of Jim Hagerty. If a reporter needed help on a major story, Powell would come on the line, whatever the hour, and was usually helpful. Furthermore, Powell, like Hagerty, could

---

*Nessen did make some valuable contributions to press conference procedures. See Chapter 3, "The Press Conference."

often speak for the President without having to check back or clear his comments.

But Powell also had his problems. For one thing, he never paid much attention to his own lids, frequently strolling into the Press Room after the lid was on to discuss the latest developments. This was especially annoying one day during the early days of the Iran-hostage crisis, when Powell disclosed the freezing of Iranian assets in United States banks about 8 A.M., before many correspondents had even arrived at the White House. He should have ordered a call-out and delayed the announcement for an hour or so. On that occasion Powell caused journalists serious trouble with their superiors, who always want to know "why weren't you there when this story broke?" So, at heavy news times such as international crises, CBS began to leave one correspondent in the Press Room even during lids, since we did not want to be caught by surprise.

As far as briefings were concerned, however, Powell maintained traditional practices; briefings are subject to the same rules that govern Presidential press conferences. Yet unlike most Presidential press conferences, which usually last about half an hour, a White House briefing is flexible (although the average duration is about an hour) and sometimes seems endless. In Watergate days, the hour was sufficient to exhaust participants on both sides, leaving the room filled with bitterness, sarcasm and unanswered questions. But the record for length was established by Powell's deputy, Rex Granum. On June 8, 1977, the briefing had been delayed while he and others on the White House staff tried to decide how to answer anticipated questions about a published report that the IRS was auditing Carter's 1976 tax returns. The session finally began at 2:25 P.M. Minutes later, someone asked about the audit. Granum confirmed the reports and said that the audit was being done at the President's request. Skeptical reporters began pelting Granum with questions. At last, in desperation, he asked us to wait in the Press Room while he checked his facts. The wait lasted one hour and eighteen minutes. Finally, Granum returned with two top

Presidential aides: Press Secretary Jody Powell and Legal Counsel Robert Lipshutz. Granum, it turned out, had made a mistake; the IRS had asked for the audit, not Carter. But the mistake and ensuing discussion brought the total briefing time to 2½ hours.

Although press secretaries try hard to control the content of briefings, they can end only when the "dean," or senior (in terms of years assigned to the White House) American wire-service person present, says loudly, "Thank you." This is not supposed to happen until all reasonable inquiries have been exhausted. But that, of course, is a subjective decision, and to avoid complaints from reporters who still need to get in their questions, the dean needs more patience than other reporters in the room. For much of the past twenty years this person has been Frank Cormier of the Associated Press. Lanky, deceptively mild-mannered, and a reporter of great integrity, Cormier takes his job very seriously. But like many of his colleagues, he sometimes became sleepy as briefing sessions droned on, heavy with esoteric and unproductive discussions between the Press Secretary and a few reporters pursuing stories of limited interest. At such times, we had to give Cormier a nudge to get him to end our misery.

The other feature that sets briefings apart from press conferences is that cameras and microphones are not permitted in briefings—although that rule can be bent if the White House desires. For example, in the spring of 1980, a few days before the New York Democratic primary in which President Carter was in a tight contest with Senator Edward Kennedy for the Jewish vote, Press Secretary Jody Powell allowed cameras and microphones to record his announcement that Mr. Carter had just invited Israel's Prime Minister Begin and Egypt's President Sadat to Washington for conferences on the Middle East.

Permitting broadcast journalists to do their job properly, however, should not be left to the President's whim. Cameras and microphones are the tools of electronic journalism, just as pencils, pens and notebooks (and increasingly, small tape recorders) are the tools of the writing press. Some reporters say that cameras should be excluded, so the Press Secretary can go "on background" or "off the record."* This is a phony charge. While the cameras and microphones do in fact record everything, so does the reporter with pencil and paper. Print journalists respect the rules of their profession, and if given the opportunity, broadcast journalists would be equally responsible.

Very early in the Carter administration, Hodding Carter, Assistant Secretary of State for Public Affairs and the widely praised spokesman for the State Department, agreed that cameras and microphones should be allowed to record his regular briefings. This system worked well, and we simply did not use the videotape of his background or off-the-record remarks. The only breakdown I know of came when Carter was giving a briefing on the hostages in Iran and forgot that he had granted permission for the networks and local stations to carry it live. He said he wanted to answer a question on background, and before anyone could remind him that he was going out over the airwaves live, he proceeded to do so. As far as can be ascertained, no damage resulted except to Carter's otherwise excellent reputation and slightly bruised ego.

Critics often say that briefings fail to produce much real news, but are instead propaganda opportunities for the White House. Actually, even if the White House puts the best possible face on each presentation, a White House correspondent's background and experience permit him to search beyond the official line. But this requires skill. Reporters must listen carefully, note nuances and omissions, and try to obtain as many facts as possible. "Reading" a press secretary is important, and the longer a White House correspondent has worked with a press secretary,

*"On background" means that reporters can use the information, but may not attribute it by name or title to the person giving it out. For example, they can attribute certain facts or quotations to "A high administration source" or a "White House official" but may not say that Press Secretary Jody Powell or a Presidential spokesman was the source of the information. "Off the record" means that the information cannot be passed on to the public in any way. Its value usually lies in preventing incorrect stories from being repeated.

the more accurately this can be done. For example, if a certain spokesman fences over a story without denying it, or denies it with hedges, this may mean the story is essentially true but that the President does not want it confirmed. If a press secretary says, "I have nothing for you on that right now," as Carter's Powell sometimes did, he usually means "That is correct but we are not ready to confirm it." After such an answer, I usually went to the press secretary privately to get further information and to ask on background if the story was true.

But no matter what impression the press secretary creates, a formal Administration statement need not and should not be accepted at face value. If the topic is totally unfamiliar, the reporter may also need extra time to put the story in proper perspective. The wire services and radio networks are particularly vulnerable in this regard, since their constant deadlines rarely leave time to check out White House assertions. As a result, they often report exactly what has been seen or heard, but not necessarily the background that makes it intelligible.

Television-network correspondents have a similar vulnerability, which press secretaries sometimes abuse. For example, in August of 1980, reporters waited most of one day for answers to questions on White House National Security Adviser Zbigniew Brzezinski's invitation the previous year to Billy Carter to bring the Libyan chargé d'affaires to the White House, where the three of them discussed the possibility of Libya's help in freeing the hostages. Since this occurred in the midst of controversial revelations regarding Billy Carter's financial dealings with the Libyans and his reluctant registration as a foreign agent, the Brzezinski invitation had stirred up considerable controversy. Finally, at 5:15 P.M. that day, Jody Powell put out a three-page single-spaced "White Paper" on Billy Carter's Libyan activities. But this paper raised even more questions, because it mentioned hitherto secret telephone calls among the President's legal counsel, Lloyd Cutler, and Billy and his lawyers.

Powell did not finish answering questions on the document until about 6 P.M., leaving network correspondents who had to do stories for the evening news no time to check with Billy, Cutler, Brzezinski, or anyone else involved. For the next two or three days, while the Billy story dominated the news, Powell repeatedly did not brief us until very late in the afternoon. As a result, my *Evening News* broadcasts were choppy, incomplete, and possibly even inaccurate. We learned later, for example, that the "White Paper" and Powell's briefings conveyed some errors and omissions.

Sometimes White House evasions fail, as we dig beneath official pronouncements to discover the truth. For example, at about 10 P.M. on Monday, March 10, 1980, Deputy Press Secretary Rex Granum surprised the few reporters still on hand by distributing to them a Presidential statement alleging that a "communications gap" had caused a highly controversial United States vote in the United Nations. Granum offered very little explanation and insisted that what he did say merely be attributed to an unnamed "White House official."

I was suspicious and began to probe, and by the next day my sources provided me with enough solid information to go on the Tuesday night Cronkite show to report why the President of the United States claimed to have discovered a major "bureaucratic error" forty-eight hours after the fact:

On Friday, March 7, Secretary of State Vance and President Carter agreed conditionally that the United States Ambassador to the United Nations, Donald McHenry, would vote in support of a UN resolution that essentially condemned Israel for permitting settlements on land seized from Jordan and occupied since the 1967 war, including East Jerusalem. The reason for the condition was that Carter did not want in the resolution several references that would be sure to inflame the Israelis. He objected particularly to one section of the resolution that dealt with the issue of access to the Jerusalem holy places of various religious groups. He wanted this section taken out of the resolution altogether, and Vance agreed. The President also suggested that the call for dismantling of certain Israeli settlements built in occupied territory was going a bit beyond previous American policy and that McHenry should note dissatisfaction with the section before approving the resolution. Even without these changes the resolution did not run counter to long-standing United States government positions, but Carter wanted it as palatable as possible to Israel and American Jews. On Saturday morning Vance telephoned the President at Camp David to say that McHenry had cleared up the Jerusalem issue, and they agreed that the United States could support the resolution. But the resolution still contained in every section a sharply worded condemnation of Israel for holding East Jerusalem, with the words "including Jerusalem" inserted directly. The President misunderstood Vance and thought that all such references had been deleted. So he approved a yes vote.

Between Saturday night and Monday, anger mounted among Jews around the United States, and the Israeli government reacted with strong disapproval. By Monday, when the President had returned from Camp David, heavy pressure was building against his Administration. Some of his own officials considered the vote to be a major error— particularly Vice-President Walter Mondale and Ambassador Sol Linowitz, who was in charge of the delicate ongoing negotiation between Israel and Egypt. Linowitz and Mondale were convinced that even if no change in United States policy had really been signaled by the UN vote, this was not the time to apply a heavy-handed public shove to Israel—which might result in Israeli Prime Minister Menachem Begin's complete refusal to continue negotiation over the future of the West Bank and the Gaza Strip. This could, they argued, jeopardize Carter's strongest foreign-policy accomplishment, the Camp David accords, just at the time when he most needed the support of Jews in the upcoming Illinois, New York and other Democratic primaries.

Late that afternoon, an emergency meeting was called at the White House. The participants included Mondale, Linowitz, McHenry, and Deputy Secretary of State Warren Christopher. Two of the Carter Administration's top figures did not participate; Secretary Vance was hurrying back from a speaking engagement in Chicago, and Chief of Staff Hamilton Jordan was preoccupied with the next day's primaries in Massachusetts and Vermont and gave the UN vote little attention. Under the eloquent persuasions of Mondale and Linowitz, the President became convinced that the UN vote was damaging to the Middle East peace process, as well as to his Jewish support in the United States. Some thought was given to placing the blame for a communications gap on Ambassador McHenry and another State Department career officer, Assistant Secretary for the Near East and South Asia Harold Saunders. But it was pointed out that blaming Saunders or McHenry would probably raise as many questions as it would resolve. McHenry happens to be black; his alleged culpability might well have resurrected the issue of his predecessor Andrew Young's forced resignation over another controversy involving the Mideast. By early evening Vance had arrived at the White House, and he and Mondale went to the President with their plan. Eventually it was decided that the White House should issue a statement saying that the UN vote was in error, due to a failure in communications and that Secretary of State Vance would take responsibility. Some discussion was devoted to the problem of President Carter's appearing to vacillate and the political damage this might cause. But Carter rejected this caution and decided to go ahead with the communications-gap ploy. That night Granum—who probably did not even know the truth—dutifully faced White House correspondents and read the President's statement.

Even had he personally known the facts, Granum's lack of candor at that briefing would not have been particularly unusual. Normal procedure is to assume that the press briefing only provides the tip of the iceberg, and at least once a week the briefings on an important story are so inadequate that we must range far wider to get the full truth. Seldom do we find it all.

Still, the UN vote stands out, because a President publicly changing his mind on such an important decision rarely happens. Perhaps because he was well aware of this, Press Secretary Powell left the briefing chore to one of his assistants. If so, this was an unusual example of reticence on his part, as he was normally quite willing to take the heat, and to dish it out too.

In fact, Powell had one of the most formidable tempers of any Press Secretary I have ever faced. I saw it for the first time shortly after Powell held a joint press briefing with Budget Director Bert Lance in which they explained how President Carter planned to cut back on the size of the White House staff. This was a boast I had heard in previous administrations, and it had never worked out before, so I was a bit skeptical now.

A few weeks later, I tried to park my car in the area behind the White House reserved for staff and press, only to find that the number of those holding parking passes had skyrocketed. No space was left, and many cars were illegally parked. For the first time in my memory, the police had started passing out warning notices, instead of the usual parking tickets. So I ordered a cameraman to take pictures of the parking problem and started mapping out a story on how the White House staff had actually grown under Carter. Since I needed some facts and figures, the White House had to be apprised of what I was after. Powell and the press office were not happy, but they provided the information. When Powell saw the story on the CBS *Evening News*, he called me on the telephone, and for over an hour he argued about it, using some very strong language and threatening not to cooperate with me in the future. However, Powell never mentioned the story again, and I saw no evidence that he ever carried out his threats.

Such run-ins and subsequent relations are important to White House correspondents, because to us press secretaries are in some respects more important than Presidents. We see more of them, hear more from them, and learn more through them than we do from those who occupy the Oval Office. White House spokemen are the daily transmission belt for information to the public about a President and his policies. If they succeed in their difficult task of pleasing two masters, press and President, they can have a profound impact on history. For weeks after Ike's

1955 heart attack, Jim Hagerty was the President in fact, if not in title. During Jimmy Carter's 1980 troubles over his brother Billy's activities with Libya, Jody Powell advised and midwifed every move. If Powell had not advocated, and carried out, a "let it all hang out" policy of candor on the President's relations with his brother, Jimmy might have lost the election before the Democratic convention. Between those two examples are dozens more, when the advice and actions of a press secretary helped a President dig himself out of a hole, or dug him in deeper.

In some respects, the best press secretaries are those who expose their Presidents most to the press, as Pierre Salinger did with John Kennedy. One of the most difficult problems a President faces is getting people to tell him things he may not want to hear. Sycophantism is a crippling disease, yet it runs rampant in the White House. Most correspondents are immune, if for no other reason than that their jobs depend on being critical of Presidents. Press secretaries are not quite so lucky, but the best are those who keep the disease under control, partly by keeping the lines of communication open between press and President.

I'm a little like Will Rogers: I never met a press secretary that I didn't like; in fact, I've liked some of them much better than the Presidents they served.

6

Television Takes Over

While serving as a war correspondent in Korea, I learned a valuable lesson the hard way: radio and television reporting of similar events can produce very different stories.

I spent the night of May 16, 1951, my twenty-sixth birthday, with an infantry company near the Hwachon Dam in Central Korea, under enemy fire—my first time on the front lines. Communist troops occupying this sector had been launching nighttime probing actions, and American Intelligence officers expected a major offensive. Despite protests from older colleagues, I talked myself into the need to test myself against both fear and gunfire. So, accompanied by an unlucky Public Information Office private who had been assigned as my guide, I set off. We were driving our own private jeep, a former Army vehicle painted a distinctive battleship gray with "CBS" emblazoned on its rickety doors in the hope that the enemy could (and would) distinguish it from military targets. It was customary for reporters to be armed, and I wore a German P-38 pistol, which I had fired several times in target practice and felt I could use in an emergency. I was scared, but also excited, because I did not know what to expect.

Big artillery guns fired occasional rounds over our heads as we passed through United States artillery positions, into the infantry units facing the no man's land where Communist troops had begun to move. We had decided to visit Fox Company of the 19th Regiment, since it happened to be astride the road and the easiest to reach. At about 11 P.M., we arrived at the bottom of the hill it occupied, parked the jeep in pitch blackness just off the road, and headed toward the ridge. I carried a rather heavy, bulky Japanese tape recorder, and hoped to record sounds of the action and my impressions of what was happening. At first not much was. We managed to stumble to Fox Company's command post, with the aid of various startled GIs, who wanted to know just what the hell a reporter was doing up there when he could be almost anywhere else. I was beginning to wonder at that myself.

Action began picking up at about the time I introduced myself to the company commander, who told me that the Chinese were creeping toward his sector, and that about seventy-five yards to our left, some GIs were already receiving fire. This news made me very nervous. Then I heard bursts of gunfire close to the road, and I began to worry that I might lose the CBS jeep and with it my last chance to escape. I think I feared the wrath of my bureau chief, George Herman, as much as I feared capture by the Communists.

I thought about leaving right away, but I had not yet done any recording, and it seemed a long way to go without getting a story. So I dutifully cranked up my recorder (at the time, recorders had spring-wound motors that had to be cranked up every seven or eight minutes), and waited.

As the tempo of rifle and machine-gun fire picked up on our left flank, the company commander radioed a request that the artillery units shell in closer, to intercept the approaching Chinese. It seemed a good time to get some sounds on my tape, so I opened the microphone. The young officer was just starting to explain the operation to me when we heard a whispering whistle and he yelled, "Look out, short round," and dived into the shallow trench beside us. I jumped in with him, tape recorder in hand. A shell exploded nearby. It sounded like a huge thunder clap and I curled myself into as tight a ball as possible as I waited for the pain I was sure would follow. It was all over in about five seconds, and as I readjusted to being unhurt I heard an incredible request over the radio: the commander of the artillery unit firing the shells wanted to know how many Chinese his guns were killing. Since it was completely dark except during explosions, and since the rifle fire to our left was getting closer, it was clearly not the optimal time to make a personal inspection. The company commander, a lieutenant, tried to explain this to his superior, who was about five miles behind the line, but to no avail. Finally in desperation he bellowed, "Oh all right, that last salvo killed eight enemy troops and wounded thirteen!" It was my first exposure to the military phenomenon of the "body count," which later became such an issue in Vietnam.

I returned safely to Division headquarters believing that my first trip to the front had been a failure. I was very unhappy with the tape documenting my Fox Company experiences, knowing that anyone could hear how nervous I had been even before that short round had gone off, and how badly shaken I was afterward. However, Ed Murrow and Fred Friendly were producing a weekly radio show, *Hear It Now,* and I knew they needed tapes of any kind, so I sent it off to Tokyo via military courier. It was a pleasant surprise a few days later to receive a warm congratulatory cable from them thanking me for my report, which they had featured as a young war correspondent enduring his baptism by fire. The drama seemed to please them, but I remained acutely aware that my fear had been obvious.

A few months later, Murrow and Friendly cabled again, saying that they were planning a television program called *See It Now,* and wanted me to repeat my performance with Fox Company—but this time with a television film crew. This proposal had serious practical shortcomings. First of all, it was not possible to film at night without bright lights, and no one in his right mind would put up lights around a line infantry company. It would have been so dangerous that the GIs themselves would have shot us in self-defense. Another problem was that Fox Company, suffering casualties and battle fatigue, was no longer in the front line, but in reserve a few miles behind it. I communicated these problems to Murrow and Friendly but they cheerfully replied that I should simply "work it out somehow."

A film crew from New York duly arrived, and we drove to the Fox Company area. Since the commanding officer and his men had enjoyed letters from home about my radio broadcast, they cooperated enthusiastically. We shot hundreds of feet of film of GIs digging trenches, building bunkers, answering mail call, eating, sleeping, griping, singing, and firing their weapons. I never actually *said* we were on the line, but it looked real. I pointedly told Murrow and Friendly to make it clear we were not near actual combat. But somehow the visual drama blurred that point. The first broadcast of *See It Now* featured my segment, and I became a temporary hero to Murrow and Friendly.

Despite this dubious success, with which I never felt quite comfortable, I had learned a valuable lesson. To cover the same stories as did radio, television, in certain circumstances, lent itself to staging. Therefore, whatever its potentialities, this new medium had to move past merely copying radio; it had to develop its own perspective on newsworthy events. Eventually we developed such techniques as filming what action we could spot while flying over enemy positions in a T-6 spotter plane. Radio could never have covered the story. People back home *saw* what the battlefield looked like, and television began to revolutionize war coverage while developing to its own fullest potential.

But the distinction between radio and TV coverage did not become crucial until the late 1950s, because until then network correspondents spent most of their time reporting for radio anyway. CBS television broadcast only a fifteen-minute nightly news show, and another fifteen-minute news show in the morning; neither was carried by all the affiliated local stations. Radio, on the other hand, had several daily newscasts, including two fifteen-minute broadcasts in the morning and Edward R. Murrow's prestigious evening report, all widely carried across the country. It was also easy to transmit radio broadcasts to New York by telephone line. Television was more cumbersome, requiring first a minimum two-member crew to produce the film, and then shipment to a film-processing center, and finally careful editing before final transmission from New York.

Yet as the persuasive powers of television became more evident, President Eisenhower and his staff devoted increasing time and attention to this new medium. By the time his tenure ended in January 1961, Secretary Jim Hagerty was treating network correspondents with the same courtesy he extended to reporters for major newspapers.

In contrast to this evenhandedness, John F. Kennedy—who instinctively understood television's potential—initiated a perceptible favoritism toward television. Press Secretary Pierre Salinger began deferring to the networks, answering television correspondents' calls more promptly, making himself more accessible to us, and inaugurating a system of frequent phone conversations and periodic meetings with network Washington bureau chiefs that became—and remains—an important behind-the-scenes tradition. President Kennedy also granted the networks other special favors, such as exclusive interviews and, for CBS a "first," Jacqueline Kennedy's televised tour of the White House.

But change came slowly in some areas, as shown by a story I tried to do shortly after the 1962 Cuban missile crisis. During the fall Congressional campaign of 1962, John Kennedy abruptly canceled an appearance in Chicago, claiming to have a cold, and headed back to Washington. For the next several days, while a series of top-level meetings were held in the White House, the Pentagon and elsewhere, reporters tried desperately to find out what was going on. Two rumors were given credence: that the United States and the Soviet Union were approaching a crisis over the Berlin Wall and a divided Germany, and that the United States and the Soviet Union were approaching a crisis over Cuba. Finally, in a nationwide television address, JFK announced that the Soviets were placing nuclear missiles in Cuba. Meeting the challenge head on, Kennedy ordered Moscow to halt further shipments of such missiles and to remove those that were already in place. It was a direct confrontation between the world's two nuclear-armed superpowers, and the risks to both sides were clearly enormous. For the next several days, while messages, warnings and threats flew back and forth, no one was sure that war would not erupt. Americans began building basement air-raid shelters, or stocking existing shelters with candles, fresh water and canned goods. Some even purchased arms, either to repel possible invaders or for protection if civilization broke down.

Several weeks after the crisis was resolved, I tried to interview President Kennedy's National Security Adviser, McGeorge Bundy. A brilliant but arrogant man, Bundy did not generally speak to reporters, even those who worked for networks. He did, however, talk to special favorites, like writer Stewart Alsop, a fellow New England WASP, whom Bundy considered more his intellectual equal.

Bundy had told Alsop about the tense and agonizing debate preceding Kennedy's demand that Soviet leaders dismantle their Cuban missile sites. Alsop—with fellow columnist Charles Bartlett, who had discussed the situation with his old friend JFK—wrote an article for *The Saturday Evening Post* revealing that Adlai Stevenson, then United States Ambassador to the United Nations, had opposed the President's decision. The Alsop-Bartlett article, obviously based on quotes from high officials, implied that Stevenson "wanted a Munich,"—that is, wanted to surrender needlessly. This raised a national controversy and deeply wounded Stevenson both personally and politically. The question arose in Washington as to who had "fingered" him.

Through discussion with my colleagues I had eliminated most of the candidates, and a close reading of the original article indicated that the source had to be in the White House or on the National Security Council "working group" handling the crisis. I began calling all the possibilities, and their denials or explanations left Bundy as the logical remaining source. Then Bundy's refusal to return my phone calls strengthened my suspicion. I was not absolutely sure, but I had enough information to believe that Bundy was the source, so I decided to try to go with the story. My final check—if only to elicit his reaction—was with Bundy himself. But Bundy still would not return my telephone calls, although I called frequently throughout an entire afternoon. His secretary, whom I knew personally, finally asked what I wanted to discuss with her boss. I explained that for that night's *Evening News* I wanted Bundy's version of his conversation with Stewart Alsop, and how it had affected Ambassador Stevenson. She promised to convey the message, hinting in the process that there had indeed been such a conversation, but no return phone call ever arrived. Bundy obviously did not believe that CBS was worth much trouble. That night, the Cronkite show carried my story.

The next morning, shortly after I arrived at the White House, Bundy's secretary called to say Mr. Bundy would see me now. With some satisfaction I said I no longer needed to talk to him. The reply came quickly, "Yes, but now he needs to talk to you!"

That afternoon, I went to see Bundy in his busy basement office by the Situation Room. I was nervous because I still had not found anyone to completely confirm my report of the previous evening. If Bundy flatly denied the story, I would have been forced to recant—on the air. One did not make many mistakes of that nature and survive in the network news business. Secondly, Bundy was a tough powerful man, and I feared that our face-to-face encounter was going to be difficult.

Bundy, however, did not deny my story. Instead, we had a fascinating conversation in which he revealed what he considered to be the most critical days, hours and problems of the Cuban missile crisis, and how they had been resolved.

I had thought that the critical moment occurred as Soviet ships with cargoes of canvas-covered missiles moved slowly toward Cuba and the United States naval blockade. I had even warned my wife that the confrontation would take place between one and three one afternoon, and that if the Soviet ships did not stop or turn back, war might break out. If she did not hear from me by 3 P.M., she and the children were to load up the station wagon and head for the mountains of western Virginia, which we had chosen as our rendezvous point.

But Bundy disclosed that this had been only the first crucial moment. The second, he said, came two days later, when an American jet plane was shot down on a reconnaisance mission over Cuba. Bundy told me there was a debate within the "working group" on what response to make. Some advocated immediate bombing of the Russian-manned antiaircraft installations. But at this point conflicting messages began arriving from Moscow. One took a hard-line approach suggesting that a fight was indeed about to begin, while another was conciliatory. Many of the President's advisers argued that the United States should bomb Cuban missile sites, where Soviet soldiers and technicians were working. But Robert Kennedy, then Attorney General and a key Presidential confidant, advised that the hard-line message be ignored and the conciliatory one acknowledged. This plan was adopted, the crisis eased, and possible nuclear war was avoided.

I did not do any direct hard-news reporting on my conversation with Bundy, since the immediate crisis was past. (A few weeks is a long time in the instant-news trade.) But during the ensuing years the information was used in various feature and documentary broadcasts, and contributed to a fuller understanding of the crisis.

Thirteen months after the Cuban missile crisis, when Lyndon Johnson took over the Presidency, network television had achieved a new level of importance in the White House. Johnson saw the camera as a flexible tool, available for almost any purpose, and began requesting regular network time to explain his latest policies to an eager (or a captive) nation. By 1966, Johnson had become so enthusiastic about these unscheduled television announcements that he persuaded the networks to construct a television studio in the White House for his personal use. He chose a room on the first floor, about fifty feet long by thirty feet wide; it is called the "theater" and is generally used to screen movies for the First Family and their guests. The three major networks dutifully installed two television cameras and a control booth, and assigned personnel to the new facilities; these technicians spent long hours in the gloomy room, mostly just waiting, but keeping the equipment ready to go on the air at a moment's notice. It was tedious for them and expensive for CBS, NBC and ABC.

The networks finally persuaded Moyers and others on the White House staff that frequent appearances on television would be counterproductive. For one thing, it was a little like the shepherd boy crying "Wolf," when there was no wolf. Viewers who saw the President suddenly appear on their screens would worry that an international emergency had erupted. When that turned out to be false, Johnson's own credibility was eroded. Furthermore, LBJ was not the best television performer in politics. On camera he tended to look like a cross between a country schoolteacher and a funeral director. This drawback was hard to convey tactfully to a ferociously sensitive President, who had visualized himself using the facilities frequently, hurrying downstairs to make announcements about troops, battles and diplomatic efforts.

The networks resisted such live "interrupts," and gradually LBJ tired of the idea. One day I went down to watch one of his reports to the nation. In this case he was trying to videotape a statement for the evening news. Every time he came to a crucial line, Johnson jumbled the words, and he became increasingly upset. No one in the room, technicians or reporters, had the temerity to laugh, or even to smile. The third time LBJ blew his lines he also blew his top. The nearest person happened to be Yoichi "Okie" Okamoto, his personal photographer, who had been snapping still pictures, and the President began to curse him using extremely vile language. A quiet, unobtrusive, highly competent professional, Okie picked up his cameras and walked out of the room. The red-faced, sweating President then resumed his efforts before his small and silent audience and eventually succeeded in an acceptable "take."

Over my objections, the White House forced CBS News to destroy the tape of Johnson's extraordinary outburst, and not long after that, LBJ closed the basement TV studio. He had been using it for about one year, and the networks who were footing the bill were more than happy to bring their technicians and equipment home.

LBJ's frustrations notwithstanding, Presidential preoccupation with television was firmly established by the time his administration ended. The President would scarcely issue a policy pronouncement or sign an important piece of legislation without contriving to televise the event. When Richard Nixon assumed power, preoccupation with television had become an accepted part of the Presidency. Nixon had watched television's increasing power throughout the Johnson years and eventually orchestrated his own versions of "coverage." During the 1968 campaign, for example, he carefully avoided any situations in which correspondents could initiate a meaningful exchange on the issues.

Thus, Nixon's campaign appearances consisted mainly of speeches before friendly audiences and studio discussions with questioners carefully selected in advance—and excluding network correspondents. Most importantly, no reporter, either network or newspaper, could ever uncover anything about Nixon's so-called "secret plan" for ending the war in Vietnam. Most correspondents suspected that no such plan existed and later events proved this suspicion to be correct. But it was a clever ploy, and it fooled many voters hungry for a solution to the bloody conflict. By the time the nation learned that his answer was no different from anyone else's, he was already President. It then took six more years and thousands of lives to bring the war to a close with a "plan" that was, in fact, defeat and withdrawal.

Once in the White House, Nixon took advantage of television in the same way Lyndon Johnson had done, using it at every opportunity to advance his policies and politics. Rose Garden ceremonies, news conferences in the East Room, photo opportunities in the Oval Office, and nationally broadcast speeches became an integral part of

everyday Presidential life, sometimes staged with remarkable creativity.

Nixon then carried this expertise into his reelection
campaign. For example, the 1972 Republican National
Convention had a minute-by-minute script designed to
maximize the benefits to Nixon from television coverage.
This script called for the President to appear the night of
his nomination, for the traditional acclamation and accep-
tance speech. We flew down from Washington the afternoon before, and he spoke at a Republican rally that night
in Marine Stadium on Key Biscayne, where he was kissed
by Sammy Davis, Jr. (That was probably in the script, as
well.) After the convention, Nixon and his propaganda
specialists initiated a somewhat unusual campaign prop
that we called "the Republican Rent-A-Crowd." Nixon's
advisers would plan a Presidential appearance at a public
place, such as a municipal airport. To ensure a large and
enthusiastically pro-Nixon crowd, and to guarantee that
no anti-Nixon pickets or anti-war protestors marred television coverage, Nixon's advance men arranged for the local Republican party to hand out invitations, and would
instruct the local police to admit to the previously public
locations only those with proper identification. Even the
Secret Service, whose agents are forbidden by law to involve themselves in political acts, sometimes assisted local
officials in keeping anti-Nixon members of the public
out.

I discovered this phenomenon at an August rally in San
Diego, the day after the President's renomination. Nixon
had already made one campaign stop on his way from
Florida to California, and he arrived at the San Diego Airport just before sundown. The press plane had landed a
few minutes earlier, so I had time to study the gathering.
Everyone in the crowd of perhaps a thousand appeared to
be a strong Nixon supporter; I found not one single anti-
war or pro-McGovern sign. This struck me as incredible
for California, particularly at a time when the President
was so controversial.

Deadline pressure made me momentarily forget about
California supporters. Nixon's speech ended close to 11

P.M. Eastern Daylight Time, when I was scheduled to feed a brief news broadcast to the network, so I had to leave the airfield with my film before the rally actually ended. Driving away from the area, I passed a big building beside the runway and abruptly discovered why no anti-Nixon picketers were at the rally. A barricade had been erected across the road, and a group of police, aided by at least one Secret Service agent whom I recognized, were keeping back a crowd of perhaps fifty people, most carrying anti-war and anti-Nixon signs. The agent cleared a path for my car, then reerected the barricade. A few minutes after my arrival at the CBS affiliate in San Diego, where I was preparing my broadcast, the local camera crews and news reporters arrived, volubly enraged. Not only had the police and Secret Service kept the pickets and protesters away from the Nixon rally, but they had apparently tried to prevent photographers from taking pictures of the barricade—a clear violation of the constitutional rights of a free press and a serious breach of the strict Secret Service regulations.

As soon as I finished my broadcast, I called the White House switchboard at San Clemente and asked for William Livingood, one of the supervisors of the Secret Service detail. I told him what had happened and asked why the Secret Service would engage in improper and illegal behavior. He promised to investigate. As is frequently the case, the answer I finally received was evasive. The agent in question claimed that he was simply assisting local police and had not meant to prevent pickets from entering a public gathering or photographers from covering a story. In any case, the Secret Service assured me that it would not happen again.

Still dissatisfied, I raised the matter at Ron Ziegler's next briefing. Ziegler pleaded ignorance and blamed the local police. Tired and distracted by the daily grind of campaign activity, we in the press corps made no further efforts to pursue it.

As later evidence proved, the practice of admitting only certified Republicans to supposedly public rallies was a deliberate strategy designed by H. R. "Bob" Haldeman and other Presidential aides. Their staging efforts were exposed the next year in a North Carolina lawsuit. Anti-war and anti-Nixon groups had been excluded from an October 1971 rally honoring the Reverend Billy Graham, which Nixon had attended. These groups later instituted a civil suit over the infringement of their constitutional rights. The trial, in which Haldeman and others were convicted, clearly proved that people attending the rally were screened carefully so that news reports and television cameras would not depict opposition to the President.

Nixon's practices set dangerous precedents, but fortunately his successors in the White House have not followed his lead. Gerald Ford, in fact, lost some of his confrontations with the networks. In 1975, for example, Ford requested live prime time coverage for an economics-policy speech he was scheduled to give in Kansas City. NBC was carrying the World Series and refused, and CBS also declined to preempt regular programming. Both networks then endured considerable pressure from the White House, and NBC gave in. Ford's speech, which was not particularly newsworthy, blacked out the baseball game for millions of Americans who were much more interested in the World Series, and left Press Secretary Nessen angry at CBS.

Despite such setbacks, Ford did an outstanding—and legal—job of manipulating television during his 1976 campaign appearances. Since the President often made similar speeches at each stop, it was not easy for his staff to get Mr. Ford on the evening news, short of encouraging him to bump his head or stumble. (Although, as Nessen once rather bitterly pointed out, Gerald Ford was one of the nation's more athletically graceful Presidents; he just didn't come across that way on camera.) So his schedulers, television advisers, and other public-relations experts laid out a series of public appearances that took advantage of meticulous staging and beautiful scenery. During a steamboat trip down the Mississippi River, for example, Ford frequently stopped at small towns. Reporters and camera crews went ashore, and then the President posed on the deck as he made a brief speech to the assembled citizens. Often, he also came ashore for a brief handshaking walk through well-wishers, with the river and the steamboat providing a picturesque background. It was excellent television and gave us pretty pictures, but told us little or nothing about why Gerald Ford should be reelected President.

One campaign appearance designed to provide more pictures backfired. President Ford was walking along a line of milk cattle on an Iowa farm when an unimpressed cow suddenly lifted her tail, splattering the Presidential pants. As he hurried to get a change of clothes, a pro-Ford Secret Service agent somewhat embittered by press treatment of his boss, mumbled, "Why not shit on him? Everyone else does."

After Ford lost the 1976 election, President-elect Jimmy Carter learned the hard way that television permeated his new life. Carter thought that New Year's Day, 1977, would be a quiet time for him, and he decided to slip out of his Plains, Georgia, home for some private quail hunting in the nearby woods. CBS News had assigned no fewer than two correspondents to cover Carter, plus two full electronic camera crews of two people each, a radio technician, two couriers, a tape editor, and a producer who acted as traveling bureau chief. Carter's efforts to elude coverage and enjoy some privacy also forced the networks to post camera crews, couriers and correspondents at each end of the street leading to his residence. Besides the walkie-talkies we used for communication among ourselves, our technicians assigned to the White House always employed an electronic device called a scanner, which monitored radio frequencies assigned to the Secret Service. Whenever a transmission came through on one of those frequencies, the scanner would automatically lock onto it so we could listen. Thus, if the Secret Service was preparing to escort the President anywhere, we were immediately alerted, and if his motorcade was already moving we could usually locate it. But on this New Year's afternoon, the President-elect escaped us. He walked through the woods to Billy Carter's house, where a friend was waiting in a four-wheel jeep, which could easily traverse the muddy back roads and rugged fields.

There had been a rumor that Carter might try to go quail hunting, so as soon as our scanner indicated Secret Service activity, we organized our forces to find the hunting site and, if possible, the hunters. One of the CBS couriers, Don Murray, is a Plains native who knew where Carter owned land that might be good for quail hunting. Sure enough, we eventually spotted a Secret Service agent about five miles out of Plains, blocking a private road. Although he was usually friendly to reporters, the agent ordered us to leave. "The Boss," he said, "doesn't want his picture taken." We explained that we were on a public road and intended to remain there. The stake-out then settled down to a long, cold wait. The temperature that New Year's Day was in the low forties with a raw wind, and the country road was *gooey* red clay. By late afternoon, perhaps a dozen carloads of newspeople had assembled, listening to football games on car radios and running relays of couriers back and forth to Plains for hot coffee and sandwiches. CBS maintained one television crew on watch there, and another cruising nearby roads hoping to cut off Carter's escape if he decided to return to Plains another way.

ABC and NBC had evolved approximately the same technique, but NBC went one step further. One of their crews guessed where Carter was hunting and drove directly onto the private land, moving right up to the President-elect for some reportedly excellent shots. (I had forbidden my crew to do the same.) No one will ever know how good the pictures were because somewhere between the rough roads, the cold, and the muddy dampness, the NBC camera broke down. When the crew got back to their trailer under the Plains water tower (all three networks rented such mobile homes where we edited and transmitted television coverage), nothing usable was on their videotape. As it was, all any of us got for our afternoon of misery— besides incurring the President-elect's wrath—was a brief shot of Carter and his friend pulling off the private road and back onto the highway. A few dead quail were visible in the jeep. The brief sequence was transmitted to New York and used on the air.

Carter's anger notwithstanding, there was certainly nothing wrong with such full coverage of the quail hunt. Nor was it bad news judgment to show such scenes, as long as this was not done at the expense of more meaningful issues. On January 1, with its many bowl games and hangovers, I'm sure most viewers preferred the quail hunt to any substantive discussion of President-elect Carter's prospective policies.

This same concern for detail goes into television's coverage of more substantive events. The public sees only a few seconds or minutes of film, but never realizes how much planning and work goes on behind the scenes. A typical example was President Carter's trip to Panama in June of 1978. The avowed purpose of the trip was the symbolic transfer of the Canal to Panama. In the early part of this century the United States government had aided and abetted a revolt by a northern province of Colombia, resulting in establishment of the independent nation of Panama. The chief United States interest in this local rebellion was Panama's desirability as the site of a projected Atlantic-Pacific canal. Because the Colombians had proven difficult in negotiations over where and who would build the canal, United States government agents helped set up a regime in Panama more amenable to negotiating terms extremely beneficial to the United States. Nearly a half century later, as post-World War II nationalism rose, Panamanians and their brethren throughout Latin America became increasingly infuriated at this clear example of big-power colonialism. Eventually, United States control over the Canal Zone became such an intense issue that President Johnson recognized the need for a new relationship. Negotiation between the United States and Panama continued during the Nixon and Ford administrations, but it was Carter who finally pushed the changes through a reluctant Congress.

The next step was an exchange of instruments of ratification, the official documents containing the terms of the new treaty. Sensing a chance to make a favorable political impression both at home and abroad, Carter decided to fly to Panama for a signing ceremony. Hence, his trip, which promoted a typical race against the clock for CBS News.

The press plane arrived in Panama City approximately one hour ahead of the President, at about 2:30 P.M. New York time. CBS had twelve employees aboard the chartered Pan American 707—about normal for an overseas trip—including three correspondents (Lee Thornton, David Dick and me), a television producer, radio producer, two camera crews of two persons each, a radio technician, and an executive who was to keep a constant watch for statements issued by the White House Press Room at our hotel.

Eight CBS News employees, as well as half a dozen drivers, interpreters and local help had already been working for days before our arrival. They had set up a complicated communications system, one part of which consisted of microwave relays from the three sites where President Carter would appear. These relays went back through a CBS switchboard at the television broadcast center owned by the Panamanian government, and from there to a satellite ground station in nearby Nicaragua, from which the "feeds" could be transmitted via satellite to the United States. The three networks shared the video parts of this system (called the "pool" line), but the audio lines from each site were separate, so that each company could use its own correspondents for narrations.

Also as part of this communication system, we were given walkie-talkie radios. These were supposed to keep us in constant touch with each other and with our base station at the broadcast center, which was to be constantly manned. (In actuality, the hot, sultry weather made the radios highly unreliable. They worked best where the parties talking were within sight of each other.)

Minutes after landing, my producers and I raced to our operating center for that evening—the sports arena where President Carter and Panama's General Omar Torrijos were to exchange the documents of ratification. The engineers had set up our communications so that each event around the city could be seen and heard on our television monitor there, and I could send live narration of that event directly into New York. The arena was crowded, hot and sticky, but the system worked perfectly, barring a few delays.

President Carter landed at 3:30 P.M., greeted by General Torrijos and a group of children bearing flowers, and singing—in Spanglish—"The Star-Spangled Banner." Watching Carter's arrival on our monitor, we decided that it should be the first element of our television story. While the President and his host were driving from the airport to the sports arena, I wrote the first part of the story and fed it to New York on our audio line. New York was already receiving the video, and it was their job to match the picture to my words: "Panamanian children with flowers from a school called 'the United States of America Elementary School' . . . the first to greet the Carters . . . a gesture planned by the government to symbolize that it is they . . . the young . . . who will inherit the benefits of the Canal when it becomes truly Panama's at the end of this century."

At about 4 P.M., the two leaders arrived at the arena, and after the introduction of visiting heads of state from neighboring Latin American nations, President Carter and General Torrijos walked on stage. The signing ceremony started at 4:30, and I could watch it both from the audience and on the television monitor, narrating the event for New York. While President Carter was still talking, I took one of our television crews outside to do a brief on-camera conclusion to the story—against the backdrop of the massive stadium and the crowd of curious Panamanians gathered outside. In the meantime, President Carter finished his speech and his motorcade headed downtown for a public rally at the Cinco de Mayo Plaza. It was to be his most important personal appearance of the day, and it indirectly created our only serious problem.

Mr. Carter and General Torrijos were to arrive about six, and the President was to speak at 6:30, exactly at our first deadline for the *Evening News*. But the huge crowds surrounding the Plaza, estimated at between 100,000 to 200,000, delayed the motorcade more than half an hour. So at about 6:15, when it seemed clear that President Carter was not going to appear in time for the first story on the *Evening News*, I narrated a segment showing only the huge crowd.

> Later, at his only public appearance here, Mr. Carter was scheduled to be presented to a huge crowd gathered in the Cinco de Mayo Square in downtown Panama City, including many government employees who had been given the afternoon off. The crowd was so densely packed, friendly and enthusiastic that the motorcade was delayed in getting through. Opponents of the treaties have been forcefully warned that there will be no demonstrations against President Carter.

The President actually arrived at the Square about 6:45. This meant we had to "update" or repeat the entire spot for the second version of the show, which goes to the affiliates at 7 P.M. But in order to keep the same general story so that New York would have to change only a few seconds of the pictures, I kept the same narration except for one minor change. Instead of saying, "Mr. Carter was scheduled to be presented," I said that, "Mr. Carter was presented" . . . with the picture changed by New York to show him actually on the balcony in front of the crowd. Because of our excellent technical facilities and the expert split-second work done by our producers in Panama and New York, it worked—the audience back home saw a three-and-a-half minute report on President Carter's first few hours in Panama. Yet the story did not make the impact that it deserved, because the White House planners had carelessly scheduled President Carter's impressive and crowd-pleasing appearance at the Cinco de Mayo too late in the day for anything but a few seconds.

As it turned out, our story was inordinately long, in part because Walter Cronkite was so touched by the Panamanian children's off-key rendition of "The Star-Spangled Banner" that he gave us an extra thirty seconds to include it.* Later that night we provided the affiliate stations with an extra "feed" (as is sometimes done for special news stories), a ninety-second spot showing the President speaking to that huge and excited crowd at the Plaza. It was sent at about 11:02, so that local 11 P.M. news shows around the country could play it immediately or tape it for later broadcast. This helped make up for our inability to show that event properly on the *Evening News*.

The next morning, one television crew and I were up early for a 7 A.M. trip to President Carter's hotel, where he planned to meet with General Torrijos for breakfast and private talks. We were scheduled to videotape the opening of these talks and be on hand in case any other pictures were allowed. As often happens, the White House changed its plans. A dozen newspeople in the pool spent three hours around the hotel dining room that morning waiting for something to happen, but nothing ever did. Finally at mid-morning, the President's motorcade departed for a nearby airfield, where we all boarded helicopters for a flight along the Canal from the Pacific to the Atlantic Ocean and back. These scenes, shot from a big Huey helicopter, constituted the first segment of our next evening report. Once we had returned to the Pacific side of Panama, the President landed at Fort Clayton to address a crowd of military personnel and "Zonians," the local term for United States civilians in the Canal Zone. We used a "cut," or excerpt, of the President's speech as the second element of my story.

From Fort Clayton President Carter drove to nearby Miraflores Lock to inspect its mechanical workings and witness the passage of a ship—also good picture material, although it added little to the substance of the story. I was reunited with the producer, Lane Venardos, and we decided to head back to the broadcast center in Panama City to begin putting together our *Evening News* piece.

*Thirty seconds is equivalent to about 80 words or 1½ inches in a newspaper.

While President Carter lunched with United States officials of the Canal Zone company and high-ranking American military officers, Venardos and I struggled with a problem. It is customary to place the correspondent on the scene at some point in a story. But in this case the pictures were so good and the story itself so anticlimactic that we could not decide where or how my appearance on camera could add anything significant to the story without detracting from the pictures. I finally wrote a close to my story over which we intended to run pictures of Carter touring the Miraflores Lock and watching the transit of a ship, perhaps adding the visual cliché of the President's departure from Panama waving goodbye and Air Force One disappearing into the blue.

But Venardos balked. A living legend for both his sense of humor and his unflappable ability to coordinate everything under deadline pressures, Venardos usually said little about editorial content, as long as he and the correspondent were in general agreement. This time, however, as he was teletyping my last paragraph to New York, he turned around and said softly, "Aren't we dismissing a bit abruptly one of the most important stories of recent years? Maybe we should think about a stronger ending." The same thought had been nagging at me. But I pointed out that a really substantive ending would "fight" our pictures; that is, not complement them, and so diminish their impact. In addition, time was fast running out on us. President Carter was by now on his way to the airport, and we had lost our last chance for a stand-up close with him on Air Force One in the background. That left us the option of using a neutral Panamanian background, such as a palm tree and a Spanish-style building, while I said something to round out the story. Finally we decided to let New York decide which ending they preferred. This was my original proposal:

> From Fort Clayton President Carter drove to the nearby Miraflores Locks, which raise ships in two steps fifty-four feet from the Pacific

Ocean to Lake Miraflores. Inside the control room Mr. Carter turned the switches which opened the first lock to the "American Apollo" . . . a container ship of the U.S. Lines . . . to leave the Pacific for the trip up the Canal. Moving to the Atlantic this way instead of around the horn of Latin America saves each ship about ten times its toll. The largest toll ever was paid by the Queen Elizabeth II in March of this year—about seventy thousand dollars. In 1928 writer-adventurer Richard Halliburton paid thirty-six cents to swim the Canal. After final turnover of the Canal in 1999 . . . *all* tolls will go to the Government of Panama. Robert Pierpoint, CBS News, Panama.

While Venardos teletyped my first close to New York, I wrote another:

As President Carter visited the Miraflores Locks today in his final act, he has now fulfilled his promise to General Torrijos and the people of Panama. The Canal will be theirs. There are still Americans who resent that, who believe that since we built it we should keep it. Some Americans working in the Zone don't believe the Panamanians can even keep the Canal operating. Some Panamanians, for their part, do not like the treaties because they want the Canal territory turned over immediately and without any possibility of American intervention to ensure its neutrality and continued operation. But what has been accomplished is a political compromise that all factions can learn to live with. As six visiting Western Hemisphere chiefs of state said in their final communiqué here today, the new Canal treaties "symbolize a fundamental respect for sovereignty and a cooperative spirit which can motivate all countries to address the difficult problems which affect all the world." Robert Pierpoint, CBS News, Panama.

Within minutes of transmission, Saturday News producer Joan Richmond and anchorman Bob Schieffer sent back word that they preferred the "substantive ending." So while Venardos coordinated the various pictures with my narration, I located David Dick's camera crew, the only crew still left in Panama, since the press plane had departed shortly after the President's plane took off. At a Spanish-style patio with some suitable flowering tropical plants, we recorded the stand-up close. It was now almost 6 P.M. Venardos was nearly finished with my piece, and had only to attach my close before sending it to New York. But we were last in line in the pool rotation, and ABC and NBC were still feeding their stories. Finally, at 6:15, our turn came, and after one false start, my three-minute piece was accepted by New York—just ten minutes before Bob Schieffer went on the air with the Saturday Evening News.

The details of our Panama coverage demonstrate the close symbiotic relationship between television and the Presidency. Presidents plan photogenic activities because television will provide coverage, and television provides coverage because the President has planned photogenic activities. In cases like Carter's Panama trip, this relationship is justifiable. But the networks often carry it too far. Night after night, they broadcast activities of the President and his family, even when there is nothing newsworthy to report. Such constant coverage is not altogether healthy; it elevates the First Family to the level of royalty by portraying as news the slightest scrap of information about its members. Of the three regular CBS News White House correspondents, one is on at least six nights and four mornings per week.

There are two reasons for this. First, it is an easy and sure way for executive producers of the news shows to have a story that will look like news, even if it is not. With twenty-two minutes to fill, they worry all day about technical breakdowns, canceled news conferences, juries that do not reach verdicts, and other unforeseeable events that may knock a story from the line-up. It is always a comfort to be able to count on a White House piece that can, if necessary, even lead off the show. No other center of "news" reliably performs this role, year after year.

Secondly, the White House provides a continual showcase for network stars. Dan Rather, Harry Reasoner, John Chancellor, Tom Brokaw, Tom Jarriel, Bob Schieffer and Ed Bradley all graduated from the White House to coveted network anchor assignments. Appearing coast-to-coast from the familiar White House lawn added immeasurably to their stature, image and recognizability.

At times, network executives even seem to use the White House as a casting couch for correspondents. It is hard to tell just how people destined for anchor positions and stardom are selected. Importance is obviously placed on writing ability, knowledge, dedication, and other basic journalistic skills. But much has to do with appearance. A television newscaster must *look* intelligent and authoritative as well as sound that way. It helps a male television broadcaster to be handsome and to dress well, and a female to be pretty and to master the art of coordinating makeup and clothes. In December of 1979, for example, CBS, NBC and ABC each had a pretty, blond woman covering the White House. They are all very competent reporters, but their attractiveness is hardly a coincidence. While the standards of appearance may not be so high for the networks' male White House correspondents (I freely admit that I was not kept on the job for my figure or handsome face), I know of at least one excellent reporter who was removed from his White House assignment because a network executive did not like his looks.

Constant television coverage undoubtedly contributes to problems associated with the Presidency. On one hand, television places the President at center stage, enhances his power, and magnifies dangers inherent in an imperial Presidency. On the other hand, continual television scrutiny of every Presidential whim and mood or wart and pimple detracts from the dignity of his office, thus making it more difficult for the Chief Executive to govern. Television brings a President and his family into every home today, but does it really enable Americans to know enough about them? We showed Amy Carter on her way to violin lessons, we covered Rosalynn Carter's carefully crafted public appearances, and we broadcast Jimmy Carter's professionally written speeches. Television can go so close up that we magnify every freckle. But what is the public learning except that Presidents have freckles? Does America, because the public has better technological devices to see its leaders, have better leadership today than it did fifty or one hundred years ago? I do not think so, and my doubts trouble me deeply.

Television does some things well—such as the live news conferences, campaign debates, and political conventions—but the daily, dramatic hard-sell on the front lawn of the White House is not enough to keep the nation properly informed. Unfortunately, nothing indicates that this situation will change in the near future. Television and the White House each benefit too much from their close-knit, mutually self-serving relationship.

7

First Ladies

During the early fall of 1963, the Kennedys appeared to be drifting apart. Jackie had flown off for a two-week Mediterranean cruise on Aristotle Onassis' 300-foot luxury yacht *Christina*. Photographs showed her on beaches and in street-front cafés with prominent, handsome, European "beautiful people." Then something changed. Suddenly Jackie came home and began acting like a politician's wife. White House correspondents never discovered what caused her transformation, but we knew that something had convinced her that President John Kennedy offered more than did the playboys across the Atlantic.

During her husband's first campaign for the Presidency, Jackie had played the loyal-wife role, but never enthusiastically. Now she appeared not only willing but anxious to accompany Jack on political trips that were the buildup to his bid for reelection the next year. In mid-November, Kennedy flew to Texas for a number of political appearances and private talks aimed at healing the bitter rift in that state's Democratic party between the conservative wing led by Governor John Connally and Vice-President Lyndon Johnson, and the liberal wing of Senator Ralph Yarborough. Texas had twenty-five electoral votes and was a key swing state, one that could go either Republican or Democratic in 1964. To win the state, Kennedy needed a united party behind him. But personal and political animosities among Texas Democrats were so intense that only personal efforts by the President could bridge their

ideological differences, or at least hide them long enough
to keep the Republicans from taking Texas in 1964. Jackie
accompanied the President on that trip, and she seemed to
be enjoying it.

On the morning of November 22 she attended a breakfast rally of Democrats in Fort Worth, where her husband
spoke. Later that morning the First Lady was radiantly
lovely, dressed in watermelon pink, as she and the President came down the ramp of Air Force One at Dallas'
Love Field. Both promptly began "working the fences," as
reporters call it, shaking hands and chatting with the
crowd that had turned out to greet them. It promised to be
a beautiful day for campaigning. A sense of excitement
over JFK's upcoming reelection effort filled even the press
buses.

As we rode into downtown Dallas on the press bus, some
of us remarked on how well the "new" Jackie was adjust-
ing to the political grind. Others read the *Dallas Morning
News*, particularly a threatening full-page advertisement
that made it clear that President Kennedy was not welcome to some citizens of Dallas. The President was perceived as too liberal, too soft on Communism, and too anxious to help blacks gain their civil rights. A few reporters
wondered whether an "incident" might occur. We all
knew that Adlai Stevenson, the United States Ambassador to the United Nations, had recently been spat upon by
demonstrators in Dallas, and that Vice-President and Mrs.
Johnson had also been verbally abused and physically jos-
tled—without Dallas community leaders showing much
concern.

The sun was shining and the sky was clear as our bus
turned the corner from Main Street to Houston Street at
Dealy Plaza, heading toward the Texas School Book De-
pository Building. I heard three sharp explosions. Suddenly the motorcade stopped; since I was sitting nearest the
front, I shouted to the driver to open the door, and I
jumped out. I had no sooner hit the pavement than I could
see the half dozen or so cars separating us from the President start to move on, so I hopped back in, looking across
the small Dealy Plaza Park perhaps fifty yards, to where

Kennedy's limousine had been. It had vanished, and in the motorcade was a sizable gap that wasn't supposed to be there. We began to argue about whether the explosions had been gunshots (my contention) or automobile backfires. As our bus started up the freeway ramp, we could see people running and a policeman on a motorcycle driving up a grassy slope. But we still weren't sure what was wrong. It wasn't until we arrived at the Trade Mart Building nearby, where Kennedy was supposed to attend a luncheon, that I knew something serious had happened. His limousine and several other cars from the front of the motorcade were missing. I ran into the building and frantically searched for the head table, where there would be at least one Secret Service agent of the advance party. Spotting an agent, I yelled, "Where's the President?"

His answer was a startled, "I don't know, I thought he was with you." Then, with hundreds of puzzled Dallas citizens sitting at their tables watching, we reporters began a wild scramble for telephones. When I finally located one and got through to CBS News, my fears were confirmed. "We have a flash from UPI saying the President has been shot and is in Parkland Memorial Hospital," said an editor agitatedly. Merriman Smith, in one of his finest journalistic performances, was already far ahead on the story, filing eyewitness reports of the assassination from a mobile phone in the pool car (wire services are always included in the pool) which is always close behind the Presidential limousine. The New York radio editor requested a quick eyewitness broadcast report of what had happened—an impossible assignment, since I had very few facts and none at all about the President's condition. Instead I proposed to go immediately to Parkland Memorial Hospital. Despite some sputtering and protests from the editor, who wanted me to continue reporting from the luncheon site, I hung up and headed out the nearest exit, looking desperately for transportation to Parkland Memorial Hospital. I was in luck. Ray Zook of the White House Transportation Office had commandeered a van. He waved me aboard along with several other reporters, and we headed for the hospital.

When we arrived I spotted Congressman Jim Wright and Senator Yarborough standing together on the sidewalk near the emergency room, looking stunned. When I asked them what they had seen, both had trouble talking, they were clearly grief-stricken and in shock. Yarborough was crying. Finally, Wright murmured that he thought a bullet had blown off the side of the President's head, and that he did not think Kennedy would survive. I remember Yarborough suggesting that the President might already be dead. When I tried to examine the Presidential limousine for evidence of what had happened, Secret Service agents and Dallas police officers barred my way. No one stopped me as I headed toward the hospital to get to a phone, but nurses and doctors saw me coming and locked their doors. No amount of pleading my need to call CBS moved them. Their fearful reaction puzzled me. Perhaps they wanted as few people around as possible for security reasons, or perhaps they wanted to keep their phones free for emergency use. But I was obviously a reporter trying to do his job.

Finally, a heavyset black woman in a white uniform, probably a nurse's aide, came up and said with calm understanding, "You need to get to a telephone, don't you? Come, follow me." She led me through the line of local police that had formed outside the emergency entrance, and to a public telephone inside, within sight of the emergency operating area. I stayed there much of the afternoon, relaying to CBS News in New York whatever I could pick up on the condition of the President. From the shocked, haggard faces of Presidential aides Kenneth O'Donnell and Ted Clifton, I knew the situation was critical, if not hopeless. O'Donnell was too choked up to speak. Clifton told me that a priest had been called in. When Father Oscar Huber emerged looking grave and troubled, he would not quite confirm that he had administered the last rites—but that conclusion seemed inescapable.

By this time, I was in mental, emotional shock and feeling physically ill, though I was trying very hard to concentrate on doing my job as professionally as possible. Then a scene of dreadful finality chilled my heart. Lyndon and

Lady Bird emerged from the operating area, hurried down the hall, and went out the door, escorted by Secret Service agents. A short while later a coffin was wheeled out, Mrs. Kennedy walking alongside, staring straight ahead, with her hand resting lightly on the coffin. Her bright-pink suit was stained with blood, which had run down onto her legs. I reported the scene over the air as best I could, but it was not good enough; I could not bring myself to describe adequately the blood-spattered widow.

During the days that followed, Jackie Kennedy was magnificent. She held up in public so well that she helped countless others to do so. Whenever she appeared on television, the young mother was poised and calm. Network correspondents worked long and difficult hours, narrating the scenes of mourning in Washington as they unfolded, or simply talking about John Kennedy as the cameras focused on the White House or the casket. CBS television suspended all regular programming for three days until the funeral was over, which placed a heavy burden on the already emotionally and physically exhausted staff. But whenever I began to falter or break down, I would recall the marvelous courage of Jacqueline Kennedy and think, "If she can go on, then certainly I can."

The assassination of her husband forced Jackie Kennedy to assume a highly visible leadership role, but in more ordinary circumstances, First Ladies are rarely taken seriously by White House correspondents. First Ladies rarely generate stories that make the network evening news programs, and reporters assigned to the First Lady generally find their task unproductive and frustrating. Furthermore, when something big does break, regular White House correspondents usually take over. For example, Jackie Kennedy had their third child, Patrick, while her husband was President. Patrick was born in Boston, fought hard against a breathing difficulty, and died within hours. We were with President Kennedy when it happened, and it was one of the sadder stories of my White House career. I will never forget sitting in a small hospital room all night, into a gray dawn, and finally phoning in a report that the President's son had failed to survive.

For correspondents like myself, contact with First Ladies comes either during such extraordinary events, or while traveling with the President. This personal contact is particularly important, because it almost always takes place in—or leads to—more relaxed gatherings with the President and key members of his Administration. With this in mind, I give colleagues newly assigned to the White House one bit of free advice: make as many trips as possible with the President, including boring weekend jaunts to otherwise forgettable places like Johnson City, Texas, and Plains, Georgia. You gain insight and good contacts this way.

Such trips gave me an invaluable chance to see two contradictory sides of Jackie Kennedy. During the 1962 Christmas holidays, the Kennedys invited the White House press and their families to a reception at their Palm Beach home. It was a delightful midafternoon affair taking place mostly in the spacious living room around the tall Christmas tree, where we could view the Kennedy family presents. A few minutes after the arrival of the Pierpoints (wife and four children from Stan, thirteen, through Eric, twelve, Kim, ten, to Marta, six months), Jackie Kennedy came downstairs. A gracious and regal hostess, she was warm and considerate, suggesting that my wife place Marta upstairs in the nursery with John-John, who was only a year or so older. She then chatted with us for quite a while, and left me impressed with the interest she had showed in each of us as individuals.

The next day, however, I saw another Jacqueline Kennedy. The leaders of the Cuban Brigade that had invaded the Bay of Pigs in 1961 were coming to visit President Kennedy. Invasion survivors had recently been ransomed from Cuban prisons for $2.5 million, raised jointly by the United States government and private sources, and their leaders were coming to thank Kennedy—not, of course, for helping to get them into trouble in the first place (nothing was said about that), but for helping to arrange their ransom. Press Secretary Salinger selected Hugh Sidey of *Time* magazine and me as the pool reporters to witness the opening of the meeting between the Kennedy and the Cuban Brigade officers.

In order to reach the living room of the beach-front mansion that the Kennedys had rented that Christmas, we had to walk up some steps off the driveway and pass through a patio. As we were entering the patio we saw Mrs. Kennedy and her sister, Lee Radziwill, setting a round table with soft drinks and cookies for the Cuban visitors. Remembering how friendly she had been the day before, I said cheerily, "Good morning, Mrs. Kennedy." I received a frozen stare and dead silence. Somewhat nonplused, I walked on into the living room to watch the President greet his Cuban guests.

It was a brief session, mainly for the photographers, and was in fact a bit awkward because Kennedy could not speak Spanish and the Cubans either were ill at ease or did not speak English. As we were ushered out, we again passed Jackie Kennedy. Aware that she had spoken fluent Spanish during a trip to Latin America earlier that year, I said, "Mrs. Kennedy, you'll get a chance to practice your Spanish, because they seem to need a translator in there."

Once again my attempt at friendly small talk was met with a cold stare and icy silence. She was a totally different person from the warm and outgoing woman I had chatted with the night before. As we walked down the driveway I said to Sidey, "What happened there?"

He laughed and said, "You just got the treatment."

"I know that," I replied, "but why?"

"Jackie's a funny lady," Sidey said. "I've known her since before she and Jack were married, but I never speak to her unless she speaks first. You just never know what kind of mood she is in."

As First Ladies go, Mamie Eisenhower was probably the most perfect in reflecting the personality and desires of her husband the President. Just as Ike ran the White House like a military officer, she conducted herself with the gracious dignity of an officer's wife. Although I have

sometimes been asked about an alleged "drinking problem," during the three years that I saw her around the
White House or on the road, I never saw one single indication of that. In fact I never saw Mrs. Eisenhower take a
drink, although on a couple of occasions when my wife was
invited to luncheons she said that Mamie had sipped wine.
Both of us felt her to be a warm, kindly person, somewhat
disinterested in politics, but nevertheless a valuable coun-
terpart to her husband.

Lady Bird Johnson, who comforted Jackie and waited
patiently while the Kennedy family took time to move out
of the White House, was an ideal politician's wife. A woman of great intelligence and charm, she was a perfect counterbalance to her husband's singleminded driving ambition. She suffered his excesses with grace and dignity.
Whatever Mrs. Johnson chose to do, she did well. As First
Lady, her beautification project—aimed at making the
District of Columbia a scenic city of flowers, trees and
shrubs—encountered financial difficulties. But she pur-
sued it as best she could, at the same time complementing
her husband's efforts in other fields. To this day Pennsylvania Avenue and other streets near the White House bear
witness to her conception of a more beautiful Washington.
Although little that Lady Bird did attracted much media attention, she always seemed to enjoy our company
whenever we were covering either her or her husband's
activities. In sharp contrast, the nation's next First Lady,
Patricia Ryan Nixon, seemed almost terrified of us. This
surprised me, because I had known her as an independent
and gregarious teacher at southern California's Whittier
Union High School. In 1941–42, while a junior at Whittier High, I was elected to what was called the Pep Committee, which mostly staged rallies for football and basket-
ball games. The committee was allowed to choose its own
faculty adviser and we selected Pat Ryan Nixon, a slim,
attractive, young typing teacher with flaming red hair who
wore bright-colored dresses. The young boys even consid-

ered her sexy. We found Mrs. Nixon to be understanding and enthusiastic, important qualities for a Pep Committee adviser. With her husband away in the Navy she devoted much time to such extracurricular activities, and was a successful choice as faculty adviser from all viewpoints.

Twelve years later, I met Pat Ryan Nixon again. By this time she was the wife of the Vice-President of the United States, and I could scarcely believe she was the same woman. I had followed Richard Nixon's career into Congress, the Senate, and finally the Vice-Presidency, but having lived abroad much of the time, I had not seen him or his wife since 1942. Now it was 1954, and Eisenhower had sent the Vice-President on a trip around the world. Their first stop was the Philippines, where President and Mrs. Ramón Magsaysay invited them on a cruise to Corregidor, the famous island in Manila Bay where in 1942 General Douglas MacArthur made his headquarters during the losing battle against the Japanese. Since Magsaysay knew a number of American reporters who had covered his own election the previous year, he invited us along on his big presidential yacht.

Traveling with the Nixons as their unofficial press secretary was a well-known former *Los Angeles Times* columnist and NBC News broadcaster, Bill Henry. During the two-hour trip out to Corregidor aboard the Philippine presidential yacht, I explained to Henry that I had known Mrs. Nixon when she taught at Whittier High and would like to talk with her. A short while later he came to the press area to say that Mrs. Nixon would be happy to meet me. We walked to the stern, where she was standing with Mrs. Magsaysay, and I was immediately struck by her tension, nervousness and drawn appearance. After Henry introduced us, I mentioned that I had been a student at Whittier while she taught there, and her reply was the safe, "I thought that name was familiar." I had not expected Pat Nixon to remember me very well, but she seemed so totally remote that I was quite rattled. It quickly became apparent that she was not very interested in chatting, so I thanked the two ladies and retreated.

Stunned at the time, on reflection I took her coolness to be a result of her fear of the press, since her husband's dealings with reporters had never been very warm. It could also have been related to her concern over proper behavior in the presence of the President of the Philippines, although I knew the Magsaysays to be informal, friendly people. But in the intervening years I have come to the conclusion that Mrs. Nixon's behavior evolved from deep-seated terror that she might do or say something to impede her husband's political ambitions. Her easiest recourse was to the obvious: clichés and silence.

We did not meet again until fourteen years later, when Pat Nixon's husband had won the Presidency. Shortly after the election, the Nixons were flying to Key Biscayne, Florida, aboard Air Force One (lent to them by LBJ), and she came into the press pool area of the plane to chat with us. Again I reminded her of our Whittier High School days, and Mrs. Nixon seemed to unwind a bit, but she was still quite tense. We next talked in June of 1970 when the President sent her to inspect the devastation caused by a terrible earthquake in the Peruvian Andes, and to bring the suffering villagers some relief supplies. CBS News assigned me to cover her trip, which gave me a chance to spend some time with her.

On the flight down, I finally persuaded the First Lady to do an on-camera interview on what she planned to do and see in Peru. It was a poor interview, because whenever the camera rolled she stiffened into a marionette playing the role of politician's wife. I doubt that any of the footage was even broadcast, but at least the ice was broken between us, and by the time we arrived in Peru she seemed to trust me.

The next day, Mrs. Nixon's party flew by helicopter from Lima high into the chilly Andes, where the earthquake had hit the hardest. It was spectacularly beautiful, with high snow-covered peaks above and lush green valleys below. But several villages had been grotesquely destroyed, their brick homes transformed into rubble. At our first stop, Mrs. Nixon was met by a group of national and local officials and led by the village priest to the town square. His small church lay largely in ruins, and chunks of the front wall had crumbled onto the square. But the cross at the top of the church and the jagged wall that led up to it were still standing.

As Mrs. Nixon and the priest talked, I saw a perfect television picture, and I suggested that they climb up on the broken stones so my camera crew could get a shot of them together beneath the jagged remains of the church, with the cross overhead. Mrs. Nixon quickly understood and followed my advice, and from that moment on, she kept an eye on me and whenever I made a suggestion she obliged immediately. She was especially warm with children, and at another village she lingered, trying to soothe some of the frightened youngsters, while I got some exceptionally touching pictures. Mrs. Nixon was also genuinely concerned about the suffering of the Peruvians, and the television stories we sent home showed a different Pat Nixon from the woman Americans were used to seeing. On the way back to the United States, I interviewed her again, and this time, while not really relaxed, she seemed much more at ease in front of the camera.

A few days later, David and Julie Eisenhower returned from a semi-official trip to Japan, and were met by her parents as well as the press corps. A bubbling Pat Nixon called me over to introduce me to her daughter and son-in-law as a former student of hers from Whittier. Since I had not taken any of her courses, this was not quite true, but she seemed so proud of me that I was not about to correct her. Shortly afterward, when the Nixons invited us to the White House to a luncheon for the wife of the President of Peru, the President also introduced me as a former student of his wife's. The First Lady seemed very pleased. Then on Inauguration Day of 1973, as the Presidential family was walking back to the White House from the high, wooden stand on Pennsylvania Avenue where they had been viewing the Inaugural Parade, Mrs. Nixon actually brought the President and the entire family over for a nice exclusive interview. It dealt mainly with the events of the day, and what they anticipated for the next four years in the White House. Since it would have spoiled the mood of an essentially human-interest story, I did not ask them about the Watergate break-in or any other serious topics.

But the Watergate scandal did overwhelm Nixon shortly afterward, and Patricia Ryan Nixon once more withdrew into her shell. Never again was I able to communicate with her on any level. Each time I saw her at the White House functions or on trips with the President, she appeared more nervous and less in touch with the outside world. As the scandal worsened, she and her husband never held hands or seemed to offer each other support. During the final days of Watergate I frequently wondered whether she might be ashamed of what Richard Nixon had done, but too deeply enmeshed in his life and career ever to express such thoughts. The report in Carl Bernstein and Bob Woodward's *The Final Days* that Mrs. Nixon took to drinking to soothe her aching heart did not surprise me.

The nation knew very little about its next First Lady, Betty Ford, but as a woman and a wife she provided a sharp contrast to her predecessor. One of the most refreshing things about Betty Ford was her determination to be her own person. She did not feel it necessary to check with her husband before expressing her views on changing American sex mores or apparently anything else, for that matter. Mrs. Ford even made occasional public declarations clearly intended to influence the President, such as her often expressed desire to see him appoint a woman to the Supreme Court. That President Ford did not always take his wife's advice did not appear to detract from their affection for each other, nor from his ability to conduct affairs of state.

The Fords broke one taboo, a situation which may have shocked some people but probably saved the lives of countless others. On the evening of September 27, 1974, I was preparing to leave the White House after a fairly quiet day, when Press Secretary Nessen announced very matter-of-factly that Mrs. Ford was in Bethesda Naval Hospital, where the next morning she would undergo surgery on her right breast. Nessen further stated that if some small nodules that doctors had located in her breast turned out to be malignant, the right breast would be removed. Within minutes I broke into the CBS radio network with a "net-alert bulletin" to report the story in detail, including several references to Mrs. Ford's right breast. After the initial excitement died down a bit, I had second thoughts about discussing such intimate details of the First Lady's anatomy. But no one at CBS News complained, and for the next several days we continued to cover the story in exactly the same frank manner initiated by the Fords themselves. We did receive some objections from the audience, but not as many as I had expected. The National Cancer Institute and the American Cancer Society later reported that the week following Mrs. Ford's surgery, ten times as many women were requesting breast examinations for cancer. Doubtless some women's lives were saved because they and their doctors caught the disease in time.

Betty Ford's candor also stirred up controversy. A number of the President's aides, and a few of Betty Ford's as well, expressed concern when the First Lady told CBS News correspondent Morley Safer on *60 Minutes* that she would not be surprised to learn that her daughter Susan was having an affair. They feared that Mrs. Ford's outspokenness on sex would hurt her husband's standing with conservative voters. I felt at the time that Betty Ford's modern, independent and forthright approach could actually win for her husband the votes of younger and more liberal voters who might otherwise never support Gerald Ford. But there can be no doubt that Betty Ford's independence endeared her to millions of Americans who saw her as a woman and mother coping with everyday problems. This humanized her husband's public image, and probably helped him substantially at the polls.

The next First Lady, Mrs. Carter, was also a tremendous political asset for her husband. Rosalynn Carter campaigned across the country for two years, often by herself, to help him win the Democratic Presidential nomination. After his inauguration, she proved to be the most politically talented and enthusiastic First Lady I ever covered. She spoke out on substantive issues with knowledge and intelligence, although she rarely took positions very different from her husband's. Mrs. Carter gave the impression that she would be perfectly capable of arguing with him forcefully and cogently in private, and not just about family matters. But their only public disagreement I saw was her gentle criticism of him for not appointing more women to high public office. Mrs. Carter seemed to believe that it was not for her, as an unelected public figure, to openly discuss her own views.

As the stories I've told here indicate, First Ladies have not occupied much of my time at the White House. First Ladies are entitled to their privacy, and whether they are strong or weak, dedicated or lazy, liberal or conservative, is only incidentally the nation's business. Perhaps there is legitimate public interest in what her views and personality may indicate about the man who wants to be—or is—President, though this tends to be a rather unreliable barometer.

First Ladies should not be treated—as they are treated now—as some sort of dotty royalty whose every move is instantly newsworthy. Of course, the White House shares a good deal of the blame for this phenomenon, since these days First Ladies invariably maintain large and active public-relations staffs. Regrettably, fascination with the First Lady merely as a reflection of her position has become a national pastime; the public seems to want all the gossip it can get.

This is not to say that First Ladies have never been in the public eye for very good and valuable reasons. Certainly Betty Ford's openness about her breast cancer allowed the media an invaluable opportunity to serve the public well. And First Ladies who inject themselves into the political process or the public arena—Eleanor Roosevelt and her many causes; Lady Bird Johnson and her beautification programs; Rosalynn Carter and her politicking during her husband's campaigns—should certainly be carefully scrutinized as far as these activities are concerned. But we must dispense with the insidious form of sexism—outdated and definitely undesirable—that a First Lady is a superficial adjunct to the President, always reflecting his desires and promoting his ends.

8

Press Ethics

In the summer of 1959, a lovely young woman friend disconsolately confided to me that she had stumbled into a summertime liaison with Senator John F. Kennedy of Massachusetts. Kennedy's wife, Jacqueline, had been away from Washington, but now she was returning and the Senator wanted to be with her.

All I could do for my distraught friend was to lend a sympathetic ear. But in view of her experience, I was not surprised to learn from young women on Kennedy's staff that during his 1960 postelection vacation in Palm Beach, Florida—approximately a year later—he was dallying with a lively and sexy college dropout.

The White House press corps must continually handle various types of Presidential peccadilloes. We must decide whether or not they are matters of legitimate public concern, and how much, if anything, to report. At the same time, the Presidents themselves often don't try especially hard to keep their personal foibles secret. For example, not long after President Kennedy's inauguration, a rather amusing incident convinced me that even Mrs. Kennedy was not unaware of her husband's extramarital activities. One afternoon, a French correspondent entered the White House Press Lobby from the direction of the Oval Office, clearly distressed and wanting to talk. Although I knew him only slightly, I was the most readily available ear, so he poured out his tale to me in fluent, if somewhat ac-

cented English. He said that he knew Jackie Kennedy personally and she had invited him to lunch that day with the
President in their private White House dining room. After
lunch, Jack Kennedy had excused himself to return to the
Oval Office, and Jackie offered my colleague a personally
conducted tour of the White House. After showing him
the Mansion, she led her guest over to the West Wing,
through the Cabinet Room, and together they entered the
small room next to the Oval Office, where the President's
secretaries usually sit. Mrs. Kennedy pointed to an attractive young woman working next to the President's personal
secretary, Evelyn Lincoln, and said in French, "There is
the girl my husband is said to be sleeping with." The
dumbfounded reporter was still searching for a reply when
the completely composed Jacqueline Kennedy showed him
the exit to the Press Lobby.

I myself became a reluctant witness to the kind of incident that fueled rumors. In March of 1962, President
Kennedy was visiting in Palm Springs, the southern California resort. His departure was set for Sunday evening
about seven, an hour or so after sundown. As one of the
pool correspondents, I had been designated to drive out to
the estate where he was staying and wait in the motorcade,
follow the President to the airport, then fly back to Washington with him on board Air Force One.

At around six-thirty the Presidential limousine pulled
up into the circular driveway and stopped by the front
door. We parked the press car a few yards away on the
opposite side of a small cactus garden. The doorway to the
house was just on the other side of the President's car.
Douglas Cornell of the Associated Press and I were sitting
quietly in the desert darkness chatting, when suddenly the
front door of the house burst open and the light streaming
out revealed JFK emerging with a woman on his arm—
clearly not Mrs. Kennedy, since she had not accompanied
him on this trip. Kennedy pulled her along toward the
limousine, and then, opening the door, laughingly shoved
her into the back seat. As the light went on inside the car,
we got a brief glimpse of his young friend just before she

disappeared into the President's arms. Then the light went out again.

After a few minutes of silence, during which Cornell and I sat peering through the dark in fascination, the front door of the house opened again and another woman came out. It was one of President Kennedy's sisters. She climbed into a fancy open convertible parked nearby, and cruised up beside the motorcade to her brother's limousine. "Come on, Mildred," she shouted, and as the light went on again in the car we could see "Mildred" (whom Cornell and I never identified more fully) disengaging herself from the President of the United States. After a brief farewell kiss she got into the other woman's car and they drove away. A moment later the motorcade headed for the airport.

"Mildred" posed an immediate problem. As a pool reporter I had to decide whether or not to include this incident in the report I would file for all other correspondents to use in their own stories. (Cornell, as a wire-service employee, was not required to participate in the pool report.) As far as I knew, nothing like that had ever been reported about the President, and to do so seemed to invade his privacy. On the other hand, Kennedy had made little effort to conceal his activity (he might not have known reporters were sitting in a nearby car), and I felt that perhaps I should pass the account on to my colleagues and let each of them decide what to do. In the end, I reported nothing about Mildred, although I might report a similar incident were I to witness it today.

This decision was not the first or last time that a White House correspondent brushed aside a troubling ethical question. The ethics of the White House press corps are roughly similar to that famous *New York Times* credo, "All the news that's fit to print." Of course, one great thing about that slogan is its flexibility: what *is* news, and what is "fit to print"?

Some reporters insist that as the public's eyes and ears at the White House, we have no right to censor ourselves; we have a duty to publish everything we learn, as long as it has suitable substantiation. The counter argument is that even public figures have some right to privacy and that voters need to know only what affects an elected official's conduct in office. But this "conduct-in-office" test presents particularly difficult problems for journalists who do not wish to engage in gossip, as shown by another issue, which confronted CBS News during the early months of Lyndon Johnson's Presidency—a President's use of alcohol. Because he was a large man, alcohol rarely affected LBJ's behavior, but there were times, especially during the 1964 Presidential campaign, when he seemed to be visibly intoxicated. That was his condition late one night, when Air Force One had landed at a small midwestern town. CBS News correspondent George Herman was on the scene, but our cameras could not record the incident because the airport was not sufficiently well lighted for the film to work. As Herman recalls, LBJ came down the ramp rather unsteadily, with a Secret Service escort on either arm to hold him up. The President tried to give his usual brief arrival-at-the-airport remarks into waiting radio microphones, but his speech rambled and he was hard to understand. Herman did a straightforward report on what the President had said, but did not mention the problem and did not use the sound tape of LBJ's actual speech. Afterward, the worried correspondent made a quick call to CBS News in New York, basically asking how to handle the situation. He was told, in effect, "Don't report it now, but we'll discuss it here and get back to you with a final decision."

But CBS ducked the issue. No such decision ever was transmitted to Herman, and the story died. (As far as I know no other correspondent reported the incident either.) I suspect that some top CBS official informed someone at the White House that the media had hard evidence that Johnson was drinking heavily. In any case, Johnson was not seen that drunk again, to my knowledge, either in public or private, and the incident was more or less forgotten.

A similar episode occurred during the Nixon administration. On the night of November 17, 1973, Nixon appeared before the Associated Press Managing Editors Association in Disneyworld at Orlando, Florida. In an emotion-charged press conference he made his often-quoted "I am not a crook" declaration. To those of us in attendance, Nixon appeared anxious, distraught, and overly fatigued. On his way to Key Biscayne later that night, the President stopped briefly to say goodbye to well-wishers at McCoy Air Force Base near Orlando. Only a small pool of reporters and cameramen accompanied Nixon, because the bulk of the press corps had stayed behind to file stories. So there were few objective eyewitnesses to clarify what actually happened.

In the course of his conversations with people standing along the runway fence, the President stepped up to Sergeant Edward Kleizo and his young son. Apparently the bright floodlights on the field obscured Nixon's vision, because he asked whether the sergeant was the seven-year-old boy's mother or grandmother. "Neither," replied the startled man, whereupon the President peered more closely, said "Of course not," and then the pool reporters standing nearby clearly heard and saw him slap Kleizo on the cheek. Unfortunately, the camera crew had positioned itself to film the President as he moved down the fence, "working" the crowd, thereby missing the incident completely.

The pool reporters, William J. Eaton, then of the *Chicago Daily News*, and Matthew Cooney of the Westinghouse Broadcasting Corporation, at first believed the incident to be of questionable importance and omitted it from their formal report. But they did mention it in personal conversations, and the next day a vague, contradictory version was added to the written pool report. The major problem then facing each of us was how to interpret what could have been a friendly gesture, a clumsy accident, or a sudden outbreak of irrational and disturbing hostility. A few correspondents wrote it up for their papers, and the White House immediately denounced these stories as "unethical," "unprofessional," "irresponsible" and "twisted."

A formal Press Office statement charged that some members of the White House press corps, solely on the basis of rumor and gossip, distorted a friendly gesture, in which the President patted a man on the face "into a slapping incident." White House officials were furious over what they considered a deliberate distortion of Nixon's mental health. Reporters contacted Sergeant Kleizo, but he was not very helpful. A strong Nixon supporter himself, he either was not sure what had actually happened or didn't want to say.

In any case, since members of the pool could not agree on what had happened, and since there was no film coverage of the incident, I chose not to report anything. However, another factor influenced my decision. In the months prior to that incident Watergate had continued to build pressures against the President and I had received increasingly hostile mail, phone calls, and even telegrams accusing me of bias against Richard Nixon. With this in mind, and being all too aware that the White House was extremely sensitive about this particular issue, I took the easy way out and chose to ignore the story. I rationalized that any way I reported the event it would appear that I was unfairly implying that Nixon was losing his self-control. After two days of checking the facts, *The New York Times* finally ran a story on the incident, including the White House denunciation of those journalists and papers that had printed the original and somewhat unclear versions. To this day, members of the White House press corps differ over how the story should have been handled.

Self-censorship on much more substantive issues still remains a serious problem. Too many reporters, myself included, assume that they must stay within the accepted mainstream of facts and assumptions. Through a kind of osmosis, reporters tune into a gradually changing agenda of taboo subjects. Twenty years ago, taboo subjects included abortion and the thin line between religion and politics. Today they include the assertion—believed by many serious analysts in the West—that the United States poses a serious, destabilizing threat to the U.S.S.R. (instead of vice versa, as was once proclaimed by the American press).

But my most painful experiences have come from widespread self-censorship involving the Middle East. Discussing the strong influence of American Jews on United States policy vis-à-vis Israel can draw on one's head an extraordinary amount of unpleasant pressure and abuse. This sometimes posed a significant dilemma for me, because of the close interaction between domestic politics and developments in the Middle East, which White House correspondents must be able to cover knowledgeably and dispassionately. But if we cross certain accepted boundaries, questioning the objectivities or dual loyalties of some Americans, an ill-planned phrase can cause severe personal or professional trauma.

A network correspondent, who does not have the luxury of writing a doctoral dissertation or a lengthy magazine article, feels this most acutely. We are constantly under deadline pressures, and even more important, most of our stories must be contained within several hundred words. Each word is thus extremely important, and to maintain a balance while discussing something emotional and controversial requires a delicate ballet.

Another perpetually unresolved ethical dilemma derives from classified information. The most likely source is oral leaks, which tend to be fragmentary and usually reveal information that never should have been classified in the first place. Reporters generally receive such information from disgruntled government employees who oppose a specific policy and hope to see it changed. In such cases our main problem is to somehow confirm the story with other reliable sources. Such confirmation is particularly important, because official denials are very troublesome and often force the journalist to make difficult decisions on whether to go with the story.

One such dilemma arose from a story I had done in Korea during 1953. Toward the end of the war, I had come to know a young Marine officer, Captain Ed Corwin (pseudonym) who was then second in command of a Marine tank company stationed near the Panmunjom truce talks. During these talks, artillery shelling and bloody struggles erupted on key hills along what was to be the demilitarized zone. Many young Marines fought and died over territory that appeared to be insignificant. Captain Corwin was particularly angry; like many other soldiers, he wanted either to roll forward to get the war over with, or pull out and quit. Corwin was outspoken and articulate, so one day he and I sat a few hundred yards from exploding Communist shells, and talked about this "police action." It made an excellent television story for Ed Murrow's *See It Now*, and the Marine officer was in hot water for some time with the Pentagon.

About ten years later, Corwin called me at the White House. Now a Lieutenant Colonel, he was assigned to the Advance Research and Projects Agency (ARPA), a federal outfit that, among other things, tries to develop new ways to win wars. The United States was becoming more involved in Vietnam, and Colonel Corwin asked if we could meet for lunch, promising that he had something important to show me. We met in a restaurant near the White House, where the Colonel, dressed in civilian clothes, pulled a large brown envelope from his briefcase and simply told me to take a look. Inside was a document perhaps thirty pages long, with a white cover and a red border. I was startled to see stamped across the cover in large red letters the word "Secret." I was in a quandary; I did not want the document, both because I did not know whether I was committing a crime by accepting it, and because I did not know his motive in showing it to me. Colonel Corwin insisted that this envelope contained a key, if not *the* key, to our success in Vietnam. He wanted my help in promoting his project, especially in selling it to my friend Ed Murrow, who was now head of the U.S. Information Agency and an influential administration figure. Corwin explained that the document was a detailed plan for defoliation designed to starve out Vietnamese villages that supported the Communists and to destroy the growth they used for ambush cover. The Marine officer was absolutely convinced that without this project the United States would lose the war, and that opposition from Murrow was blocking it. Corwin said that Averell Harriman, then Assistant Secretary of State for Southeast Asia, also opposed the plan. But Corwin maintained that if Harriman or Murrow could be persuaded, President Kennedy would probably agree to implement it.

After some hesitation, I agreed to read the document and pass it on to Murrow without my personal endorsement. That afternoon, I called Murrow to make an urgent appointment, and then I went home to study the secret papers.

What I saw created a dilemma for me: It was morally reprehensible to attempt to win the war by starving civilians, and yet my experiences with the military (both during the Korean War and after) had led me to be cynical whenever the military classified something as "Secret." Usually the censors were simply trying to hide or cover up a deficiency. For example, after the Korean War, while I was still based in Japan, two U.S. Air Force officers had come to see me. They did not want their names used, and I agreed to this condition. They then told me that the particular plane they were flying, a low-level B-26 Night Marauder Bomber, had developed a design problem. Several of them had crashed, killing their crews. So the Air Force had grounded these bombers all over the world, and for the past month none had been allowed to fly. The two pilots believed that the Air Force was not moving fast enough in correcting the problem, mainly because the higher-ups who had approved the plane's design did not want to admit their mistake.

After a brief preliminary check at the Air Force Headquarters in Tokyo, I sent Edward R. Murrow a long cable outlining what I had learned. I said I had no reason to doubt the two pilots, but that the Air Force in Japan had refused to either confirm or deny anything, and that I wanted Murrow to check with his sources at the Pentagon. He did so, and quickly cabled back that my story was correct, but that the Air Force would try to keep it off the air.

Almost simultaneously, I received a call from the Air Force command office in Tokyo, asking that I meet with the top general in the area. He and his staff conceded to me that the story was true but argued that to publicize the facts would "give aid and comfort to the enemy," and possibly entice the Soviets into attacking us. This was nonsense, and I told them so. We were not at war with the Soviets or anyone else at that moment, so legally there was no "enemy." But more important, the Japanese Communists had spies all over the country. Among other things, they could count every American plane that took off, as well as those that did not. I also had to assume that they had spies in other countries who were doing the same thing. Therefore I was certain the Soviets knew as much about the B-26 as I did, and that the so-called enemy knew a great deal more than did American taxpayers.

That night, Murrow asked if I were willing to do the story. I said "yes," and we broadcast it. Several weeks later, the two pilots came by again to say that there had been a great furor over the leak and a remarkable speedup in the redesign of the aircraft—which was now much safer and back in the air.

Against that background, I felt that any self-proclaimed military "secret" deserved close scrutiny. But I was happy when Murrow returned the secret papers to me along with the observation that making war on civilians by destroying their food supplies was not the way he thought the Vietnam war should be fought. I returned the envelope to Colonel Corwin, along with Murrow's reaction, which was not exactly what he had hoped to hear.

At the time I did not realize what a controversial and important story defoliation would turn out to be,* so I let the whole situation drop. I had incorrectly assumed that the colonel was desperate to revive a dead issue, that the Pentagon and the White House had already considered

---

*A defoliation plan *was* put into effect a year or so later without much public discussion, although the Pentagon now claims top officials never approved the policy of destroying crops. Defoliation was used mainly to clear areas where guerrillas could hide, and even that was not notably successful.

and rejected defoliation. Had I known that it was still a viable option, I would have reported the program as "under consideration by the Kennedy Administration" and thus brought it into the open for the public to consider.

On another occasion, however, I did broadcast a story based upon restricted information. In the winter of 1962, the United States government was planning to begin disarmament discussions with the Soviet Union and other governments in Geneva. One still-undecided issue was whether to hold the conference at the foreign-minister level, or as a summit conference involving chiefs of state. In a message from Soviet Premier Nikita Khrushchev, the Soviets had formally proposed a summit conference, but President Kennedy and other Western leaders had responded that it would be premature at this early stage of negotiation.

Within the Kennedy Administration, however, there was some fear that Khrushchev would appear unannounced and dramatically upstage the less prestigious American delegation—thus creating the impression of greater Soviet commitment to world peace. So United States foreign-policy experts began to think that perhaps Kennedy should attend the start of the conference, throw his weight on the Western side of the arguments and thus demonstrate his own peaceable intentions. The situation eventually evolved into a cat-and-mouse game, with the United States government waiting and hoping that the Soviets would say whether or not Khrushchev would go, and Kennedy standing by to make his decision. I then learned through an oral leak that the President had definitely decided to go to Geneva if Khrushchev did; I wrote a story to that effect for television and composed a similar story for radio to be aired shortly before the TV news. At that time, the CBS TV *Evening News*—anchored by Douglas Edwards—went live at 7:15 P.M. from New York. We had no way to do live television broadcasts from the White House without elaborate and time-consuming preparations.

I double-checked my story as carefully as possible, and

it was not ready for airing until almost 6 P.M. After recording my radio piece, I raced to our television studio seven miles from the White House, arriving only moments before air time.

In the meantime, the wire services had picked up my radio broadcast, and White House aides who read the wires rushed to the President. JFK was furious—he felt that my broadcast made it appear that he had left the initiative to Khrushchev—and ordered White House operators to locate his old friend and Harvard classmate, CBS News Vice-President Blair Clark.

At the time, I knew nothing of this. I was seated behind a small desk in the studio with a glass of water and a microphone in front of me, and the camera pointed in my direction. In those days going "live" was still a new and unsettling experience, and I was nervous. Then the director's voice came booming through the loudspeaker, telling me that the President of the United States had refuted my story. Although my nervousness increased immeasurably, I followed my instincts, which were to simply say, "The hell with the President, I stand by my story." I was convinced that my source was reliable and that Kennedy was simply trying to save himself from embarrassment, so I began to argue over the microphone with the director, who was sitting in the control room with Blair Clark waiting on an open telephone line. The director relayed my reaction to Clark, and eventually we compromised.

As the second hand crept toward my spot on the *Evening News*, I wrote a one-sentence denial by the President. Only seconds later, a production assistant removed the glass of water and pointed to me; I took a deep breath and began my broadcast. Nowadays disputing the President of the United States is not so difficult, at least for me. But I was glad when this particular one minute and fifteen seconds ended. I fully expected to hear directly from JFK himself, but never did. Presumably the story was accurate, or he would have made more of a personal fuss with me about it. In the end, Khrushchev never went to Geneva, and neither did Kennedy.

Not all security "leaks" are entirely serious. One day

during the Johnson Presidency, my superiors ordered me to cover a Pentagon briefing on Vietnam. It did not produce much of a story, but as my camera crew and I were leaving, we saw hundreds of pieces of paper scattered on the wide lawns bordering the access roads into the big building.

Then we noticed a few men frantically scrambling around grabbing at the pieces of paper which the wind was tossing out of their reach. I suggested we stop and pick up one for ourselves, which we did. As I had suspected, all were stamped "Secret." Some of the men chasing the papers were clearly Pentagon employees, and others seemed to be curious tourists. Our cameraman had a field day filming the wild scene.

It seemed like a grand comedy to me, but Defense Department security agents apparently did not agree. At first they said we should stop gathering secret government documents, but when we pointed out that the papers were on public park land and that there was no law against picking up scraps of paper on public land, they gave up. In fact, we handed them most of the papers we had gathered, keeping only a couple of pages for the story I planned to do on that evening's television news.

Back at the studio, I read them. Each page was dated, and they clearly dealt with some form of rocketry outdated by at least ten years. When I called the Pentagon to say that I had some of their secret papers, a spokesman explained that they were a part of an old file that was being taken to a storage warehouse. Several cartons had fallen off a truck and broken open. The spokesman was extremely unhappy that I was about to do a story complete with pictures of security agents running around gathering up secret documents. He pointed out that showing the documents would be a violation of national security. I asked if he really believed these ten-year-old papers were still vital to national security. He refused to answer, on the grounds that even to discuss the papers would be a violation of current security. I thought the Pentagon's case extremely weak, to say the least, since Soviet knowledge of rocketry had unquestionably surpassed ours of ten years earlier.

Suspecting that he simply did not want the Pentagon to be embarrassed, I insisted that I would do the story.

During the next half hour before air time, two Pentagon officers of higher rank called, trying to block the report. Finally I agreed that we would not photograph the documents on television in any way that disclosed their contents, we would simply show the "secret" stamp. For over an hour they had been demanding that I immediately return the documents, so I told them to send a messenger to the CBS studio at 7 P.M. We then went ahead with the story, which made the Pentagon look rather silly, but certainly compromised no national security. The military messenger eventually retrieved the documents, and I received a letter of commendation from the Defense Department for having helped preserve national security by returning some "lost" Pentagon papers.

Even when a source is undeniably reliable, classified documents can be extremely risky. My colleague Daniel Schorr's CBS News career was terminated partly because of his questionable handling of just such a document.

In late January 1976, Schorr obtained the House Intelligence Committee's final report on widespread and sometimes illegal Central Intelligence Agency activities since World War II. These included assassination attempts, misuse of government funds and recruitment of journalists to act as spies. Under strong Ford Administration pressures, especially from within the CIA, Committee members agreed that the public should not be told what had been learned. Fortunately, someone with access to the report believed that the public should be told what was being done in its name and gave a copy to Schorr. One of the hardest-working, brightest and most aggressive reporters in the profession, Schorr had already distinguished himself with his excellent coverage of Watergate and the various investigations of United States intelligence activities that followed the Watergate revelations. Like most good journalists, Schorr had no hesitation about what to do with that kind of classified document. He broadcast it, or as much as CBS News deemed newsworthy. His handling of the report afterward, however, is open to varying judgments.

CBS News executives (who believe that any material an employee uncovers in the course of professional activities belongs to the company) were incensed to discover that in a rather murky manner the Committee's report managed to find its way from Schorr's hands onto the pages of New York's *Village Voice*. Schorr still maintains that his duty was to see the report published *somewhere* in its entirety. This was not the first time Schorr and CBS News executives held divergent views on a controversial issue. But it was the last time. The House Committee, upset about the CBS broadcast as well as the *Voice* publication, tried to force Schorr to reveal his source; Schorr refused, and in a protracted legal struggle CBS backed its correspondent completely, paying his considerable legal fees. But after the Committee dropped its attempt to learn Schorr's source or cite him for contempt, CBS forced him to resign. I applaud Schorr for having obtained the report, but not his handling of it after his broadcasts. Nevertheless, it is unfortunate that this incident deprived CBS of a very able broadcaster.

Of course, when national security is really concerned, the public does not always have a right to know. For example, during the 1979–81 Iran hostage crisis, reporters deliberately withheld some information. The best-known case is the story of the six Americans who hid in the Canadian Embassy and certain other locations in Teheran. Many news organizations knew about the situation, but none reported it until after the Americans had escaped. My colleague at NBC, Richard Valeriani, put it best: "It was easy," he said. "Would you have reported to the Nazis the hiding place of Anne Frank?"

Not all government secrecy, however, is related to national security or even to affairs of state. Political motivation guides much of what the White House tries to hide. For example, one night during the middle of the Watergate crisis (the late winter of 1973), reporter Alan Lidow, who worked for a California radio-TV organization, spotted a large limousine parked near the hideaway office (located next to the White House in the Executive Office Building) used by President Nixon. Lidow checked the license number through police sources and found it registered to a famous Washington criminal lawyer named John Wilson. Lidow suggested to me that the heavy clout of CBS might be useful in pursuing the story, so I asked Press Secretary Ron Ziegler what Wilson might be doing around the White House late at night. This forced Ziegler to disclose that the President's two closest aides, Haldeman and Erlichman, had hired the lawyer. I immediately suspected that Wilson was coordinating a three-way defense for the President and his two advisers. Later that summer, I asked the President at one of his infrequent press conferences if this was the case, and predictably he denied it. In the meantime, Haldeman and Erlichman had resigned, but they continued to retain Wilson as their Washington lawyer.

From bits and pieces of information, I became convinced that they also maintained fairly close contact with the President—but I had no real evidence. Then over lunch one day a woman who worked in the White House asked if I was aware that Haldeman held constant phone conversations with the White House. Some calls, she said, went directly to the President, but most went through Ziegler, who was more and more acting, together with General Haig, as chief coordinator for Richard Nixon's defense efforts. She further claimed that Haldeman still exercised enormous influence over the President. I tried to check the story with several sources, but I had no success. Few White House employees in those days were talking much to reporters, and many refused even to return phone calls.

Alexander Haig, a bright and carefully correct career Army officer who had replaced Haldeman as Chief of Staff, was among those who did not return my calls that afternoon. Finally, about 5:30, I decided to inform Ziegler that on the 6:30 CBS *Evening News* I intended to report that Haldeman still had great influence with Nixon. Although I wanted to give him a chance for official reaction, this was a ploy, since I was not yet certain that I would use the story. When I tried to reach Ziegler, the Press Secretary happened to be with the President, but his deputy, Gerald Warren, realized that they had to be interrupted. Ziegler then phoned me from the private quarters of the Nixon family. He was shouting and swearing. He knew, as I did, that public knowledge of the continued Haldeman connection would hurt the politically pressed President.

At first, Ziegler flatly denied the story. But under questioning he calmed down somewhat and said that Nixon had held "perhaps six or eight" phone conversations with Haldeman in the months since the Presidential aide had resigned. To me, this tended to confirm the story, although out of fairness and accuracy I did put Ziegler's qualified denial in my piece. About 7:15, after the story had aired (in Washington, D.C., the *Evening News* is seen at 7 P.M.), Al Haig returned my phone call. I casually asked about a possible tennis date, as if that was all I had originally phoned about. But I was certain he wanted to discuss something else. Sure enough, after declining my invitation, Haig said not quite so casually, "Bob, I don't think that broadcast you did about Haldeman's continuing White House influence is correct."

"Al," I asked, "are you always around when the President and Ziegler talk?"

"Not always," he admitted. I could tell from his tone that my story had touched upon some serious problems among those close to the President.

"Then, isn't it possible that without your knowledge Haldeman is relaying ideas and suggestions through Ziegler to the President?" I asked.

"Around this White House anything is possible," he conceded.

During that same Watergate period I picked up another story, which caused me momentary panic. Presidential counsel John Dean had never been very visible around the White House and was largely inaccessible to reporters. But as his name began surfacing more and more prominently in the winter and early spring of 1973, CBS News urged that I get him to grant a television interview. One truism of television reporting is that most people are not worth interviewing if they are not known to the public, and that once known, they often don't want to be interviewed. This was definitely the case with Dean, who kept refusing to talk to me, even on the telephone. By early April, it was apparent that President Nixon was shifting blame for Watergate to Dean; so on April 18 I made yet another ritual call. Rebuffed again, I told his secretary that if ever he did want to talk, CBS News would be readily available.

The very next day, at about 11:45 A.M. I received a phone call from a young woman who said she had a statement from John Dean. Expecting a routine explanation of why he refused to be interviewed, I casually put a piece of paper in the typewriter and said, "Go ahead." She dictated in a trembling, nervous voice, and from the first sentence it began to appear that Dean was defecting. My CBS colleague Phil Jones was in our White House cubicle with me, and I covered the phone to tell him to alert our executives, radio editors and TV producers. The woman's dictation of about half a dozen sentences, which I transcribed furiously on the typewriter, took perhaps two minutes.

"Some may hope or think that I may become a scapegoat in the Watergate case," Dean announced. "Anyone who believes this does not know me."

Thanking the woman hastily, I hung up and told Jones to phone the producer of the CBS New York 11:54 A.M. TV news to prepare for a bulletin, and also to alert CBS radio news for a live insert at noon. At exactly 11:54 I relayed to New York a couple of key sentences indicating that the Watergate case appeared to be breaking open with a defection by John Dean. Five minutes later, I dashed into our radio booth for a one-minute live broadcast. When I emerged, feeling excited and triumphant, Phil said to me with a smile, "How do you really know that was John Dean's secretary?"

Since Jones is a persistent practical joker, I froze with

fear. Had he pulled one on me? Then I realized that even Jones would not have let me go quite that far. Still, his question was absolutely on target: I did not know for sure who had been on the phone, although the voice sounded like the same woman in Dean's office I had spoken to just one day earlier. For a story of such magnitude I should have hung up after getting her name and phone number, then called her back. Still dazed, I gave my story to the wire services, since my fate was sealed. I knew that they would check my facts and come up with a verdict very soon. The wires usually credit the news organization that first breaks such a story; so, if it was true, CBS would be doubly happy, and if not, the blame might be divided and deflected. But before the wire-service reporters had finished reading my copy of the John Dean statement, the same secretary was on the phone to their offices delivering the same statement. Fortunately for me, it was not a false leak, but a legitimate Watergate story that I had broken a few minutes before my colleagues.

Like all journalists, I have occasionally, if unwittingly, been used by sources, but this does not necessarily mean that I was led to broadcast falsehoods. In the spring of 1980, for example, the Carter Administration was conducting a broad campaign against the Soviet Union's invasion of Afghanistan. Carter's aim was to persuade as many nations as possible not to attend the Olympic games, and to cut back the shipment of grain and high technology to the Soviet Union. The President particularly wanted the American Olympic Committee to boycott the games. During that period, Press Secretary Jody Powell called a number of us into his office one afternoon and proceeded to provide an intelligence briefing on Soviet activities in Afghanistan. Among other things, Powell said that intelligence sources had evidence that the Soviets were suffering heavier casualties than expected, that several hundred of their soldiers had died and about two thousand had been wounded. Powell also claimed that Soviet troops had been seen executing Afghan civilians. There was, of course, no way we could check these stories, and Powell would not let his name be used. The result was that we put out the story and attributed it to a "high Administration source." The information presented by Powell was probably true, but it also served the Administration's purposes by spreading adverse information about the Soviet Union's activities in Afghanistan.

As in the case cited above, almost all information provided as background, instead of on the record, is given out for some reason that benefits the source. Usually the source also believes that he or she is serving the national interest. The key question is not whether the reporter is being used, but whether the public interest is served by publication of the information.

Of course, we reporters also have our tricks. One technique in manipulating a source is to pretend that you know more than you actually do. Here's how it works: I once suspected that Hamilton Jordan, President Carter's Chief of Staff, had been in Panama or Paris negotiating freedom for the American hostages in Iran. But no one in the White House would even discuss the subject, let alone confirm my suspicions. So I called Jordan's office and left a message saying I wished to discuss his "trip abroad on the Iran situation." Because Jordan was now aware that I knew something, he returned my call. Taking a gamble, I said that I understood he had been in Panama meeting with officials of that government and with the Shah's representatives. What could he tell me about his trip? Although Jordan denied that he had been in Panama, he revealed that there had indeed been such meetings. He would not discuss exactly what was decided, but because extradition of the Shah from Panama was in the headlines at the time, I knew it must have been one topic. Jordan indirectly confirmed this by saying that the Panamanians definitely would not extradite the Shah. But he would not reveal the location of his meetings, and he insisted that he had not left the country.

I had started the story with practically nothing, and yet I now had enough facts to report a new development: that top White House aide Hamilton Jordan had been holding secret meetings somewhere inside the United States with

Panamanian officials and representatives of the Shah and that part of the negotiation dealt with the hostage situation. I then went to other high-ranking sources* and filled out the story, indicating that I had talked to Jordan and knew what he had been doing. From them I added the fact that the future of the Shah's considerable financial assets had also been discussed. Of course, most top officials are well aware of these techniques, as Jordan was when I talked to him. But they usually cannot be sure just how much a reporter knows, and thus will say or least confirm something that adds to a story.

Although the process of reporters and their sources using each other is well understood by all concerned, a very difficult ethical question is just how close to sources of information and objects of his news coverage a journalist should—and can afford to—get. At some point, it is impossible to determine exactly when or how public officials may become friends to be protected rather than covered.

Lines are difficult to draw. For example, the adversary relationship is necessary and proper during the give-and-take of press briefings, but does this mean the Press Secretary and the correspondent must keep at arm's length at all other times? Or what about the President himself? How much camaraderie should a President permit himself with the press corps? This problem has plagued White House correspondents, dating at least from the times when Harry Truman strolled into the Press Room for a few rounds of poker. The reporters couldn't turn Truman away, any more than today they can resist an invitation to a White House social function. We never know when the President may drop some nugget of news.

Even strictly social occasions are hard to decline, espe-

---

*By "high-ranking sources" I mean political appointees, at Cabinet, subcabinet or White-House-adviser level. The Press Secretary would be included, as would the President's Legal Counsel, his National Security Adviser, and top political people such as a Hamilton Jordan or a Robert Strauss in the Carter Administration. There is no hard and fast rule, but I would not use "high-ranking" to describe a civil servant or foreign-service officer unless he or she were at the very top of the trade, as an ambassador.

cially when that impressive embossed White House card with its gold lettering arrives. Although reporters may be tempted to RSVP No for ethical or personal reasons, their spouses are apt to intervene with a quick Yes, since such coveted invitations are not common.

During one summer vacation at Rehoboth Beach, Delaware, I had planned a deep-sea fishing trip with friends, when a sudden summons came to join President and Mrs. Nixon for a noon luncheon. Rare as such opportunities were, I had no desire to drive the three hours back to Washington just for lunch. My Washington Bureau Chief, who had relayed the telegraphed invitation, left the decision to me. I made the mistake of asking my wife, who had also been invited. We went. I missed the fishing trip—which, I learned later, was a huge success. The luncheon turned out to be a large affair with over one hundred guests assembled hastily for the wife of the President of Peru, and it resulted in no news.

Another time, ABC's Tom Jarriel and I received invitations to one of President Nixon's politically oriented Sunday morning religious services in the White House. We talked it over without telling our wives and decided that in principle we were opposed to using the White House for religious services—on the grounds that this breached the constitutional separation of church and state. So on this high moral basis we declined the invitation and instead played tennis.

The question of social relations between press and President can be fairly serious, however, when a President tries to influence reporters through such contacts. There is nothing intrinsically evil about politicians trying to influence reporters. It happens every day. But the issuing or withdrawing of social privileges can enhance or impede a journalist's ability to cover the Presidency. For example, those who attend such functions, particularly Presidential aides, can readily see whom their boss finds acceptable. This in turn can open doors and telephone lines, facilitating contact with sources; never being included when colleagues are invited can make work difficult for the socially spurned correspondent. Furthermore, if a reporter and a

White House official have socialized by playing tennis, drinking a beer together, or eating in a relaxed atmosphere, their subsequent professional interchanges can give the reporter a better "feel" for subsequent stories. At the same time, this kind of reporting can be overdone, and the correspondent can become merely a gossip. Stories that get on the network evening news are seldom gleaned from chitchat or social events. So I can easily justify avoiding most of them to spend more time with my family, then catching up the next morning by a careful reading of the Style section of the *Post*—a must in Washington. That's where you find out most often who is doing what to whom.

When the journalist happens to be a personal friend of the President, still more problems present themselves. John Kennedy, for example, had close relationships with Ben Bradlee of *Newsweek* (and later editor of the *Washington Post*), columnist Charles Bartlett, *Time* magazine's Hugh Sidey, Sander Vanocur (then of NBC), and others. The large and socially prominent Kennedy family was constantly entertaining, and they almost always included various members of the press corps. The relationships put a particular strain on those of us not close to the President; we feared that we would be frozen out. But this did not happen often, and I don't think I missed any major stories because I lacked the proper social connections.

Even in the absence of close—or distant—social ties, a correspondent's political sympathy with the President may pose a dilemma, especially when the President or one of his aides asks for advice or an opinion. Shortly after the 1960 Presidential election, half a dozen reporters invited Robert Kennedy to a private dinner, during which he asked us if we thought his brother should name him Attorney General. I was so surprised and flattered at being asked that I gave Robert Kennedy my honest opinion, that the appointment would be a clear-cut case of nepotism and as such politically damaging. In retrospect, I have to admit that I was wrong. Robert Kennedy turned out to be a good, tough Attorney General, with the major exception of his unwillingness to fire J. Edgar Hoover. His relationship with his brother made him more effective, although it did set an unattractive precedent. But as a supposedly objective journalist, I never should have responded to his question. After all, I would be expected to cover the appointment if it occurred, which means that I would be reporting on the validity of my own advice.

Perhaps ethics in such instances must be decided on a case-by-case basis. Yet, clearly, limits exist. In 1964, Clark Mollenhoff, who was covering Barry Goldwater's campaign for the *Minneapolis Tribune* and the *Des Moines Register*, sat on Goldwater's campaign plane and wrote memos for the candidate's speeches.* Such surprising public breaches of professional ethics are easy to identify. But unfortunately, when most ethical questions arise, right is not so easily separable from wrong, nor even so visible when they occur.

---

*Mollenhoff later joined Richard Nixon's White House staff, where his conservative politics were welcome. But it turned out that his blunt honesty was not, and Mollenhoff resigned in just over a year. Like most reporters who join government, he found the transition difficult.

9

Anatomy of an Award

Network reporters assigned to cover the White House experience peculiar challenges and rewards, as demonstrated by the two Emmies awarded to me and my colleagues in 1974. The first Emmy went to the producers and correspondents responsible for the CBS *Evening News* on October 10, 1973, the day on which Spiro Agnew resigned as Vice-President. What I believe happened is this: in going through the evening news broadcasts of that year, CBS decided to enter the entire show for an Emmy on the day Agnew resigned. When Cronkite's show won the Emmy for that night, every correspondent who had contributed a story relevant to the Agnew resignation received a separate Emmy. I had done a brief report from the White House that evening, detailing the President's role and the White House reaction to the resignation. This is the kind of story that one does almost daily and quickly forgets. It had probably taken me a total of three hours to gather the information, write my 75-second story, and film it on the front lawn of the White House. For that minor effort I received nationwide recognition and an impressive gold-plated statuette.

Ed Bliss, a former professor of journalism at American University and before that a colleague of mine and a writer for Edward R. Murrow, once suggested that the public believes the White House "is the answer to an enterprising reporter's dream—that it fairly teems with stories that can be dug out—whereas in reality there is little exclusive news to be had, since most stories come out of news conferences and briefings (shared by everyone) and handouts." My experience proves Bliss to be absolutely correct. The story of Agnew's departure was more the product of handouts and briefings available to all White House correspondents than of any direct reportorial effort.

White House correspondents, especially those representing the networks, are not encouraged to attempt prolonged investigative reporting; covering daily events surrounding the President and his staff can easily provide more than a full day's work. Time, however, is far from the only problem; at the White House, where every appointment is logged and every corridor guarded by police, we have very little freedom of action. Telephone calls are difficult, since most desks in the crowded Press Room are within easy hearing distance of the others. Even when I found myself on the trail of a hot story, it was sometimes nearly impossible to keep my investigations private.*

Another factor mitigating against investigative reporting is that the rewards in television journalism do not come so much from reporting as from performing. The nation's best-known (and best-paid) television journalists, the men and women who anchor the nightly newscasts, do very little or no reporting. Many (such as Walter Cronkite, Dan Rather, Roger Mudd, John Chancellor, Charles Kuralt and Frank Reynolds) have been excellent reporters. But the way to get a lucrative and prestigious anchor job is certainly not to devote weeks to an investigation that may produce only three minutes on the air—therein lies the surest way to oblivion. The fastest way up the ladder is to grab a beat with plenty of exposure, such as the White House, the Congress, or the Pentagon, and to perform well, get your facts right, get yourself some exclusive interviews with newsworthy public figures, dress appro-

---

*The networks have semisoundproof booths. But because we need to project our voices, broadcasts easily penetrate to nearby cubicles. Sometimes even routine telephone conversations inside the closed cubicles can be overheard.

priately, speak clearly and authoritatively, and project a
suitable image.

Beyond this, the giant corporations that control the networks are basically entertainment institutions, designed to
make money. They are reluctant to invest in reporting,
investigative or otherwise. Despite the sizable profits from
their news divisions,* CBS, NBC and ABC maintain dis-
hearteningly small news staffs. In Washington, for example, the CBS News Bureau has twenty-three reporters,
while *The New York Times* employs about thirty-five. Yet
the CBS News audience is at least fifty times larger.

Over the years, I have worked on two investigative reports that required a great deal of time, energy and money, and yet failed to yield a story. But in both cases I *still*
believe a story exists. Each involved a President very directly, and each took some travel within the United States
and also overseas. In both cases we gathered evidence over
a period of several months. In one instance, which dealt
with illegal funds being channeled to a President's reelection campaign, I even managed to locate the courier who
was handling the money. I spoke to him on the phone, and
he admitted that he was doing a great deal of traveling for
mysterious reasons—which he would not identify—and
that he was depositing some of the funds under different
names in various banks. But he would go no further. He
also refused to see me face to face, and since journalists do
not have subpoena powers or other law-enforcement methods to force compliance, we had to give up. The other case
involved the efforts of a rich foreigner to influence a President. We tracked down the man's business, his home, and
even managed to get television pictures of him at a restaurant where he had just entertained the President and
members of his family. I also acquired evidence of lavish
gifts being distributed to the President's family by the foreigner, although I could get no pictures of real proof. (I
was shown what appeared to be a diamond bracelet of

---

*Each network's news division keeps its expense and profit figures a
closely held secret.

great value by one member of the President's family, who told me the foreigner had given it to her.) In both cases, despite extensive efforts on the part of many people within CBS News, we could not verify the stories to my satisfaction.

But sometimes such efforts do succeed. The same night that CBS received Emmies for the Agnew broadcasts, CBS Washington producer Ed Fouhy and I were awarded a joint Emmy for a three-part *Evening News* series describing the favorable treatment that Richard Nixon's friend Charles "Bebe" Rebozo had received from the federal government in his banking and savings-and-loan businesses. That series had required more than eleven months of investigative reporting and filled ten minutes and five seconds of air time.

Throughout these months, Fouhy and I had the complete cooperation of CBS News executives, but we also had to perform most of our normal duties. Fouhy's production staff filled in for him on occasion, while Dan Rather was supportive in assuming some of my work at the White House. Both of us put in many extra hours, but part-time investigative reporting is clearly not the best way to work.

The Rebozo story started during a tennis game at Key Biscayne. We spent so many weekends there during the Nixon years that I had made some friends among the tennis players who lived on the Key and played at a local club. One winter day in 1972, after a friendly doubles match, Wilber Gasner, a retired vice-president of Levitt Corporation, asked if I had any idea how hard it was to get a federal bank charter for a new bank on Key Biscayne in view of the fact that the President's friend "Bebe" Rebozo had a banking monopoly on the island. He was both needling me and trying to get me interested. Like most businessmen, he was somewhat conservative and felt that the press was a rather naïve, liberal institution. His approach was that of a concerned citizen who knew how things worked and suspected that most politicians were crooked. He was trying to prove his point by demonstrating from his own experience that even Presidents helped their friends to make money. But I suspect that in the back of his mind was the hope that somehow I could aid his projected enterprise by doing a story.

Intrigued, I asked if he could provide more information. He could. Very shortly, I was introduced to Richard Sherlock, a small, neatly attired federal bank examiner who spoke with a clipped accent and looked and spoke just like the movie image of a bank examiner. Sherlock told me that he had studied the economic profile of Key Biscayne, talked to people in business there, and examined the data submitted by both those requesting and those opposing a new bank charter. This included information on the number of businesses in the area, the total population, the average income, the availability of other banking facilities, and the record of the existing bank in providing financial services. His conclusion was that the Key could use—in fact, needed—another federally chartered bank. But his recommendation had been overruled by someone in the chain of command in the Treasury Department, and the charter was denied. Although Sherlock did not quite say so, he clearly agreed that favoritism was being shown Rebozo because he was widely known as the President's closest friend.

On my return to Washington a few days later, I approached Fouhy with my belief that this group had a legitimate grievance and that we might have a story, although it was quite likely we might find nothing. Denial of a second charter might have been justified on the ground that Key Biscayne simply could not support another bank.

Our first task was to verify information about Gasner's friends' efforts to obtain a charter. They provided us with all their data—statistics on population, income, and availability of banking facilities at Rebozo's bank and elsewhere in the area, plus names and addresses of Key Biscayne residents who did not feel that Rebozo's bank offered the kind of service they needed. For example, consumer loans, even for such obvious needs as automobiles or such common items as boats, were extremely difficult to get. But when we approached many of the people who had told the rival group they were interested in a new bank, they refused to talk. Some claimed that they did not want publicity, and others either said or hinted that they were afraid to criticize the President's friend. Nevertheless, we did find a few people who were willing to openly declare that they thought Key Biscayne needed and could afford another bank. In addition, I phoned the bank myself several times asking about auto and boat loans. Bank officers repeatedly told me that the Key Biscayne bank was not interested in making consumer loans. The officers did not even suggest where I could go to get loans for such purchases. In any case, all other lending institutions are on the mainland in Miami, fifteen to thirty minutes away.

A careful check of state and other public banking documents confirmed another of the rival group's charges: that Rebozo's bank was happy to take deposits from the affluent folk who dominate Key Biscayne, and to manage their estates, but was reluctant to lend that money out again to them or others in the community. Rebozo and his friends operated their bank very conservatively, investing most deposits in high-grade government bonds. Members of the community clearly needed more extensive banking services.

Why, then, did the Comptroller rule against another federally chartered bank? We turned for answers to the Comptroller's office itself, which is in the Treasury Building directly across East Executive Avenue from the White House. This was convenient to me, and I spent several lunch hours at Comptroller William B. Camp's headquarters trying to elicit information. The public-relations officer for the Comptroller, William Foster, provided only a few innocuous documents on Rebozo's bank and on the attempt of the rival group to get a federal charter—primarily the same statistical studies that I had already obtained. We were stymied. We knew other documents existed, but could not gain access to them.

This was a short time after enactment of the Freedom of Information law enabling reporters to gain access to most government documents, with the right to sue if denied such access. CBS Washington Bureau Chief Small had participated in the efforts to get such a law passed, and he

suggested that we invoke the new act. So Fouhy and I
wrote to the Comptroller of the Currency, demanding certain documents revealing why the rival group had been
refused a federal bank charter. At first, Public Relations
Officer Foster told us that we would have to sue to get the
documents, but two days later he phoned to say the Comptroller had changed his mind and the documents would be
available immediately. I asked if I could copy them for
study elsewhere and was given permission to do so.

A careful check showed that most of the information we
had asked for seemed to be present, except for a key document showing the actual name of the person who had
recommended to Camp that the rival group's charter be
denied. Internal memos and letters referred to this person,
but I could not find the name anywhere. After closely ex-
amining the documents I pointed this out to Foster. He
claimed that there must have been an oversight and came
up with the missing document the next day. It revealed
that following a hearing in Atlanta, at which Rebozo had
"observed" while prominently displaying his cuff links
with the Presidential seal, the Comptroller's Regional Administrator, Joseph Ream, had made the negative recommendation. Ream cited as reasons lack of need and the
Key Biscayne's economic inability to support another
bank. The documents proved Ream had overruled not only
Sherlock's recommendation, but that of an additional investigation that corroborated Sherlock's findings.

Fouhy and I now began a series of telephone conversations with Ream, who maintained that Rebozo's friendship with the President had not influenced him and that he
simply did not believe the examiners' reports. A civil servant and not a political appointee, Ream took full responsibility for the decision, confirming that the Comptroller
had simply gone along with his recommendation. (The
Comptroller could, of course, have overruled the Regional
Administrator and supported his examiners by deciding to
grant a charter to a group in competition with the President's closest friend, but somehow that did not happen.)
We now faced a difficult decision. Our strong suspicions

that Rebozo's influence had kept out the rival bank were based on circumstantial evidence. We could not prove anything. After six months of hard work, Fouhy and I had no story to run.

Although we continued to nibble at its edges now and then, we had essentially given up our Rebozo investigation when a Federal Home Loan Bank informant—someone who had previously provided us with reliable inside information—called. He said that Rebozo and several associates within his bank were seeking a state charter for a savings-and-loan association, to provide needed financial services to the community and to be located right next door to Rebozo's bank. The Federal Home Loan Bank Board as well as state agencies had been approached, because under Florida regulations a state savings-and-loan association must be federally insured.

It turned out that Rebozo and his associates were using almost the same—in some cases actually identical—statistics used by the rival group in their efforts to get another bank on the Key. Within a couple of months, Rebozo had his new charter and we had our story. We could not prove that anyone had done anything illegal. But there was plenty of circumstantial evidence that a highly publicized friendship with a President had given Rebozo unfair influence. As a result of our story, the House Banking and Currency Committee began an investigation aimed at tightening regulations that govern the granting of lucrative federal bank and savings-and-loan charters. A staff investigator was dispatched to Florida to talk to Rebozo, who was not under oath, not under threat of subpoena, and not very helpful.

In the meantime, Comptroller Camp suffered a heart attack and retired. In his place, President Nixon appointed a former lobbyist for the American Bankers Association, James Smith. A small-town banker from South Dakota who had been brought to Washington by that state's longtime conservative Republican Senator Karl Mundt, Smith undertook a review of the entire Rebozo case. In early 1974, he upheld his predecessor's decision, and the rival banking group was again denied the charter to compete with the President's friend. But Smith, troubled by charges leveled against the loose method by which charters are granted, ordered an outside investigation and evaluation of the process.

The Comptroller was clearly encouraged by crusty old Wright Patman, Chairman of the House Banking and Currency Committee. Patman and his staff prodded Smith to explain just how Rebozo could have received such privileged treatment. While a full explanation was never forthcoming from Smith, he did institute some internal changes, opening to public scrutiny how requests for bank charters move from the local scene to the Treasury Department in Washington and what procedures are employed in granting or refusing these requests. Our investigative reporting also exposed to public and Congressional scrutiny some questionable practices, such as permitting a President's friend to display himself prominently at a hearing even though he is not called upon to participate. Just how much the controversy prompted real changes is a judgment for experts to make. One such expert, Joseph Christopher "Jake" Lewis, a staff member of the Banking and Currency Committee, said that the CBS News stories on Rebozo's influence "definitely started a process of opening up" the Comptroller's office and the Federal Home Loan Bank Board.

But Lewis maintained that much still needs to be done to remove what he called "the conspiracy of silence between the banks and the government regulators." He pointed to the whole affair of Bert Lance, President Carter's first Director of Management and the Budget, and Lance's ability to indulge in some highly questionable banking practices, as evidence of the need for more light in the shaded corners of the banking regulatory agencies. Lance had first run a state-chartered bank in the small town of Calhoun, Georgia, and was accustomed to operating in the rather loose "old boy" manner of that state's laws and establishment. When he moved to Atlanta and became an officer of a larger bank, he continued some of those practices, which included questionable loans to friends and relatives. After Lance moved to Washington with his close friend Jimmy Carter, some of those questionable loans went sour. At that point the Senate and the Justice Department began investigating, and Lance was forced to resign. Back in his native Georgia, where the "old boy" image is still acceptable, Lance was acquitted of all charges of wrongdoing.

Some time after the Key Biscayne bank story, I received a call one afternoon from a banker-lawyer involved in the earlier effort to get a bank charter. He told me that he had just learned from friends in the financial community that the Comptroller of the Treasury was about to close down the U.S. National Bank of San Diego. That bank was controlled by an old friend and supporter of Richard Nixon's and was one of the top banks in the nation. If true, this was a very significant story. But I needed confirmation. I put in a quick call to Comptroller Smith, whom I had come to know and respect through the Rebozo story. But his deputy said he was away on vacation. Since I knew that Smith's home was in Pierre, South Dakota, and that this was pheasant-hunting season out there, I called his parents' home and reached him on the phone. Smith conceded that there had been some problems with the U.S. National Bank, but he led me to believe that they were not particularly serious. He also reminded me of the laws concerning dissemination of information that could lead to a run on a bank, and which might make me liable for criminal prosecution if I broadcast such a story. But Smith assured me that when he got out to the West Coast in a day or two, he would look into the U.S. National Bank situation and let me know the outcome. I was suspicious, and I tried to make a few more phone calls. But by this time it was a few minutes before deadline for the *Evening News* show, and we had to make a decision: either we trusted my original source and went with the story, or we dropped it until the next day. It was not really much of a choice, since my one source was outside government and possibly had a vested interest.

The next day I called our Los Angeles Bureau, which

sent a man to San Diego to look into the story. By evening I had determined that the Comptroller was already in California working on the U.S. National Bank problem and that federal examiners were also at the bank. But still I could not be certain enough of the outcome to broadcast that the bank was going to be closed. So, once again the Cronkite show was broadcast without any mention of the story, although this time producer Sanford Socolow and I were tempted to go with it. We should have done so. About eight-thirty that evening I received a call from the Deputy Comptroller at the Treasury Department informing me that the Comptroller was closing the U.S. National Bank of San Diego. He said that Smith sent his apologies to me for having lied, but that my learning about the story had forced him to divert me from the truth while he hurriedly arranged for some other bank to take over U.S. National's assets and save its depositors' money. He also wanted me to be the first to get the official announcement. I was bitterly disappointed to miss such a story, although I did recoup a bit by doing a quick radio broadcast from my study at home, by telephone, for the 9 P.M. hourly radio news. That, of course, is 6 P.M. in California, and the report had some impact there. But it was basically a couple of days late.

CBS obviously could have done a better job of breaking and covering such stories if more investigative resources had been available. Assigning a full-time investigative correspondent to the White House would be unproductive because not enough opportunities arise. But we should maintain an investigative team, with "quick strike" capacity, to look into any situation that appears potentially fruitful. Instead, we have one investigative reporter in Washington, Robert Schakne, an excellent journalist but overworked covering almost every federal scandal that comes along.

Public-opinion polls consistently show that most Americans regard television as their principal and most trusted source of news. This gives us a special responsibility that we have yet to fulfill, because no news coverage is complete without adequate investigative work. Furthermore, network correspondents are among the best journalists in the business; given the opportunity, we could handle inves-tigative journalism as well as anyone. The problem is that we are not given the chance. In receiving the 1974 Emmy for our Rebozo series, we were singled out somewhat like Dr. Johnson's apocryphal dog that danced—rewarded not because we had done something extraordinarily well, but because we had done it at all.

Conclusion

At the end of each television report that I have done from the White House during these last twenty-three years, I have added a final paragraph that in broadcast journalism is called "The Close." In a few words spoken directly into the camera, I have tried to add a thought or observation that leaves the listener with a sense of balance, fairness and continuance, something to ponder beyond the hard news itself. This, then, is the close of my book.

The question I am most often asked about my years at the White House is: Which President was "the best"—usually followed by which President I liked the best. Obviously these are two separate issues; the first is difficult to answer, the second is easy. I liked John F. Kennedy the best. The reasons are completely subjective. Kennedy was young, vigorous, jaunty and fascinating. He was fun to be around. He did not fear reporters or the press. In fact, he alone among Presidents I have covered seemed to enjoy and thrive on give-and-take with us, whether in live television press conferences or in the relative privacy of his vacation homes in Palm Beach and Hyannisport.

Part of the reason for JFK's rapport with us seemed to stem from his own brief experience as a journalist working for the Hearst newspapers. Journalists like to joke about all these public-relations people and politicians who invariably inject into the conversation "I used to be a reporter myself." It is usually said half apologetically, and more frequently it is received that way by correspondents, who consider anyone who has abandoned the trade a bit of a traitor. But John Kennedy never mentioned his career in journalism.

Obviously, Kennedy used reporters, just as all politicians do. But it was never dull around the White House in those days. Away from Washington, life was even better. The President, his family and his traveling staff seemed aware that the White House press is made up of human beings, people who did not want to be away from home at such family times as Christmas and Thanksgiving. Therefore they included us with a spirit of fellowship and friendship that was thoroughly enjoyable and probably profitable for both sides. Professionally, it was sometimes impossible to view with complete objectivity the person mainly responsible for this warmth. Journalists always hope that at the end of a twenty-hour day they can still put exhaustion and personal feelings aside and produce a story that is fair and complete. But this is asking a bit much of anyone, even an experienced member of the normally fair-minded White House press corps.

After thus admitting to occasional lapses in objectivity, I shall now undertake the more serious part of this close— which President that I covered was "the best." After years of professionally imposed restrictions, one begins to qualify judgments. Therefore, I must break down my answer into two separate areas, most qualified and most popular. I believe that Lyndon Johnson was the most qualified. He genuinely cared about the poor and underprivileged, those who needed the federal government to fight for them in a generally uncaring society. Johnson set specific goals and knew how to use power to achieve them. Having served so long in Washington, he skillfully manipulated the various levers in Congress, the bureaucracy and the White House itself. In domestic affairs, he inherited the slow start of John Kennedy and went on to achieve some remarkable breakthroughs. His accomplishments in civil rights, health care, education and the war on poverty were the most important since Franklin D. Roosevelt. In my view, Lyndon

Johnson will be regarded by history as one of America's outstanding Presidents, for his domestic accomplishments.

But this success only serves to highlight Johnson's failure in foreign affairs. Like millions of his countrymen, he never understood that Asian Communism was a complex mixture, including Asian Marxism, Asian nationalism and anticolonialism. Johnson assumed that the Soviet brand of Marxism posed the basic problem, and that all aggression originated in the Kremlin. To Lyndon Johnson, Marxism was Godless, evil and imperialist. I think he actually believed that if the forces of Ho Chi Minh captured Saigon, they would eventually attack Hawaii and San Francisco. This serious misreading of the enemy led to Johnson's downfall, and more tragically to the needless deaths of thousands of Americans, Asians and others. President Johnson alone is not to blame, of course. A majority of Americans supported the Vietnam war for many years, and Richard Nixon and Henry Kissinger prolonged it four more years after LBJ left office. But the war drove LBJ from the White House and will, in my judgment, prevent him from being viewed by historians as a truly great President.

One can argue that Johnson inherited the war, as well as many of his domestic policies from John Kennedy. It is true that, when Kennedy died, close to twenty thousand American troops were already in Vietnam, some of them engaged in the fighting. But there is a tremendous difference between twenty thousand and the half a million Americans who served in Vietnam at the peak of the Johnson administration. I personally remain convinced that Kennedy would have seen the light sooner than did Johnson. But of course I cannot prove it. I do feel that Johnson eventually confused the possibility of defeat in Vietnam with the defeat of his own manhood, exhibiting that strange *machismo* complex that would cause him to say on occasion, "I'm not goin' to let those commies cut my balls off!"

Although Johnson did the best job in domestic policies,

I'd like to suggest an unpopular choice—Richard Nixon—as having done the best job in foreign affairs. While Nixon took too long to extricate the United States from that land war in Asia (as well as helping to spread the carnage into Cambodia) he did show exceptional ability in several other areas of foreign policy. The best example is his decision to reopen relations with China, a surprising move for a man who had built a sizable part of his political foundation on support for the Nationalist government of Chiang Kai-shek and the so-called China Lobby. For years Nixon had taken money and political help from those who had an almost fanatical commitment to the weak and venal government on Taiwan. But when he came to power, encouraged by the urging of Henry Kissinger and others who were ready to face reality, President Nixon did an about-face. His trip to China and his signature on the Shanghai Communiqué (formalizing a Sino-U.S. dialogue) were master strokes that historians may view as important enough to wipe out some of the disgrace of Watergate. Not coincidentally, Richard Nixon's dramatic trip to China was so timed as to boost him to an overwhelming reelection in 1972, proving that he could read the American electorate in some respects better than many of his political colleagues. He knew that the nation was ready for the "China Card."

Other Nixon accomplishments in foreign affairs deserve to be mentioned, although once again the Machiavellian brilliance of Henry Kissinger may have brought them about. Nixon's two trips to the Soviet Union, as part of his effort to smooth relations and achieve détente with the Kremlin, would have been worthy of praise if done by any American President—but especially for one who had been a long-time professional anti-Communist. The signing of the SALT I Treaty was the culmination of a drive toward nuclear disarmament actually begun by John F. Kennedy many years before. Nevertheless, it ranks as an important achievement of the Nixon years.

Another important Nixon action—the initiation of an "even-handed" Middle East policy—opened the door for the Camp David agreements between Israel and Egypt negotiated under Jimmy Carter's leadership. Carter too deserves special mention in terms of foreign affairs. He finished another Nixon project by formalizing full diplomatic relations with China, and he also turned the Panama Canal back to Panama, granted immediate diplomatic recognition to the new government in Zimbabwe (Rhodesia), and managed to help maneuver Anastasio Somoza out of his dictatorship in Nicaragua, without seeing that country go Communist. None of these foreign-policy accomplishments made Carter more popular at home, but they were the right things to do for the future of the country and of the world, and he did them despite domestic opposition. This is an essential quality that many American Presidents lack—doing what is right for the country in the long run, even though it is not supported by the emotions of the moment, by the Congress, or even by a majority of the people.

Without question the most popular President I have covered was Dwight D. Eisenhower. He commanded a respect and even an affection that none of his successors could ever achieve. In my view, this had little to do with his abilities as Chief Executive; it grew from his fatherly image, his benign public personality and his war record. He was unquestionably what most Americans wanted at that time, a chairman of the board, who let his aides do much of the work while he took the credit. Secretary of State Dulles, for example, largely controlled our foreign policy, and with his missionary zeal against neutrality and Communism, he came across as the "heavy," while Ike alternately smiled or frowned in the background. There is a new and rather revisionist school of thought that says President Eisenhower was really much more clever and manipulative than the public and the press realized.

That may be, although I never saw much of this side of Ike. I did, however, have one interesting and revealing experience with him. This came much later, in 1965, when Lyndon Johnson was President. I drove up to Gettysburg one day to interview the retired President at the small college in that town where he had his office. After we had finished discussing racial problems, Ike wanted to chat about politics. A believer in the eventual goodness of man but of moving slowly—if at all—to force such goodness by law, Eisenhower was not enthusiastic about the civil-rights measures then being pushed by President Johnson. Yet in the late fifties, Ike himself had helped maneuver some mild civil-rights reforms through Congress. With a twinkle in his eyes, Ike said to me, "I can remember a certain Senator from Texas who wasn't nearly so enthusiastic about civil rights in those days." He was referring, of course, to Johnson, who as Majority Leader had a very different approach to civil rights than he did when he became President. It was an illustration that Ike had a more caustic view of politics and politicians than he cared to let on. Certainly he knew enough to have been reelected as long as he cared to, had it not been for the two-term limit in the Twenty-second Amendment to the Constitution.

One of the unique things about Dwight Eisenhower's Presidency was that he became more popular at the end of his second term than when first elected—in contrast to Presidents since then, who seem to wane in public esteem the longer they remain in office. During the years that I have been at the White House I have undergone a change in my own attitude toward Presidents, and I have seen that change reflected to some extent in public perception of the nation's leaders. One of the first traditions I learned after joining the White House press corps was to stand when the President entered the room. As reporters, we did not applaud a President. But it was explained to me that to rise is to show respect for the office, even though we in journalism may not show partisan reaction to the person who occupies that office. This made sense to me. In those days a President was an institution, one that I viewed with a certain amount of awe and even fear. But the more I saw of Presidents, the more I came to consider them politicians who for one reason or another, including skill and luck, had scrambled to the top.

Perhaps it is a bit of that old axiom about familiarity

breeding contempt, although that would be far too strong a word for my opinion of any of them. Even Richard Nixon I now regard more with pity than with anger for his betrayal of the public trust. (Age and distance mellow even the nastiest reporters.) I was disappointed in Eisenhower's dogged determination to back Richard Nixon, even though Ike clearly had his private doubts about his Vice-President's integrity. John Kennedy knew full well what an autocratic schemer and ruthlessly powerful manipulator J. Edgar Hoover really was, yet he allowed Hoover to continue the FBI's illegal excesses against fellow Americans.

Lyndon Johnson not only escalated the war in Vietnam far beyond its strategic worth, but he lacked the courage to call for the heavier taxes to pay for it; Johnson's war-based inflation continues to plague us today. Gerald Ford made a great national epic out of ordering a U.S. military strike against Cambodia's meager forces for having seized the *Mayaguez,* an American merchant vessel, in disputed waters. Those on the *Mayaguez* might well have been released in a matter of hours, and more people died in the subsequent United States military rescue than were actually aboard. Jimmy Carter was a classic anti-Washington "outsider" who never understood that the President of the United States must become the ultimate insider. Furthermore, each of these Presidents thirsted, at times, to prove his manhood through military actions. From Eisenhower's Marine landing in Lebanon to Kennedy's Bay of Pigs invasion of Cuba to Richard Nixon's Cambodia incursions, they often were unable to resist hard-line advisers who insisted that they use some of that marvelous military hardware.

I don't know whether it is maturity or cynicism, but I no longer feel the sense of awe that I once felt in the presence of a President. Perhaps it would be different if the man were a Franklin Roosevelt or an Abraham Lincoln. I hope so, but I am not sure.

I am sure, however, that things have changed in these twenty-three years. I can see it in my younger colleagues, who have been nurtured by—and now anticipate—today's skepticism and innate distrust of public officials. Perhaps this is a step in the right direction. Possibly journalistic mistakes can be avoided by a healthy cynicism. Maybe the unquestioning esteem given past Presidents was unhealthy for democracy. At the same time, I cannot help but wonder what would happen were a Lincoln or an FDR to come along these days; would his talents have room to reveal themselves and grow, or would he inevitably be buried beneath an impenetrable national apathy and distrust? I wish I knew the answers to these questions, for I think they are important items for the nation's long-range political agenda.

However, the cynicism is already having an impact. In the twenty years after the departure of Dwight Eisenhower, no United States President has served two full terms. A decade or more ago, observers began noticing that governors were toppling regularly after only one term in the statehouse. Now the federal government appears to be entering a similar era, when Presidents fall or fail after a single term in the White House.

In addition to a broad undefinable dissatisfaction with government, the chief explanation for this phenomenon, I believe, is that the nation's problems are so deep and complex that no political leader, however astute, can hope to solve most of them. Therefore, the longer a President stays in office, the more disappointments he engenders and the more enemies he makes.

The mass media, particularly television, constantly contribute to this. On the one hand, broadcasters have helped to expand the President's power by focusing the nation's attention so intently upon him. Our unblinking gaze has brought him into the life of each citizen, and it has made him the only true spokesman for the entire nation. But at the same time, this media attention corrodes the President's power by raising too many expectations about what he can and should do, and by making him too familiar to the ordinary American. Charles de Gaulle, who parceled out his television exposure carefully, once noted that "mystery is power." It is a lesson American Presidents, at first seduced by television's availability, may have had to learn for themselves the hard way.

As the number of Presidential primaries has escalated, from fifteen in 1968 to thirty-seven in 1980, the media have also become increasingly important in the selection of Presidential candidates. For example, we have made such an important horse race out of the early primaries in such states as New Hampshire and Florida, that those candidates who lose are virtually ruled out as losers long before most primary voters even have a chance to cast their ballots. By the time a candidate has won a few opening primaries and has been "crowned" by the media, he is on his way to the national convention and is expected to arrive with a majority of the delegates wrapped up. The political professionals and citizen activists who have been working in the vineyards on a local level for many years then don't have a thing to say about who their national leader will be. The result is that largely via the media a candidate can reach the White House ignoring party leaders, local politicians, and members of Congress without whom he cannot govern effectively. This is precisely the problem Jimmy Carter faced when he entered the White House.

Another factor contributing to short-lived Presidencies is the exhaustion, despair and even bitterness that seem to creep into a President as he faces the enormous, ever more complex problems of the nation and the world. Lyndon Johnson, for example, surrendered the office in the face of the Vietnam war. He still believed that he was correct in pursuing that war, and he still thought he could have defeated Richard Nixon. But Johnson also knew that a nationwide political campaign, with anti-Vietnam protests blocking the streets and antiwar chants interrupting his every appearance, could have resulted in serious domestic violence. Rather than face that baleful prospect, Johnson simply gave up. He thought it was best for the country that he do so, and he was probably correct.

Whatever the exact causes, these short-term or truncated Presidencies have produced a lack of continuity in both domestic and foreign policies. The nation is governed in fits and starts, as leadership at the top frequently changes both in personality and party. Bureaucrats, those much-maligned but often dedicated public servants who try to make the system work, find that they are spending a great deal of time and energy trying to figure out which conflicting policies and orders they are to administer. As Henry Kissinger, former Secretary of State, pointed out during the 1980 Presidential campaign, changing Presidents and foreign policies every few years makes it very difficult for even the best foreign-service officers to conceptualize and carry out a coherent strategy for any of the world's many flash points. It also makes it almost impossible for America's allies to figure out what United States foreign policy may be the day after tomorrow, let alone a few years from now.

The same fate—a short-lived Presidency—may very well await Ronald Reagan. (Leaving aside for a moment his age—he will be seventy-three in 1984. Despite America's prejudices against aging, Reagan could be a physically vigorous, viable candidate for reelection.) The American voter is in a state of rebellion that shows little sign of ending. Reagan will have to deal with an increasing population and decreasing natural resources, with inflation and unemployment that seem to feed on each other, with his own promises to reduce taxes while increasing military strength, with a Soviet Union possessing as much capacity to destroy us as we to destroy them, and with an increasingly powerful Third World fully able and willing to disrupt the carefully laid plans of both superpowers.

The simple and unavoidable truth is that these problems will persist no matter who is President. No easy answers will magically appear, and large segments of the American people will be dissatisfied no matter what Ronald Reagan does. But as the Reagan era begins, we—press and public alike—must remember that our best hopes for a better future and our most dangerous capacities for self-destruction still reside at the White House.